Discovering the Geology
of Baja California

Discovering the Geology of Baja California

Six Hikes on the Southern Gulf Coast

Markes E. Johnson

The University of Arizona Press
Tucson

The University of Arizona Press

© 2002 Arizona Board of Regents

All rights reserved

⊖ This book is printed on acid-free, archival-quality paper.

Manufactured in the United States of America

First Printing

07   06   05   04   03   02   6   5   4   3   2   1

Library of Congress Cataloging-in-Publication Data

Johnson, Markes E.

   Discovering the geology of Baja California : six hikes on
the southern gulf coast / Markes E. Johnson.

        p. cm.

Includes bibliographical references and index.

   ISBN 0-8165-2228-6 (cloth) — ISBN 0-8165-2229-4 (pbk.)

   1. Geology—Mexico—Baja California (Peninsula)—Guidebooks.

2. Baja California (Mexico : Peninsula)—Guidebooks. I. Title.

   QE203.B34 J64 2002

557.2'24—dc21   2002001047

British Library Cataloguing-in-Publication Data

A catalogue record for this book is available from the British Library.

For mothers everywhere, but especially for Agnes Carey Johnson,
Alzira C. Castro Amarante, and Gudveig Baarli

Contents

Illustrations

Maps

Figures

Acknowledgments

My travels in Baja California were undertaken in the company of others, most often my professional colleagues and students. I owe an immense debt to my field partner and friend, Professor Jorge Ledesma-Vázquez, of the Universidad Autónoma de Baja California in Ensenada. Without his invitation, I would not have found my way to Baja California. Without his wise counsel, I would see and understand the geology of Baja California less clearly. Without his hearty friendship, I would be a much poorer human being. I am much indebted to Marge and Jere Summers for their warm hospitality at Punta Chivato and for their help and encouragement in the writing of this book. They have never failed to welcome me other than as someone returning to his natural abode. Parts of chapters 6 and 8 were written in their Punta Chivato home, which they graciously made available to me in early May 2000. I am grateful to Francisco Escandón Valle, director general, Minera Curator, S.A. de C.V., for permission to reproduce data on annual precipitation in the Santa Rosalía district. Preliminary drafts of the book were read and edited by Marge Summers and my patient wife, Gudveig Baarli. An early version of chapter 5, on the Ensenada El Muerto, was reviewed and improved by my colleague at Williams College, William T. Fox. Lauren R. Stevens was my consultant on the penultimate draft. His insight as a writer, environmentalist, and experienced hiker was most helpful. Credit is due to Yvonne Reineke, acquiring editor at the University of Arizona Press, for helping to give the manuscript its final shape. Jane Kepp applied her considerable craft as a copyeditor to clarify the most persistent offenses of my tangled prose.

I am a significant beneficiary of student involvement in my research. More eyes see all the better, and my students deserve high praise. In particular, my former students Laura Libbey Blackmore, Marshall L. Hayes, Cordelia Ransom, Patrick Russell, and Maximino E. Simian played important roles in this story about Punta Chivato. Many other students from Williams College accompanied me to other parts of the Baja California peninsula, sometimes making a brief call at Punta Chivato. Most of the hikes described in this book were tried out on them. They survived, happily, I believe. Funding for the original research conducted at Punta Chivato during the 1990s was provided by the donors of the Petroleum Research Fund (administered by the American Chemical Society) and occasional grants from the Anderson Fund for Latin American Studies at Williams College. Finally, the Office of the Dean of Faculty at Williams College contributed a generous subsidy to the University of Arizona Press that helped make this book a reality.

Advice to the Reader

This book tells the geological story of a place called Punta Chivato on the gulf coast of Baja California Sur, Mexico, through six nature hikes. Here is found a remarkable landscape, which I revisit as often as possible. Although I have carried out research elsewhere around the world and have traveled widely through the rest of the Baja California peninsula, this spot holds a powerful attraction for me. Each time I return, I take away a richer understanding of the complex web of relationships in nature, particularly their linkages to the distant past.

The Punta Chivato region covers approximately 9.5 square miles (25 km²), jutting like an elbow into the Gulf of California above the entrance to scenic Bahía Concepción (map 1). A growing number of homes cluster around the Hotel Punta Chivato on the southeast corner of the peninsula. An airstrip for small planes serves the area, but it is also accessible by road from Palo Verde off Mexican Federal Highway 1. The principal town, Santa Rosalía, lies 28 miles (45 km) to the northwest, and the village of Mulegé, 12.5 miles (20 km) south, as the crow flies. From January to April, the local climate is welcoming— especially for anyone eager to escape the rigors of a northern winter, as I am. Punta Chivato sits just above 27° north latitude, similar to Sarasota, Florida.

The region includes three small islands, the Islas Santa Inés, one of which is the site of a sea lion colony. Four distinctive mesas, three of which bear formal map names, dominate the mainland's topography. They are more ridgelike than table-topped. These features rise in elevation from 260 to more than 330 feet (80–100 m) above present sea level. The largest and most commanding is the broad Punta Chivato promontory, which covers approximately 2.5 square miles (7 km²) and affords sweeping views of the surrounding gulf. The four mesas and the Islas Santa Inés formed an archipelago in the nascent Gulf of California about 5 million years ago, during the early Pliocene Epoch. In response to regional tectonic forces, changes in global sea level, and the ceaseless effects of erosion by wind, waves, and rain, the islands changed their size and shape through time. Gradually they foundered below the gulf waters, eventually to rise again and join, in part, with the peninsular mainland. The story of these ancient islands, rich in marine life, makes up only part of the region's geological history. The origin of the Gulf of California itself is shrouded in the older basement rocks of the Pliocene Santa Inés archipelago and the surrounding landscape.

Because Baja California was and is a popular adventure destination, the peninsula has been vividly described by a wide range of visitors—generic vagabonds, novelists, teachers, and naturalists (somewhat like myself), as well as people who achieved extraordinary feats of long-distance hiking and kayaking

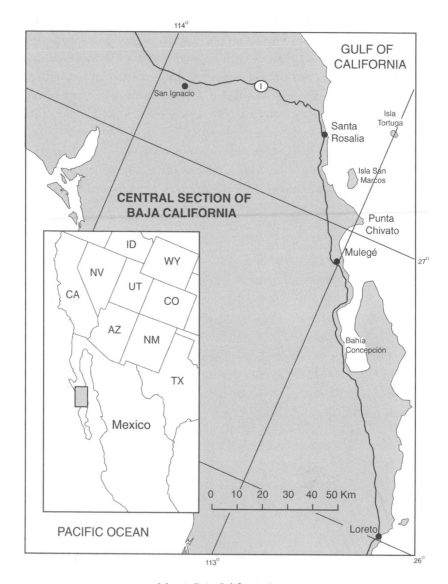

Map 1. Baja California Sur.

and lived to tell their story. None of the popular accounts of life, nature, and travel in Baja California, however, has been written from the perspective of a geologist. My viewpoint is informed by geomorphology and historical geology. Geomorphology is the study of landforms and the processes of erosion responsible for their sculpture. Historical geology is a discipline that seeks to order the physical and biological changes on planet Earth through time.

Fossils and the layered sedimentary rocks in which they are preserved provide many of the clues that bring meaning to the pages of this all-encompassing and still unfinished epic. Our planet has a tangible geological history spanning more than 4 billion years, but the gulf coast of the Baja California peninsula is young by comparison. Its geological history stretches back less than 80 million years to the Cretaceous Period, at best. Indeed, rocks younger than 15 million years, beginning with the later Miocene Epoch, tell most of the relevant story of the Gulf of California.

Geomorphology seeks rational explanations to show why a particular valley is located where it is, for example, or why a certain hilltop stands up in bold relief. The landscape of a given district is dependent entirely on its underlying bedrock. Some rocks are harder, denser, or better cemented than others and thus more resistant to erosion by wind and running water. A geomorphologist must be familiar with the full range of possible rock types: sedimentary, igneous, and metamorphic. Baja California provides fertile ground for consideration because, although it is still a comparatively young landscape, it exposes a profusion of rock types to a desert climate subject to occasional rainstorms and regularly shifting wind patterns. Though often tranquil, the gulf coast can face sudden winter winds that feed vigorous and erosive waves. In short, Baja California presents a veritable marketplace of delights in historical geology and geomorphology, because the sparse vegetation and thin soil cover cannot obscure the goods on display. Knowledge derived from paleontology, stratigraphy, and volcanology can help us appreciate and understand this unique gulf coast landscape and its former shorelines.

When I read accounts by travelers such as the long-distance hiker Graham Mackintosh, who walked the entire coast of Baja California, or the marathon kayaker Jonathan Waterman, who paddled the full length of the Gulf of California along its peninsular shores, I become envious. The coastline of Baja California stretches over a distance of 3,000 miles (4,800 km), including both the gulf and Pacific shores. The length of the gulf coast alone is about 800 miles (1,280 km). Part of me longs for the sheer physical stamina such adventures demand. More, I covet the opportunities to see intimately all aspects of the passing landscape experienced by their eyes. Much of the most interesting and dramatic geology of Baja California is exposed along its rugged coastline. In their books, Mackintosh and Waterman both describe the aching beauty and isolation of the peninsular coast, sharing with us the emotions of meeting daunting physical challenges and infusing us with a sense of how it feels to abandon all the comforts of civilization and return to the wild. Through their stories, we understand just how unforgiving the harsh country is, just how rough the seas may turn, and how tenaciously life clings to mere survival. Through them, we experience an intensely personal metamorphosis of spirit.

But these feats of daring leave many secrets of the landscape unrevealed. Where did the Baja California peninsula come from? How did life take hold there? How have the geography and its native ecosystems changed through time? From my geologist's point of view, a successful traverse of the complete Baja California shoreline would be undertaken not for the record books but to cull from the whole the most prized discoveries—the most telling of natural histories.

My landscape envy extends to my cousin's husband, who routinely flies jet aircraft back and forth over the length of Baja California. How wonderful to see the entire countryside unroll before your eyes like a movie. On commercial flights, I refuse to pull down the window shade for the in-flight film, for the show outside is much superior. Distance gives me the big overview, but I also need to see and experience the terrain up close. During my field visits, I have done some stretches of the gulf coast by motorized *panga,* an open boat of local design, and by small aircraft. But walking or paddling is better, because I need time to think about the landscape and sort out the potential answers to the questions it poses. My ideas about a piece of landscape are usually in flux. I look, I ponder, I go away and return to find more pieces of the puzzle revealed on another day. A rich landscape must grow on me gradually and be nourished by many different and sometimes competing considerations.

I knew I had found something special on my first visit to Punta Chivato. Over time, I came to realize that the main promontory and its immediate environs embody a rich microcosm of the greater lands surrounding the Gulf of California and all its islands. One need not see everything to understand and fully appreciate a whole territory. The trick to understanding a complex piece of geography is to travel enough to recognize the ghostly traces of possible patterns and the potential for a good story.

A rough-cut jewel of a place, Punta Chivato offers many advantages to the traveler. It can be reached within 24 to 48 hours by some combination of air, ferry, and ground transportation from almost any substantial population center in North or South America. The local hotel and its associated campground provide excellent to adequate headquarters. At the same time, complete peace and solitude are never more than a few footsteps away. Almost everything described in this book can be seen, experienced, and pondered by foot. Most importantly, the fundamental structural and environmental patterns that govern the ecology of other headlands and islands in the Gulf of California can be understood by unlocking the geological secrets of Punta Chivato.

In *Pilgrim at Tinker Creek,* Annie Dillard asserts that "landscape consists in the multiple, overlapping intricacies and forms that exist in a given space at a moment in time." The landscape of Punta Chivato has evolved yet remained surprisingly constant over many moments in geologic time. Dillard presents a three-dimensional impression of her subject that is essentially ecological. My goal in writing this guidebook was to render a landscape in four dimensions—the fourth being time—and, in doing so, to link the ecology of the past with that of the present.

The plan of this book leads readers through a series of six daylong hikes. All tours begin at the southeast corner of the Punta Chivato promontory, the terminus of passable roads leading to the hotel. Each in turn loops out in a different direction from this center, like the petals of a flower. Each circuit is designed to minimize overlap with other, adjacent hikes and to maximize exposure to instructive variations in the landscape while bringing you back to the same point at day's end. The hikes progress from a relatively short, easy hike on flat land during the first day to the longest hike, traversing the roughest, most pathless terrain, on the fifth. The sixth day takes you to the largest of the Santa Inés islands and involves almost no climbing. Geological precepts ranging from simple to more intricate accompany the excursions, allowing you to grasp the larger geological history of the Gulf of California.

Like any other science, geology and its associated disciplines have evolved through contributions from one thinker building on another. Even if they set out to explore virgin territory, all trained geologists go into the field following in other geologists' footsteps. These intellectual forebears have given us a set of conceptual tools with which to solve the problems that stir our innate curiosity. In chapters 1–7 and on each walk, a guide from the past joins us to share his insights.

My overriding motivation for this book was to describe the Punta Chivato area before it is consumed by commercial development. This landscape interacts with weather, wind, and waves to knit together an intricate and varied web of life. Such a landscape, and all its interactions through time, has its own natural history—its very own pattern of growth, decay, and possible rejuvenation. It has a past, a present, and a future. My fondest hope is that its future will include land conservation and ecotourism.

For visitors to Punta Chivato, I have some words of advice. The maps for the walking tours in each chapter come from the topographic sheet for San José de Magdalena (G12A46). The scale of this map, produced by the National Institute of Statistics, Geography, and Information (a branch of the Mexican federal government), is 1:50,000. The standard contour interval for a topographic map at this scale in Baja California is 20 meters. The metric system is used exclusively in Mexico; for Americans unaccustomed to it, every contour represents a rise of about 65 feet. You may wish to carry your own copy of the official map, which covers the region well beyond Punta Chivato. The maps by which my students and I navigate the wilds of Baja California are photocopied from the original government topo sheets and enlarged significantly. You do not need your own copy of the San José de Magdalena sheet, but before you head for the mesas of Punta Chivato, I recommend making large photocopies of the maps in this book. They are easier to orient yourself by and allow more space for comments about interesting spots to which you might wish to return. In addition to a map, you should carry a reliable compass and know how to use it. Unlike on conventional nature trails, no markers delineate the pathways in this guide.

The six hiking guides may each require an hour or less of reading time, but they are designed to keep you outside for as much as six hours a day. You will easily find yourself too far from the hotel at Punta Chivato or from the nearby *tienda* (small grocery store) to acquire lunch or a cold drink. Be sure to carry whatever food and water you require. *Agua purificada,* or purified water, is available at the local shop. During the winter, the temperature will be cool in the mornings but will rise to 80° Fahrenheit (27° C) by early afternoon. Most days are sunny, even when the weather turns windy. A hat with a visor to protect your head and a light windbreaker are strongly recommended, along with liberal use of sunblock. Once the sun sets, by six o'clock in January, the temperature plummets. Long trousers and a light but long-sleeved shirt protect against wind, sun, and ubiquitous thorny vegetation.

With any exertion, you will certainly become hot and sweaty, but you will rarely be far from the cooling gulf waters. I usually carry a towel and a swimsuit on my coastal explorations. In fact, most of the hikes described in this book offer a daily swim at a choice and geologically interesting spot. The water temperature during January is 60° to 62° Fahrenheit (16° to 18° C). During the summer, the water temperature may exceed 82° Fahrenheit (29° C). At the very least, beachcombing and shallow wading are always agreeable in January. The shores of the Gulf of California are superb shelling grounds. For more serious exploration, pack some swim goggles and water slippers. Finally, bringing a small first-aid kit to treat the inevitable cuts and scrapes is always a good idea. Your gear and supplies can be carried in a small and comfortable backpack.

Most importantly, it is absolutely necessary to wear well-soled boots with adequate ankle support during your hikes, for two reasons. First, much of the terrain you will cross is volcanic. The rocks are sharp. If you are not walking on igneous rocks, you will likely be walking on limestone that has weathered under karstic conditions (for a definition of which, please see the glossary near the end of the book). Those surfaces, too, are sharp. Or you may step on a piece of cactus. These easily pass through the thin rubber soles of sneakers. Ordinary sneakers or running shoes would last for no more than a few days of extensive walking. Even the best field boots rarely give me more than two months of service in Baja California.

The second reason for proper footwear is scorpions and rattlesnakes. January is an especially good time to visit Baja California because they tend to be in hibernation, or at least in a state of lethargy. In more than 10 years of winter travel in Baja California, I have never had a problem with either of these creatures. Only rarely have I spotted them in the field, although the scorpions are rather more abundant than the rattlesnakes. A rancher once tried to sell me a shot of tequila from an enormous glass jar with a pickled rattlesnake inside, informing me that venom extract mixed with tequila was medically proven to clear the cholesterol from your arteries. He kept an identical jar with a live rattlesnake imprisoned in it. The live one tried to strike through the glass. Involuntarily, I leapt backward. He went on to tell me that I would live to be an old man if I took a shot of the venom-fortified tequila once a week. I did not take the treatment. Those are the only two rattlesnakes that have come within striking distance of me, so far as I know. My life always feels more secure, however, when I'm wearing a pair of good boots.

My parting word of advice is to resist the temptation to hike the mesas and coastline of the Punta Chivato area alone. Should you decide to go there, and especially if you are inclined to follow my unmarked path, it is always wise to hike with a companion. A fall onto rocky rubble from even the lowest cliffs could lead to a broken bone. Besides having someone along who can go for help, there is an additional benefit. Two heads are nearly always better at figuring things out than one. Field geologists rarely do their research solo.

Punta Chivato serves as the ideal key to unlock some of the major themes in the natural history of the Gulf of California and to trace their continuity with the geological past. The same key may open the way to a deeper appreciation of countless other headlands and islands along the gulf shores of Baja California, from San Felipe in the north to San José del Cabo in the south. Whether you incline more to an armchair tour of Punta Chivato or determine to visit the place for yourself, my earnest hope is that you become inspired to seek out other landscapes for your own exploration.

Recommended Travel Accounts of Baja California

Berger, B. 1998. *Almost an Island: Travels in Baja California.* University of Arizona Press, Tucson, 213 pp.

Janovy, J., Jr. 1992. *Vermilion Sea: A Naturalist's Journey in Baja California.* Houghton Mifflin, Boston, 226 pp.

Johnson, W. W. 1972. *Baja California.* Time-Life Books, New York, 184 pp.

MacKintosh, G. 1988. *Into a Desert Place: A 3000-Mile Walk around the Coast of Baja California.* Unwin Hyman, London, 312 pp.

Krutch, J. W., and E. Porter. 1967. *Baja California and the Geography of Hope.* Sierra Club, San Francisco, 168 pp.

—— 1986. *The Forgotten Peninsula: A Naturalist in Baja California.* University of Arizona Press, Tucson, 277 pp.

Steinbeck, J. 1941. *The Log from the Sea of Cortez.* Viking, New York, 282 pp.

Waterman, J. 1995. *Kayaking the Vermilion Sea: Eight Hundred Miles Down the Baja.* Simon and Schuster, New York, 223 pp.

Zwinger, A. 1983. *A Desert Country near the Sea.* University of Arizona Press, Tucson, 399 pp.

Discovering the Geology
of Baja California

Ancient Shorelines and the Meanings of Landscape

Pulchra sunt, qvae videntur. Pulchriora, qvae scinuntur.
Longe pulcherrima, qvae ingnorantur.—Nicolaus Steno, 1673

Stand apart from your private world for a moment, from the place you presently occupy, and consult an atlas that shows the entire physical geography of our planet on a single page. Let your eyes wander over this miniaturized, flattened likeness of the greater world. A map on such a scale lends a feeling of omnipresence, of being able to see into every corner of a place at once. Forget the political lines that divide the continents. Banish from your thoughts all the cultures that separate us. Look at the terrestrial world only in terms of its raw distribution and the cut of the land.

If you have not noticed them before, let me draw your attention to three improbably elongated appendages that exaggerate what we might otherwise regard as the classically proportioned Roman peninsula. They are the Malay Peninsula of Indochina, the Kamchatka Peninsula of far eastern Siberia, and the Baja California peninsula of North America. If the physical arrangement of any land possessed the power to compel someone to abandon home and family and repair to that place, then the raw shape of those lands should draw inquisitive people from far and wide. Some places are easier to reach than others. The adventuresome might succeed in exploring such novel places. But this does not prevent the rest of us from wondering what processes molded the shape of such land.

Now shift your gaze from land to sea. We spend most of our lives on land, and we accept its geography as something innately positive. But the boundaries of the marine realm also present distinct profiles. Why should any sea have the shape that it does? The Gulf of Siam off the Malay Peninsula and the Sea of Okhotsk that isolates the Kamchatka Peninsula from the rest of Siberia are not so strange in shape as the slender Gulf of California that separates Baja California from mainland Mexico. Why should such a long and narrow peninsula be situated adjacent to such a long and narrow body of water? As a geologist, this double conundrum amazed me. What did its apparent randomness mean? What answers awaited me on the far peninsular shores of such a place?

Let me begin by saying I never expected to travel anywhere south of the border between the United States of America and the United States of Mexico. I first saw these gulf waters on January 12, 1990, as I descended the winding road leading down the steep escarpment—dropping nearly 1,000 feet (300 m) in elevation—onto the narrow coastal plain north of Santa Rosalía. I felt electric with anticipation. I had expected the precipitous descent to Santa Rosalía, but the stunning blue of that sea is something not easily conveyed by any map. John Steinbeck, who sailed the Gulf of California with the biologist Ed Ricketts on the *Western Flyer* in 1940, claimed that the deep waters surrounding the Baja peninsula were something more than ultramarine in color, likening the tone to the flat uniformity of blue dye in a washbasin.[1] This color startled my sensibilities, pulling me farther into the landscape than I'd thought possible at the journey's start.

Prior to my ten years of visiting Baja California, I had considered myself a person of northern temperament, and I typically undertook research that would afford crisp summer days and long twilight shadows in higher latitudes, such as Canada, Scandinavia, and even Siberia. An avid map-gazer, I had been drawn to other landscapes and shorelines on the globe. The size and shape of Hudson Bay, for instance, eventually lured me to its Manitoba shores. Scandinavia, too, remains a place I visit frequently, although now more due to connections by marriage. Arctic Siberia is etched in my memory as a place of great danger where one must have faith in the people and means of transport to get to remote spots. Through my travels and research, I know how political boundaries and cultural differences are stubbornly difficult to separate from our notions of geography. Nevertheless, a thinking person can develop a deep, passionate relationship with a landscape based only on its physical terms, devoid of other considerations of birth or culture.

Landscapes exist. It follows that we may grow to love a place, almost any place, because we are mentally capable of reaching an understanding of how that place came to be. We can explore and discover what a place represents in terms of its natural heritage. Nature places its own boundary lines across the landscape and has done so throughout time. Our gift as an uncommonly perceptive and curious species is to wonder how nature has done so.

Is love too strong a word to describe our relationship to landscape? Consider the preamble to the national anthem of Norway:

Ja, vi elsker dette landet	Yes, we love this land
Som det stiger frem	As it rises forth
Furet, vaerbitt over vannet	Furrowed, weather-beaten over the water
Med de tusen hjem	With the thousand homes.[2]

Here is a statement in song that exceeds patriotic pride. It begins directly with an affirmation of love for the landscape. Clearly invoked is the image of the coastland arising from the ocean in the shape of steeply eroded fjords and their associated valleys. Although not Norwegian by birth, I recall my emotions at first hearing those words sung by a mixed chorus on the steps before the old

University Aula in Oslo on the opening day of the academic year. The melody, the blending of strong voices, and my comprehension of the words all combined instantly to bring tears to my eyes. At that time in my career, I had already spent a year living and working in Norway. I was becoming fluent in Norwegian language and culture, and I was much aware of how Norwegians enjoy their landscape both summer and winter, hiking and cross-country skiing. The sudden ease with which my emotions were stirred told me that I had been successfully absorbed by a culture with a strong nature ethic.

As I waited to board a flight on my first leg homeward from Norlisk in north-central Russia, a member of the geological party I had lived and worked with for the previous month made a bold inquiry. Did I know anything finer in America than the combination of rocks and landscape we had just experienced together on the wild rivers in Arctic Siberia? I answered that some landscapes simpler in geological structure and certainly less dramatic than the Anabar Dome might still be central to interpreting the prehistoric world. My colleague's corner of Arctic Siberia is a unique and thrilling combination of terrain and geology. Yet it is an apple that cannot easily be compared with an orange on another continent. This was a complicated idea to translate. We had been communicating in a mixed vocabulary of "Russlish," but it always fell to our official translator to add precision to our deliberations. Not infrequently, her analysis of the situation called for a dash of missing grace. I saw that she understood my predicament but also recognized the native pride felt by my colleague. Before I turned to leave, the translator took my arm and offered a tactful observation: "East or west," she said, "home is best." In order to love a landscape on its own terms, we must be willing to loosen ourselves from our national strictures and explore beyond our cultural safety net.

We can be attracted to foreign landscapes via different routes. The printed word draws some. The nature writer John Janovy was so inspired by John Steinbeck's pure descriptions in *The Log from the Sea of Cortez* that he was compelled to visit the Gulf of California. He subsequently wrote his own book on the region, *Vermilion Sea*. It begins with his departure by airplane from the Great Plains of Nebraska and his thoughts about what awaits him.[3] He speaks of Steinbeck's gulf as a mythical place surrounded by a magical landscape, contrasting it to the net of country roads that tamed his prairie home.

During the decade I have explored the landscapes and geology of Baja California, my host and field partner has been fellow geologist Jorge Ledesma, from the university in Ensenada. The intensity of field studies and life outdoors often transforms what might be only a professional acquaintance into a solid friendship. A good field partner is not easy to find. The relationship requires trusting another for your personal safety and thrives on the kind of give-and-take that allows each to offer ideas and interpretations (however wild) without fear of ridicule from the other. When it works to its best potential, a good field partnership helps you analyze all the vagaries of a landscape more expediently than would ever be possible alone.

Early on, I learned that the 1989 film *Dances with Wolves* had made a strong impression on Jorge. It celebrates the Great Plains as they were in 1865, just after the American Civil War. The hero is a young military officer who is drawn to the yet unspoiled terrain of the northern plains and is befriended by Sioux Indians. The movie inspired in Jorge a strong desire to experience the topography of the plains and see what was left of the once endless buffalo herds. Around a campfire under the shadows of spectacular scenery in his Baja California homeland, the irony struck me that Jorge Ledesma was lured by the artifice of a fictional film to see the flatlands, while from the other end of the axis, John Janovy's desire to see a humpback whale brought him to the Gulf of California. Jorge's dream was to ride horseback over the crest of a rolling hill and encounter a vast herd of buffalo.

My own path to Baja California took a circuitous route. I grew up on the former edge of the long-grass prairie in eastern Iowa. Flat sedimentary bedrock makes for a relatively level landscape there, and the rolling hills reflect little more than a three- or four-degree slope of interbedded sandstone, shale, and limestone dipping regionally to the southwest. The geomorphology of the prairie landscape is controlled by the changing surface expression of the bedrock, but the succession of sedimentary layers tells quite another story, about changes in ecosystems hundreds of millions of years ago. The limestone layers in eastern Iowa are full of fossils that caught my attention at an impressionable age. My father was a high-school biology teacher. When I showed him the fossils I had collected from a road construction site near our home, he explained how they represented the remains of marine life from a shallow salt sea that had covered the land long ago. Iowa is far from the nearest ocean, and the thought of so profound a change took an unyielding hold on my imagination.

One thing led to another, and I became a geologist and paleontologist intent on learning all I could about the marine life that populated those seaways of the Paleozoic Era. The general extent of flooding at any given time period during the Paleozoic is not complicated to show, but the actual water depth of the mid-continental Paleozoic seas is hard to appraise. I soon became embroiled in an arcane academic dispute over the rhythm and magnitude of sea-level fluctuations that long ago inundated the central core of North America.

As a map-gazer, I was drawn to the edge of Canada's expansive Hudson Bay, where some answers to the debate lay. Hardly an ordinary bay, it is the nearest embodiment to a huge inland salt sea anywhere in our present-day world. Hudson Bay makes a great indentation on the continent, covering 316,000 square miles (819,000 km²) with an average water depth of only 330 feet (100 m). The sea bottom is relatively smooth and flat. I was determined to see the bay in order to conceptualize, even vaguely, the Paleozoic seas of the upper Mississippi River valley. I made several summer trips to Churchill, Manitoba, between 1984 and 1987, where my students and I found superimposed on the present coast a former rocky shoreline dating from the seaway's early incursion about 445 million years ago.[4]

Three aspects of this spot enthralled me. First, the onshore marine rocks that bank against a hard bluff of Precambrian quartzite consist of limestone with eroded quartzite boulders and pebbles admixed. Today, thick limestone deposits accumulate mainly in the tropics and subtropics, indicating that the ancient Hudson Bay (and much of North America) was located far to the south during the Paleozoic Era. Second, we began to find fossil corals attached in growth position on the larger shore boulders. The old coastline had possessed its own ecosystem, complete with intertidal life. Third, the intact preservation of the former shoreline and the way in which it was gradually drowned showed that ancient water depth could be measured in a coastal setting. In the sinking of the old shore, we had a virtual meter stick to go by.

The limestone layers of eastern Iowa are as endless as the cornfields in their lateral extent, or so it seems. No former shoreline is exposed nearby, probably owing to the smoothness and fundamental flatness of the ancient seafloor. Without preservation of the Iowan coastline and its relationship to changing sea level, it is difficult to gauge in absolute numbers the changing depth of the marine waters that lapped onto and off the core of the North American continent during mid-Paleozoic times. I became obsessed with finding examples of other documented ancient shorelines. It soon became apparent that few such examples were known, compelling me to write a report titled "Why Are Ancient Rocky Shores So Uncommon?"[5] I expected to get some reaction from readers.

Not long afterward, I began to hear from Jorge Ledesma at the satellite campus of the Autonomous University of Baja California in Ensenada. He sent me a photo of a nearby rock outcrop with a caption on the back that read, "Are ancient rocky shores uncommon? Not here!" The accompanying letter came directly to the point: "Get a good [travel] grant and enjoy Baja California soon." That was it. Jorge was sure that the photographic evidence from a single good spot would prove irresistible. That is how I was lured to the "forgotten peninsula," as it was so aptly described by Joseph Wood Krutch.

The living landscape at any place on Earth's surface may or may not be directly connected with the former landscapes and ecosystems entombed in the underlying bedrock. We require some basic conceptual tools to unravel the ancient secrets of any landscape. Some coastal landscapes, such as the Norwegian fjords, are much easier to read than others, such as the karst topography around Gascoyne Junction in Western Australia.

The last remaining ice fields still cast an unmistakable morphological spell over the Norwegian landscape. Great ice sheets abandoned Scandinavia not long before the beginning of Holocene time, only 10,000 years ago. Multiple cycles of advancing and retreating ice ravaged the landscape for 2 million years, but the last great thaw in global temperature melted back the ice, leaving trademark signs that are geologically as fresh as yesterday. It was the flowing ice that sculpted the long fjords and their connected side valleys, leaving characteristic U-shaped profiles. Not all the ice has vanished; the Jostedal Glacier of southern Norway is the largest remaining ice field in continental Europe. It occupies a plateau 188 square miles (487 km^2) in area, with glacial ice that reaches a maximum thickness of 1,524 feet (500 m).[6] This glacier is only one of 1,593 scattered around Norway, but it dwarfs all of the other remnants. Although the total area of ice fields accounts for only 1 percent of the Norwegian landscape,[7] one need not travel far to see a live glacier.

The concept that describes this process is known to geologists as uniformitarianism.[8] The term refers to the idea that physical processes put into play by the likes of advancing glaciers, flowing rivers, or blowing wind are limited within a natural range of uniform rates essentially the same in the remote past as now. Physical geology students sometimes hear their teachers express this concept with the mantra, "The present is the key to the past." According to uniformitarianism, if you are able to see how the ice works in a living glacier, then you can understand how it formerly caused the erosion that created nearby U-shaped valleys and fjords.

In contrast to Norwegians, Australians might find the landscapes of their homeland puzzling. The bedrock geology of Australia disguises a more complex relationship with geologically older ecosystems. Unlike the central mountainous spine of Norway, which looms over the Scandinavian peninsula, vast lowlands dominate Australia, and fully one-third of the continent is taken up by desert.[9] A red residual soil called laterite is widespread in Australia, a characteristic that bespeaks a time some 30–60 million years ago when the entire continent experienced a far more humid environment, not unlike that of the Congo or Amazon River basin, where lateritic soils form today. The principle of uniformitarianism tells us that much.

The bedrock beneath the soils of Australia harks back even farther in time to an astonishing array of former environments and landscapes. One example illustrates the great complexity of superimposed landscapes. It involves limestone, a sedimentary rock that, under exposure to moderate to heavy rainfall, allows groundwater to dissolve and widen preexisting joints and fissures in the bedrock into a regular grid of open passageways. Below ground, the development of karst geomorphology may eventually form extensive caves. Above ground are features that sometimes assume the shape of orderly city blocks layered in concrete.

The most picturesque spot in Australia typical of such morphology lies on the north side of the Gascoyne River near a well site named Coronation bore, the only human landmark in the vicinity. Streetlike corridors cross at right angles along straight lines separated by rectangular limestone towers the size of two-story houses. Larger passages traverse the district like boulevards. An occasional limestone tower thrusts skyward as high as 98 feet (30 m). My exploration of these karst-eroded passages gave me the uncanny feeling of moving about an oddly deserted city. Only the sound of the wind brought an eerie, subdued voice to the empty passages.

The most important clue to this bizarre landscape is not the architectural limestone blocks but the altogether different rocks of the intervening alleyways. The corridors are paved with sandstone. On the outskirts of this stone city, it is possible to see where limestone towers stand half embedded in a sandstone matrix, as if a giant hand had filled the gridwork with tons of beach sand. Remarkably, this boxy landscape is now being exhumed from a protective sandstone cover by wind erosion. The natural cement that binds together grains of sand in the covering sandstone layers is weak compared with the bonds that harden the older limestone layers. Therefore, the sandstone erodes more readily than the exhumed limestone. The karst towers are the products of water seepage and dissolution, but under a former climate, long vanished. They stand now partially unveiled, like finished monuments from the landscape of a distant past. Today, coastal limestone towers of similar size and shape are found along Haiphong Bay in Vietnam and the Langkawi Islands of Malaysia and Thailand. Indeed, the present does provide us with needed insight in discerning improbable landscapes from the past. The remarkable work of early geologists gives us indispensable tools for interpreting such landscapes.

FEATURE / Nicolaus Steno and the First Laws of Stratigraphy

Uniformitarianism is a powerful tool that allows geologists and geomorphologists to understand the rock record and nature's limits in the development of landscapes. Other, more fundamental tools, however, are needed to understand nature's cumulative handiwork through geologic time. One of these is stratigraphy, or the study of layered rocks, primarily sedimentary rocks such as limestone, sandstone, and shale but also some volcanic rocks such as basalt flows and ash beds. The word "strata" refers to a sequence of layered rocks. A stratum is an individual bed within the sequence.

The earliest clearly articulated laws of stratigraphy date to the cogent field investigations of Niels Steensen (1631–1686), better known by the Latin version of his name, Nicolaus Steno. Niels Steensen grew up in Copenhagen, Denmark, where he was a precocious student who preferred the company of adults to that of children his own age.[10] Eventually, as a student of medicine, he became especially adept at the art of dissection, using animals and human cadavers. His education in anatomy continued in Amsterdam, Leyden, and Paris. In 1665, at the age of 27, Steno arrived in Florence, where he was soon awarded the post of court physician to the Grand Duke of Tuscany, Ferdinand II of the House of Medici. There, he joined the company of other scholars under Medici patronage in the Accademia del Cimento. None other than Galileo Galilei, who struggled to champion the heliocentric universe, had tutored Ferdinand II. The Tuscan environment nurtured scientific inquiry. Steno's court appointment and membership in the academy permitted him to travel locally and engage in varied researches. It was from Florence that the immigrant scholar explored the landscapes of the Arno River valley and surrounding hills of Tuscany, far from his native Denmark.

Two years after arriving in Florence, Steno wrote a pivotal paper on his dissection of an enormous shark's head.[11] Recorded as weighing 3,000 pounds, the animal was captured by fishermen near the port city of Livorno. What struck Steno was that the shark's abundant teeth were comparable in size and shape to objects commonly found buried in the hills far from the sea. The Roman naturalist Pliny the Elder (A.D. 23–79) had known about such objects and gave them the name *glossoptra,* or tongue stones. He maintained that "they resemble a man's tongue and grow not in the ground, but fall from the heavens during the eclipse of the moon." No one from Pliny's time recognized that the objects frequently exhibited a serrated edge, effective for cutting flesh, nor had anyone searched for an analogous structure in living animals. Steno clearly recognized the connection between glossoptra and living sharks but was puzzled over how an organic relic should come to be contained within another object as hard as stone.

So it happened that Steno launched himself on an inquiry that led to the publication in Latin in 1669 of his famous *Prodromus* (or preliminary treatise), otherwise known by its full and awkward title, *Dissertation Concerning a Solid Body Enclosed by Process of Nature Within a Solid.* In it Steno asserted that stony objects dug out of the ground that resemble sharks' teeth, shelled mollusks, or even plants differ from those objects only in color or weight. He went on to enunciate four observations of far-reaching importance about layered rocks with such reason and clarity that he speaks with a voice almost indistinguishable from a thinker contemporary with us. In translation from the original Latin, Steno argues:

1. If all the particles in a stony stratum are seen to be of the same character, and fine, it can in no wise be denied that this stratum was produced . . . from a fluid which at the time covered all things.
2. The comminuted matter of the strata could not have been reduced to that form unless, having been mixed with some fluid and then falling from its own weight, it had been spread out by the movement of the same superincumbent fluid.
3. At the time when any given stratum was being formed, all the matter resting upon it was fluid, and therefore, at the time when the lowest stratum was being formed, none of the upper strata existed.
4. At the time when one of the upper strata was being formed, the lower strata had already gained the consistency of a solid.[12]

The first two of these statements describe the law of original horizontality, which asserts that layered rocks originate as sediments that fall out evenly from a turbid fluid and come to rest as flat-lying deposits. The last two statements are regarded as the law of superposition, which infuses layered rocks with a sense of relative time. The layer at the bottom in a stack of horizontal strata was deposited first, and therefore is the oldest. The layer at the top was deposited last, and therefore is the youngest. In the original, Steno ordered the statements differently in different parts of the text. Nonetheless, it stands to reason that organic relics find their way to burial within strata during the process of sedimentation in an aqueous setting such as a river, lake, or sea. Moreover, it is clear that strata no longer found recumbent in a horizontal position were subsequently shifted and tilted by other processes at work within the Earth.

One of the few illustrations in Steno's *Prodromus* is a series of six cartoonlike panels depicting his interpretation of landscape development in the Arno River valley as related to stratified rock layers and their postdepositional modification (fig. 1). The series begins at the bottom of the page with a simple cross section through a complete sequence of horizontal strata, with the oldest layer on the bottom and the youngest on the top. The second panel, placed directly above the first, shows a large cavity eroded from the center of the section, perhaps by some agency of groundwater, but with the uppermost stratum still in place above the cavity like a roof. The third panel shows how the roof has collapsed into the cavity, causing parts of the layer to tilt downward along its walls. The fourth panel indicates how a new succession of strata may fill up the cavity with sedimentary rocks derived from waters that flood into the open trough. The latter demonstrates an important step, because it marks a natural break in the story, where a new chapter begins. The final two panels elaborate on the previous themes of cavity formation and collapse of tilted strata, as developed in the second and third panels. The ordering of Steno's panels from page bottom to page top is not accidental. Like the law of super-position he so clearly announced, the panels follow time, with the oldest scenario at the bottom and the most recent at the top.

When I view Steno's remarkable diagram, I am awed by the originality of a rational person who traveled far from home with an open mind and invested himself in an unfamiliar landscape. The diagram summarizes his interpretation of the relationships among horizontal and tilted sedimentary layers in the foothills bordering the Arno River valley. He was not fully confident about what forces in nature might have led the region's strata to tilt, but he mentioned the forces of water and fire, meaning volcanic activity. Steno did not record features of a karst topography, which involves the dissolution of limestone, in northern Italy. Instead, he clearly stated that most of the strata in the Arno Valley were composed of sandy beds with some clay intermixed.

Minus the development of tilted strata, the sequence of events Steno outlined may be applied to the landscape of the Gascoyne River area in Western Australia as a story told in two chapters. In the first, flat-lying sedimentary units are laid down in an aqueous environment. Later, they are uplifted and exposed to the air, then eroded by natural agents such that local topographic relief emerges. This topography is the staging ground for the second chapter, in which the landscape surface subsides, is reflooded, and inherits a new set of flat-lying strata that occupy the low ground. Renewed uplift and continued erosion are the climax of that chapter. The two subsets of stratified rock represented by the chapters meet at a physical junction separated only by an erosional surface. As I show later for coastal Baja California, Steno's basic outline, inclusive of tilted strata, may be adopted, with certain qualifications, to account for the birth of the Gulf of California.

In short, Nicolaus Steno used his keen intuition to tell a geological story both specific to a given place and universal in its applicability. It was a loss to the geological sciences that Steno quit his investigations on fossils and stratified rocks not long after publication of his *Prodromus*. He had been unable to comprehend the amount of geological time required for stratification to occur and for landscapes to be altered by erosion. An anatomist at heart, Steno returned home when he was offered a post at the university in his native Copenhagen. During his stay in Tuscany, however, the Dane had converted to Catholicism.

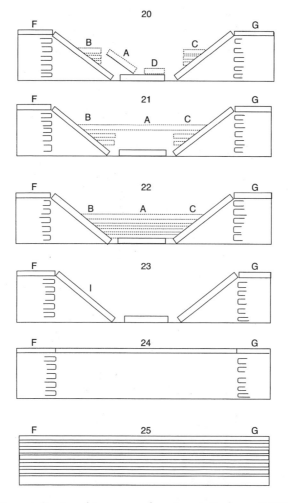

Figure 1. Stratigraphic sequence from Steno's *Prodromus* (1669).

Back at home in Denmark, religious intolerance made his new post untenable, and he resigned. Steno later took holy orders and ended his life as a prelate and vicar in Schwerin, northern Germany. His grave is located at the cloister of San Lorenzo in Florence, where a medallion portrait and an inscription in honor of his contributions to geology and anatomy were erected in 1881.[13]

A particular landscape at a given place may be so perfect in its shape and may so clearly outline the various chapters in its natural history that it becomes a standard by which to compare and contrast other, related landscapes. Such a spot may define the natural history of an entire region or all such analogous regions around the world, linking its distant past with its present so inexorably that we escape our limited sense of time and become inspired by the greater time scale of Earth's ecosystems.

The journey to Punta Chivato offers a look beyond the reflections of a beautiful sunset or a pleasing vista. Although Punta Chivato is a single point of land among hundreds, larger or smaller, that thrust into the Gulf of California, it is a rich microcosm that mirrors the major patterns of the more expansive gulf at its doorstep. Punta Chivato's landscape is neither as easy to decipher as Norway's recent glacial landscape nor as remote in time and difficult to interpret as the ancient landscapes of Australia. It is something more intermediate in complexity.

During his inaugural lecture as royal anatomist in Copenhagen in 1673, Nicolaus Steno spoke on the improvement of knowledge. "What we see is beautiful," he said, and "what we know more beautiful." But to this he added, "What we cannot grasp [is] most beautiful."[14] In seeking to understand a thing, let us say a landscape, do we commit a sacrilegious act against nature or some higher authority? There are those who do not wish to know how the mountain is made, for fear that knowledge of it will spoil its beauty. There are those who are afraid to explore the unknown, for fear that comprehension of it will spoil its place in our cosmology. Nicolaus Steno rejected that argument. Although deeply religious, he was not a close-minded person who refused to look through a telescope at the heavens because the sights so revealed might alter his worldview.[15] The property of mystery that makes a thing beautiful also attracts our untiring intellect. The most beautiful things in our universe drive us forward precisely because we have not yet taken their full measure.

The house of nature is full of inspiring landscapes. My reflections on the natural history of Punta Chivato trace an odyssey in a desert landscape on the edge of a new and bountiful sea. In making this journey, I relied on others, such as Nicolaus Steno, who stood behind me to remind me of the conceptual tools I would need to complete the search. My annual visits to Punta Chivato became explorations of time and place that took me in directions I never dreamed possible when I set out. For me, the experience was and is akin to watching the building of a great natural edifice by time-lapse photography. All the central secrets of its construction are revealed, except that you are an active participant because you can find and read the clues left buried in the scenery. It is an elegant nature film, and yet you realize, however faintly, that the film has no ending.

South Shore: Playa La Palmita on Bahía Santa Inés

This desert about us was once a vast sea, he said.
Can such a thing vanish? Of what are seas made? Or I? Or you?
—Cormac McCarthy, *Cities of the Plain*

It was a still, clear morning in April 1957, but the sun was already high. The tide was well out when the single-engine Ercoupe circled above Bahía Santa Inés and dropped over the low dark cliffs on Punta Mezquitito from the east to land on the empty stretch of a pocket beach. The small tires held firm on the wet sand. It was a tight fit, but there was some space left at the far end of the beach as the plane taxied to a stop near the brown slabs of sandstone that jutted into the water. From the air, Jim Johanson had seen only a single dwelling, the place called Casa Grande. He understood why someone might want to build here. He'd found nothing to surpass this place during the several years he'd been flying to the Gulf of California from Van Nuys in Alto (upper) California. Jim was a rocket-propulsion engineer for Rockwell International, devoted to his work but intensely attracted to the primitive lands on both shores of the Gulf of California. Every chance he had, he would make the two-day flight south to the midriff of the gulf, stopping over in San Felipe. Tall and lanky, Jim pulled himself from the cockpit of his aircraft. It was a beautiful day for a swim.

The view from the small beach across Bahía Santa Inés took in the remote tip of the Concepción Peninsula 16 miles (25 km) to the southeast. The white sands on nearby Playa La Palmita curved gently off to the southwest and melded into the craggy landscape, with the village of Mulegé in the far distance. Directly between these flanking vistas yawned the open mouth of Bahía Concepción, a place the naturalist Joseph Wood Krutch proclaimed "surely one of the great beauty spots of the world."[1] Jim would need to leave before the tide turned and advanced too far landward. When he swung the little Ercoupe around to face back down the beach, he promised himself that he would return someday to make his own home here. Forty years later, Jim Johanson finished his dream house. Set in the wall above the fireplace is a stained-glass window that depicts the majesty of the view from the south shore. No church window I know captures the essence of so tranquil a view.

At the beginning of the twenty-first century, the hotel launched by the original builders of the Casa Grande now stands in its fourth renaissance on the low cliffs at Punta Mezquitito. For most of its years it has gone by the name Hotel Punta Chivato. A dirt airstrip cuts across the plain above the south shore, but below the sheltering promontory to the north. Jim Johanson now has several expatriate American neighbors who, like himself, built their homes along the south shore. Smaller, less imposing homes dot the far end of Playa La Palmita as well. Before the paving of Mexican Federal Highway 1 was completed in 1971, it required two weeks of hard driving to come overland on perilous tracks from Tijuana in the north to La Paz in the south. That's how Joseph Wood Krutch arrived in Mulegé and how he continued south along the west side of Bahía Concepción over a path passable around the headlands on the beach only at low tide. The new transpeninsular highway opened the country and made the place more accessible to all sorts of people, including tourists, long-haul truckers, and naturalists.

Technically, Punta Chivato (Goat Point) is the name for the northeast corner of the larger peninsula that butts its way into the Gulf of California on an east-west axis. If you ask the way to Punta Mezquitito (Little Mesquite Point), the official map name for the southeast corner of the peninsula, where the hotel sits, no one will oblige you. Punta Chivato has become the name synonymous with the entire area. For me it has come to represent the promontory that looms above the nearby airstrip. This most prominent rise of land, too, has an official map name, Mesa Atravesada, denoting something that sits crosswise. Indeed, the land pushes itself squarely into the gulf. Viewed from here, however, the promontory rises like the broad, stooped shoulders of an old man facing north into the wind with head bowed out of sight.

Names are significant. They are affixed to the land by mapmakers, and they usually give the land some meaning. The American residents of Punta Chivato tend to ignore the names given by Mexican mapmakers. Standing in the shadows of the hotel on the cliff line, one may gaze west across the small beach where Jim Johanson first landed and follow the graceful curve of Playa La Palmita (Little Palm Beach) to the southeast. The Americans call the place Shell Beach, and that is where our walk takes us this morning (map 2). The only palm trees in sight are those planted around the hotel or the groomed gardens of the American homeowners. The full circuit will bring us over mostly level ground for a hike of about 4.3 miles (7 km). The name "Little Mesquite" for the rib of rock where we begin serves as a reminder that fresh water does not flow naturally in this land; mesquite is a drought-resistant native tree. Hotel Punta Chivato depends entirely on fresh water piped from wells some seven miles (11.25 km) away. Water availability is the dominant factor of human commerce in this region, but the wind is a close second.

Yesterday the wind was up. It has been blowing hard for the last three days, the locals tell me. This morning three shrimp trawlers and a sailboat lie at anchor in Bahía Santa Inés under the shelter of the Punta Chivato promontory.

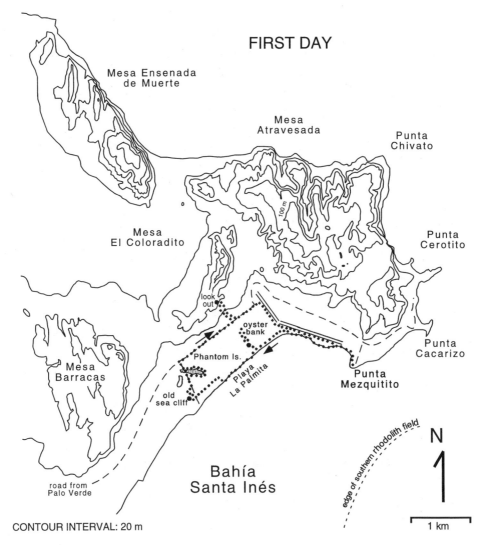

FIRST DAY

Mesa Ensenada
de Muerte

Mesa
Atravesada

Punta
Chivato

Mesa
El Coloradito

100 m

Punta
Cerotito

look
out

oyster
bank

Mesa
Barracas

Phantom Is.

Playa
La Palmita

Punta
Cacarizo

old
sea cliff

Punta
Mezquitito

edge of southern rhodolith field

N

Bahía
Santa Inés

road from
Palo Verde

CONTOUR INTERVAL: 20 m

1 km

Map 2. Route for Playa La Palmita.

Even if the wind continues to bluster today, our tour of the lowlands behind the treeless Playa La Palmita will remain comfortable. I tug against the visor of my hat, shoulder my backpack, and descend the road westward toward Jim Johanson's little beach. A boat ramp now resides there, and the sport fishermen have a cleaning station on the adjoining jetty, where pelicans flock at the sight of an incoming *panga*. In the darkness of the predawn hours, my light slumber was unbroken by the whine of outboard engines, and it appears that the fishermen stayed home today. The water on the bay is becalmed, and the vessels ride easy at anchor. Atop the sailboat in the outer part of the bay, a pennant barely flutters in a southerly direction.

A small rock exposure at the bottom of the hill reveals the structure of Punta Mezquitito and the entire rise on which the hotel sits. The rocks are dark in color, almost black when wetted by the waves, but show a reddish color under strong sunlight. Charles A. Anderson was the first geologist to set foot here. He spent all of one day late in 1940 in the vicinity of this headland on Bahía Santa Inés and never returned.[2] I imagine no signs of human occupation were evident when he disembarked from the research schooner *E. W. Scripps* for his traverse. Anderson identified the dark rocks at Punta Mezquitito as volcanic flows made of basalt with flecks of the green mineral olivine. Basalt is a rock more characteristic of the ocean floor and oceanic islands such as Hawaii. Basaltic rocks would not normally form a bay attached to a continent. This is perhaps our first hint of something special. Anderson allowed, however, that most of the igneous rocks in the region belonged to another type, andesite, lacking the olivine but including a dash of silica not present in basalt.

Below the road where it meets the beach are traces of brown sandstone in close contact with Anderson's basalt. These strata were originally muddy sands that washed against the shores of Punta Mezquitito. The sandstone extends inland to the north beneath the airstrip and along the base of the low rise that forms the spine of Punta Mezquitito. Outcrops of sandstone are clearly visible on the other side of the boat ramp and beach area farther to the west. We must pass this way along the south shore to reach the inner beach of Bahía Santa Inés. Water laps against the rocky slabs and washes gently back and forth along deep fissures that fracture the rock vertically. Now and then, it is possible to hear the gurgle of water beneath us, where the sandstone has been undercut. A blue heron *(Ardea herodias)* stands silently, like a mime artist, in the shallow water just off the blocky sandstone shore. He is there every morning and I greet him with a nod, like an old friend.

Along the shore about 1,500 feet (460 m) from the hotel, distinct patterns appear on the bedding surface of the sandstone. They look like trails, only 2 inches (5 cm) wide, permanently embossed in the rock. In fact they are the traces of burrows tunneled in soft muddy sands that later hardened into strata. There is no hint of the animal that made the burrows, but similar structures found today in warm-water lagoons are made by a small crustacean called the ghost shrimp. The burrows are typically horizontal, except for the short vertical entrance, where the shrimp creates a cone of surface debris scraped out from the tunnel network. These rocks and their trace fossils represent part of the ancient tidal flats of Bahía Santa Inés. Had it been possible to walk here long ago, only the cone-shaped mounds marking the entrances to the burrows would have been visible. We would sink ankle-deep into the dark sediments.

Near the end of low cliffs along the south shore, the first body fossils are exposed on the bedding surface of a tan sandstone. The fossils are sea biscuits, or heart urchins, echinoderms related to starfish but with a durable outer shell called a test. In life, these animals are covered by a stubble of spines, but only the test is preserved here. The scattered specimens are small—1 inch (1.5 cm) in diameter—and easy to overlook. I am reminded of plump candy drops, each unmistakably stamped with a design of five radiating petals. The raised attachment sites for the absent spines resemble sugar grains dusted across the test. The scientific name for this species is *Agassizia scorbiculata,* honoring the Swiss geologist-paleontologist Louis Agassiz (1807–1873), who established the Museum of Comparative Anatomy at Harvard University in 1860 but is most remembered for his contributions to glacial geology and his coinage of the term "ice age."[3] Unfortunately, this particular fossil tells us nothing about the age of the sandstone, because the species is still alive today. I leave the fossils to their slumber, for hammer and chisel leave ugly scars in the rocks. I prefer to collect photographs instead and leave the specimens behind for others to discover.

The orange windsock belonging to the airstrip rests limp on its staff in the distance to the west, beyond the last house and next pocket beach. We are well within the shelter of the bay. On the other side of the beach, thick layers of tan, silty sandstone beg to be climbed and explored. There, a single huge, exposed bedding plane reveals almost 200 fossil sand dollars stuck to the rock like saucers firmly nailed down on a table. These are much larger than the sea biscuits, about 3.5 inches (9 cm) in diameter, and easier to spot. Because the delicate echinoderms were sheltered from waves, many are perfectly preserved, showing a flat surface of five petal-like loops (fig. 2). These fossils reveal more than the sea biscuits, because they represent an extinct species limited to Lower Pliocene strata deposited between 3.5 million and 5 million years ago. The paleontologist J. Wyatt Durham, who accompanied Charles Anderson to the Gulf of California on the 1940 cruise of the *E. W. Scripps,* sorted out the vertical distribution of fossils through the sequence of sedimentary rock layers in this region.[4] As I look at the strata, I literally can see the layers of time from past to present: from Lower, Middle, and Upper Pliocene into the overlying Pleistocene. The upper layers include contemporary invertebrates.

This visual chronology helps reveal the structure of Bahía Santa Inés. The tan-brown sandstone along the south shore that includes the fossil sea urchins and sand dollars overlaps and abuts the dark basaltic rocks of Punta Mezquitito. If the sandstone is early Pliocene in age, then the abutting and underlying

Figure 2. Fossil sand dollars (Pliocene). Photo by author.

igneous rock must be older—probably late Miocene in age. The relationship is divulged like an intricate wood inlay. The volcanics are like a dense oak base, and the edging of Lower Pliocene sandstone beveled to fit its contour has the grain and hue of dusky ash.

South over Playa La Palmita, the landscape behind the beach sits below the margin of the Lower Pliocene sandstone. To reach the north corner of the beach and the lowlands beyond, one must follow a bench cut into the side of the sandstone strata or descend the steep track beyond the airfield windsock. Under a cloudless sky, the reflection of strong sunlight off the ground behind the beach dazzles me with its whiteness. The low, moundlike bluffs are not solid but consist of a stunning quantity of bleached and fragmented shells and other debris. This is a vast but uncemented rock ledge in the making, which geologists call an unconsolidated deposit. In terms of our structural inlay, the effect is rather like that of pine shavings and sawdust filling the contour of a half-bowl confined on the north by the ashen woodwork. On the skyline to the west looms a rocky ridge of reddish andesite called Mesa El Coloradito (Little Red Table). From our present vantage at the start of Playa La Palmita, I surmise that the muddy sandstone on our northern flank likely borders the unconsolidated deposit and dips underneath it to the south. Likewise, the volcanics of El

Coloradito in the background presumably disappear beneath both the loose shell deposit and the Lower Pliocene sandstone.

The vast shell deposit fronted by Playa La Palmita fascinates me. This white interior covers a sizable area of one-half square mile (1.5 km²). Any arroyo cutting across the low landscape to the beach will bring you to the center of this extraordinary place. In this case, I take the eighth arroyo on our southerly march—2,300 feet (700 m) down the beach—and head inland to where I camped on my first magical visit to Punta Chivato in 1991. This stream-dissected landscape was the extension of Bahía Santa Inés when sea level stood at least 20 feet (6 m) higher than today, some 125,000 years ago.[5] When global sea level fell rapidly during the last great glaciation to grip the Northern Hemisphere, only 21,000 years ago, this shallow seabed was abandoned to the sky, leaving everything precisely in place.

My fascination with this place stems from my childhood. Growing up in landlocked Iowa, I not only dreamed of visiting the ocean but wondered what it might be like to explore a seabed entirely drained of saltwater. Diving gear played no role in my vision, despite the boyhood allure of Captain Nemo's submarine, the *Nautilus,* and other fabulous equipment in Jules Verne's *Twenty Thousand Leagues under the Sea.* Instead, I wanted to walk unhampered on the exposed seabed and to hold its treasures up to the unfiltered light of day. The lowlands behind Playa La Palmita comprise the least disturbed fossil seabed I have ever explored. Here my childhood wish merges with my profession. Others, both paleontologists and marine biologists, who have accompanied me to this place never fail to leave without being deeply impressed by this snapshot of bygone life and the forces of nature that shaped such a vast deposit.

Chalky white shells of marine mollusks are strewn about the landscape, a child's and geologist's dream collection. In no time at all, it is possible to gather up a sampling representing more than a dozen species (fig. 3). The biggest clam is a Venus shell *(Dosinia ponderosa),* its valves as large as a salad plate. Growth lines clearly visible on the shell suggest that some individuals lived to the age of 15 years. Other thick-shelled bivalves include an ark shell *(Anadara multicostata),* a bittersweet shell *(Glycymeris maculata),* and a cockle *(Trachycardium consors).* Pronouncing the Latin names gives a pleasant jingle to my ears. Abundant pecten shells are scattered about, each with a prominent scar showing the attachment site of its circular muscle, stirring my hunger for fresh seafood. The more delicate jackknife clams belong to a larger species *(Tegelus californianus)* and a smaller species *(Tegelus politus).* Like the broader but streamlined tellen shells *(Tellina cumingii),* these are especially adapted for movement below the sediment surface. Open gaps in the paired shells enable the extrusion of a siphon from one end and a muscular foot from the other (the latter also very

Figure 3. Fossil shells (Pleistocene). Photo by author.

tasty). The rare occurrence of a mussel *(Modiolus capax)* is the only hint of a species adapted for life attached to boulders or a rocky shoreline. All the others represent shallow-water species typical of sandy flats.

The story told by the most common sea snails (gastropods) is much the same. You can easily pick out a conch *(Strombus gracilior),* a delicately spiny rock shell *(Murex tricoronis)*, a bullet-shaped cone shell *(Conus princeps)*, and a surprisingly high-spired auger shell *(Turritella gonostoma)*. A turban shell *(Turbo fluctuosus)* is the only abundant species often associated with rocky shores. Also found loose on the surface and fairly common are perfect sand dollars. The giant keyhole sand dollar *(Encope grandis)* is recognized by five notches on the circumference of the test and a single, large opening through the test. A related species *(Encope californica)* is distinguished by six open holes, all of which perforate the test. Virtually all of the fossil invertebrates from this expansive deposit are found readily alive today in the adjacent shallow waters of Bahía Santa Inés.

The few shells cited barely reflect the tremendous marine biodiversity of Bahía Santa Inés and the adjacent Gulf of California. As for the fossil shell beds, marine biologists studied this locality and counted more than 86 species of extant marine invertebrates. An early visitor impressed by this place, William Beebe (1877–1962), visited Bahía Santa Inés in 1936 aboard the yacht *Zaca* and later commented on the abundance of Late Pleistocene fossils behind the beach.[6] He was an experienced hose-and-helmet diver, as well as the co-inventor of the bathysphere. With his partner Otis Barton, Beebe had set a new diving record of 3,028 feet (923 m) two years before, in 1934.[7] He was a genuine flesh-and-blood explorer and promoter of the ocean depths, the scientific likes of Jules Verne's fictional Captain Nemo. Apparently, life in the deep sea kept Beebe sufficiently occupied that nothing directly developed from his visit to Bahía Santa Inés. It was not until 1953 that G. D. Hanna and J. R. Slevin gathered the fossils from which the most accurate species count from the shell beds at Playa La Palmita was eventually made. Their collection of 86 species now resides with the California Academy of Sciences in San Francisco.

The raw numbers are important, but there are more striking ecological aspects of the Playa La Palmita deposit. In particular, the mass of shells is not extensively fragmented, winnowed, or heaped about at random. Rather, the deposit retains much of its original context of habitat zones, so that as you wander around, you may recognize even today the distribution of species with their associated environments. The adventure in exploring this abandoned seabed is heightened by the many dry streambeds that dissect it. These create cross sections that provide the means to piece together a three-dimensional picture of the old embayment that no dry species list can match.

The eighth arroyo from the north is the longest to cross the plain behind Playa La Palmita. It extends for about 0.3 mile (0.5 kilometer) inland and eventually intersects the former shoreline of Bahía Santa Inés. The arroyo mouth cuts almost 10 feet (3 m) into the old seabed near the present beach, exposing only poorly consolidated material. A short distance up the arroyo, however, an oval-shaped mound of bedrock about 100 feet long (some 30 m) is profiled on the south bank. The mound is oriented perpendicular to the present shoreline of Bahía Santa Inés and is composed of brown, silty sandstone of the same kind as on the south shore. The bay is indeed a half basin unevenly scooped out from Lower Pliocene bedrock. The mound is draped with intact fossil oysters with valves united and in growth position. Thousands of individuals stare back blankly from this once great oyster bar. Small islands of sandstone provided a hard surface for the development of colonies slightly elevated above the surrounding seafloor. Once the pioneer colony was anchored in place, subsequent generations settled atop the shells of their parents. The oyster bank is 22 inches (40 cm) thick. Allowing a dozen years per layer of colonizing individuals, the bank was replenished over no less than a 50-year interval. Traces of similar oyster banks occur in adjacent arroyos.

Directly above the great oyster colony rests a layer of volcanic pebbles and cobbles mixed with shells. Almost all the clasts are composed of dark basalt or andesite, but a few pebbles consist of granite of a salt-and-pepper complexion. This cobble layer may be traced far inland as a finger along the arroyo walls. The coarse layer marks the doom of the oyster colony by suffocation from debris swept off the slopes of nearby Mesa El Coloradito during a flash flood. The oyster colony never recovered. What is mysterious about the granite pebbles is that none of the surrounding countryside reveals obvious exposures of granite uplands that might have served as a source. Not every peculiarity has a ready solution, and the answer to this small problem must await the unexpected evidence that will surface on another day.

Above the distinctive line of cobbles, the loose shell beds of the old embayment are well exposed along the arroyo walls. The shells rest in a finely broken matrix. Now and then in this matrix, it is possible to find an oddly shaped organic relic known as a rhodolith (see fig. 4), a ball-like colony in the tribe of red coralline algae, not reported by Hanna and Slevin in their master taxonomic list. These calcareous colonies are reminiscent of delicate corals, with fine to stumpy branches that radiate to the size of a golf ball or somewhat larger. Whereas related algae simply encrust the surfaces of shells or boulders, these colonies roll about the seafloor with the gentle push and pull of bottom currents or waves at depths between about 6.5 and 40 feet (2 to 12 m). They are skeletal algae that grow into a spherical shape because the colony is in more or less constant motion under clear, sunlit water.[8] Fully 60 percent of the bleached bulk mass of the shell deposit exposed in this arroyo is derived from crushed rhodoliths. Because the skeletons of these algae are composed of calcium carbonate ($CaCO_3$), as are the shells of all the associated marine invertebrates, the entire deposit of unconsolidated material is forming a massive limestone shelf above the Lower Pliocene bedrock. The debris represents rhodolith colonies that were washed shoreward and subsequently fragmented under their own weight and the violence of occasional storms. Thus, the structure of this old embayment was created by a continuous importation of crushed rhodoliths from the sea and the occasional rapid expulsion of volcanic pebbles and cobbles from the surrounding land.

The dry streambed follows a winding path that leads ever closer to the old shoreline. I uneasily skirt a thorny palo Adán *(Fouquieria diguetii),* a treelike shrub in the ocotillo family, preferring the friendlier and decidedly more aromatic copal *(Bursera hindsiana),* a small tree in the torchwood family. These plants enjoy the protection of the arroyo and its occasional channeled water. But the trees give me the unwelcome reminder that I am on dry land. I don't want the spell of my visitation to the old seabed broken, and the branches of the vegetation obscure the arroyo walls. Suddenly, however, I encounter a stretch of arroyo wall in which numerous articulated jackknife clams are exposed in their characteristic vertical burrows. These bivalves are closely related to the family of razor clams, so called because of their resemblance to an old-fashioned straight-edge razor folded back in its slightly curved, elongated handle. Razor and jackknife clams burrow by extending their fleshy feet into the seabed and gaining a purchase on the surrounding sediments by engorging the foot with blood. In withdrawing the extended foot into the shell, the clam winches itself downward.

By repeatedly extending and withdrawing the foot, these clams can swiftly retreat from predators or other natural disturbances on the seafloor. Seeing them tells me this is the former zone of shoal water on the old embayment, but it also returns me to one of my earliest recollections of the seashore. When I was 17, I had the good fortune to spend the summer with a warm and caring family in Portugal. Members of this extended family made frequent trips from Lisbon to the seashore and gave me my first prolonged exposure to the ocean. Somewhere near Nazaré my hosts took me on an expedition to gather razor clams on the tidal flats. It is impossible to dig the clams out by hand. They are too fast. By baiting the opening to their burrows with the dried essence of ocean from a salt shaker, we could trick the clams into extruding their siphon above the surface. One at a time, they were assured that the tide had turned and it was safe once again to take in fresh seawater. My Portuguese brother, sister, and cousins waited with ready fingers to pull them up like carrots from the garden. Fried in olive oil with a dash of garlic, those clams offered my first taste of the molluscan fruit of the sea.

Farther along the streambed, the walls of the arroyo dwindle to knee height or less and merge onto the open plain. Here and there, patches of the limey ground are cemented as a pavement. The frequent wetting and drying of fine carbonate sand under intertidal conditions produced these pavements, sometimes called beach rock by geologists. Tiny vertical holes less than an inch (1.5 cm) in diameter puncture the pavements, and each reveals the siphonal end of a pholad bivalve *(Thracia curta)*. Unlike jackknife clams, which burrow into soft sediment, these clams are capable of boring into a hard substrate. Penetration is achieved through mechanical abrasion, assisted in some species by the secretion of a weak organic acid sufficient to dissolve or loosen material from the bedrock. Nearby, andesite pebbles are scattered along the former shoreline. Each is partially encrusted by thin layers of red coralline algae, added as the pebbles rolled in now-vanished waves.

It is late morning and the sun is overhead. Returning through the arroyo to present-day Shell Beach, I thankfully shed hot boots and sweaty socks and cool off in the gently lapping waves. Beachcombing offers the perfect excuse to seek out the descendants of the same chalky species observed as fossils in the arroyo. Every day is a little different. Today, many of the high-spired shells belonging to the auger shell *(Turritella gonostoma)* are washed up on the beach. Their purplish brown with mottled checks of cream is fresh and vibrant. Their color is like a splash of cold water, rousing me from a dream of many thousand yesteryears. Now and again, there is a small conch *(Strombus gracilior),* yellowish brown overall with the aperture white but edged in orange brown. At a distance, a mussel *(Modiolus capax)* is easy to spot, its shell a shocking orange brown color. Only the occasional Venus shell *(Dosinia ponderosa)* turns up as purely white as the fossils of its bleached forebears. Sampled in the adjacent shell beds and subjected to radiometric dating in the laboratory, Venus shells reveal the decay of tiny amounts of radioactive lead that dates the fossils to the last interglacial epoch of the late Pleistocene, about 125,000 years ago.

Making my way down Playa La Palmita, crossing the width of the beach to the water's edge and back again, I am forcibly reminded that the berm is a place where occasional storms and the highest tides lay down a shingle of shells. Back on go my boots. The narrow, chaotic deposit of wave-tossed shells on the berm is entirely contrary to the expansive, undisturbed fossil beds just explored.

Three-quarters of the way farther along Playa La Palmita, another prominent arroyo leads onto the Late Pleistocene seabed. It is the fifteenth arroyo from the north end of the beach. Although it would take too long to explore the plain to the northwest, stopping to look at the fossil composition at the arroyo opening is worthwhile. As before, the arroyo walls reach to about 10 feet (3 m), but instead of continuing on a winding path the arroyo quickly opens into a broad depression. Shade from a wall facing northeast provides some relief from

Figure 4. A fossil rhodolith and dense rhodolith debris (Pleistocene).
Photo by author.

the intense sunshine. The outcrop here is different. In making our way south along the curve of the beach, we have moved more centrally into the outer part of the Late Pleistocene seabed. Whereas the unconsolidated material examined earlier is 60-percent composed of rhodolith debris by bulk, here the percentage is 90 or better (fig. 4). These sediments also contain more silt.

Here, in this part of the old seabed, the diversity of species is much diminished, and it is difficult to spot any fossil shells. Where a sizable piece of shell protrudes from the arroyo wall, I use the pick end of my geology hammer to dig it out. It is a giant clam known as the geoduck. This species *(Panopea globosa)* has a shell that reaches more than 6 inches (16 cm) in length. By habit, it is a deep burrower capable of digging permanent dwelling places up to 4.25 feet (1.3 m) deep. The specimen is complete, with both valves preserved. The paired shells resemble a section of heavy industrial tubing parted lengthwise in two matching halves. The large gaps in the articulated shells provide space for extrusion of the clam's massive digging foot at one end and long siphons at the other. In life, the siphons are permanently extruded and may reach a length more than twice that of the shell. The edible geoduck is not especially common in the Gulf of California; it is far better known from temperate latitudes along the Pacific shores of North America. The name is believed to derive from the words for "dig deep" in the language of the Nisqually Indians of British Columbia, where the clam typically dwells in the sandy mud of protected bays.[9] This particular species has a known range today from San Felipe in the north of Baja California to this vicinity in the south.[10]

Here is another mystery the likes of which were noted by Steinbeck. How does a temperate marine species come to inhabit the upper reaches of the Gulf of California when the lower gulf is home mainly to tropical species? Steinbeck cited the example of a cold-water crab *(Pachygrapsus crassipes)* that commonly ranges from Oregon south to California on the Pacific coast but also occurs north of Loreto in the Gulf of California. "These animals are apparently trapped in a blind alley with no members of their kind to the south of them," he wrote.[11] Whether a crab or a geoduck, how did these animals shift south from relatively cold waters to relatively warm waters at the tip of Baja California and then move north again into the upper part of the gulf to colonize cooler waters? One explanation advanced by a marine biologist who thought about the problem early on was that a marine passage once crossed the peninsula far to the north. Such a geographic shortcut would obviate the need for the long trip around the end of the peninsula. Steinbeck noted that the mountainous ridges of the northern peninsula and their geological record did not support the hypothesis. He had no other answer to the riddle. A likely solution is climatic shifts associated with the advance and retreat of the great Northern Hemisphere glaciers. Louis Agassiz mistakenly believed there was only a single great Ice Age, but there were in fact several during the last 2 million years.

The geoducks must have arrived in Bahía Santa Inés prior to the last great glacial epoch, because we find its fossil remains buried in the abandoned seabed that dates from the last interglacial epoch. The exact timing of its arrival is less important than the hypothesis that the waters around the tip of Baja California were colder during intervals of extensive Northern Hemisphere glaciation than they are today. The periodic chilling of those waters would have permitted more temperate marine species to migrate around the tip of the peninsula into the Gulf of California. With the return of semitropical to tropical climates in the south during interglacial epochs, the immigrants, accustomed to temperate waters, would have been trapped in the gulf, where we find them today. Indeed, if global temperatures were to warm significantly, the geoduck and other temperate species might well go locally extinct because they have no place to retreat. The present habitat of geoducks in the Gulf of California ranges from shallow to offshore waters at a maximum depth of almost 200 feet (60 m).[12] By whatever means the geoduck first arrived in Bahía Santa Inés, its ancestor lived closer to shore than the species does today.

Even the most casual traveler in these parts must wonder why the beaches are filled with white sand when the landscape is so overshadowed by dark, igneous rocks such as basalt or the more pervasive andesite. It is the scant transport of terrestrial material from the uplands to the gulf coast, along with the high input of organic material onshore from the bountiful sea, that creates these startling beaches. Rainfall in the central desert adjacent to the Gulf of California amounts to only 2 inches (5 cm) in an average year.[13] Tropical hurricanes (called *chubascos* by the locals) may drop more significant local rainfall; such a downpour in Late Pliocene times caused the heavy runoff that smothered the oyster bank. Nonetheless, erosion by running water in a desert environment is minimal over the short term. The white beaches along this part of the gulf are composed not of silica sand (SiO_2), derived from the erosion of silica-rich rocks, but of calcium carbonate ($CaCo_3$) from the breakdown of shells and skeletons of marine organisms.

Michael Foster, from the Moss Landing Marine Laboratories in California, taught me the importance of rhodoliths as an unheralded source of calcium-carbonate sand. We met by chance during my second trip to Baja California Sur, in 1991. I was camped with my family and a research student, Marshall Hayes, on a scenic stretch of beach connecting Isla Requesón to the peninsular mainland in nearby Bahía Concepción. Marshall was my first research student in Baja California, and together we studied the intertidal zonation of marine invertebrates on rocky shorelines in the gulf. Every morning, he and I would cross over to the small island to map its shoreline and take a census of the abundant organisms living on the rocky shores. If the tide was out, we could walk the full length of the beach to the island. If the tide was in, we had to wade across the middle section of the spit. After a week's time, we were surprised by several vehicles that crossed to the far end of the beach, where no one ever camped. We laughed, knowing that the group would be cut off by the tide in the morning.

Next morning the new campsite was cut off by the tide, just as we had predicted, but the vehicles and tents were dry at the water's edge. This was my introduction to the flamboyant Mike Foster, whose California plates on his pickup truck read "Captn Kelp." Mike is an algologist, a marine biologist who specializes in the study of algae. He had been to Isla Requesón before and knew what he was doing. On this trip, he was leading an expedition from Moss Landing to map and study the living rhodolith beds in water 20–40 feet (6–12 m) deep around the island. Mike showed me my first rhodolith, and I instantly understood where the white carbonate sand on our beach had come from and how it was replenished. The tips of the rhodolith branches typically have a pustular or lumpy appearance that looks something like cottage cheese. When the broken rhodoliths wash ashore, they lose their pink coloration and soon are bleached white by the sun. In Spanish, as I was soon to discover, *requesón* refers to "curdled milk," or cottage cheese. The local inhabitants well know the meaning of Isla Requesón.

Mike is an inventive fellow. When he needed to retrieve a core sample from one of his rhodolith beds, he jury-rigged a coring device from a tequila bottle. I convinced him to publish on Gulf of California rhodoliths in a technical volume that I helped to edit. The black-and-white photo in the article shows Mike's tequila bottle perfectly filled with rhodoliths in life position, as neat and pretty as a model ship in a bottle. The core demonstrates that the living beds form a surface layer only 2–4 inches (5–10 cm) thick that rapidly grades into a rubble of broken rhodoliths and finally dark, oxygen-starved sediments. Mike had cut away the bottom of the bottle and used the neck to push the device into the seabed.

Mike's total enthusiasm for his research is such that we became good friends and correspondents. When I first found and recognized fossil rhodoliths and their abundant debris in the Playa La Palmita deposit, I urged him to visit me at Punta Chivato. We walked the arroyos with our students and sat on the ancient seabed at Playa La Palmita. Mike had never seen fossil rhodoliths outside of museum collections. He was delighted with the abandoned seabed, but he was more than doubtful when I pressed him to search for living rhodolith beds just offshore in Bahía Santa Inés. A year later, the initial search was still unsuccessful, because the beds are located farther offshore than I had anticipated. Eventually Mike found the bay to harbor three immense rhodolith beds, the largest yet known in the Gulf of California. Two of them measure each more than a half mile (0.8 km) across and greater than 2.5 miles (4 km) long. The precise dimensions of the beds are impractical to define using scuba gear. Mike believes that more sophisticated use of side-scan radar and towed video equipment may be necessary to complete the investigation. Here, then, is a case of uniformitarianism in reverse—the past was key to the present. Someday, I will don scuba equipment and visit the rhodolith fields of Bahía Santa Inés.

Rested now, we are ready to continue our exploration of the old seabed. Several new homes congest the far end of the beach, and it is best to skirt around the rear of these structures to the southwest. No permanent building stood here in 1995. Our goal is to reach the south margin of the fossil beds situated in the last arroyo, about 1,300 feet (400 m) away. We climb the west bank of the large depression, traverse the plain, and cross another arroyo and another flat stretch interrupted by a dirt road before reaching our destination. Once across the road, it is clear that something different awaits us in the next arroyo. The coloration of the landscape supplies the clue. The previous arroyo embankments, the surface of the plain, and the road are white. Ahead, the red stain of andesite rocks is splashed across the ground. The southern edge of the abandoned seabed is wedged against volcanic rocks; the Lower Pliocene sandstone that underlies the Pleistocene basin and forms its northern margin is absent from this side of the embayment.

About 1,000 feet (300 m) from the beach, the present arroyo exposes an ancient sea cliff with 6.5 feet (2 m) of relief. The dry streambed meanders, like all the others that dissect the plain. In this arroyo, the west wall often exposes solid volcanics, while the opposite wall cuts through the loose, white carbonates of the old seabed. Here the streambed twists in just the right way to produce a superb cross section that shows how the 125,000 year old carbonate sediments bank directly against the volcanics. I grin because I recall my first visit to Isla Requesón, when I saw white carbonate sands brush against red volcanic cliffs in the living world. There, Marshall Hayes and I predicted the kinds of fossils that might be preserved in a sea cliff buried by sand derived from adjacent rhodolith fields. Before us now is the materialization of that prophecy. Marshall, who went on to his own graduate studies, never had the opportunity to visit this spot. Another student, Laura Libbey, discovered this place. She knew she had struck intellectual gold the moment she rounded the bend in the arroyo.

Both the ancient cliff face and the eroded andesite boulders associated with it are densely encrusted by coralline red algae, various articulated bivalves, barnacles, and one species of tiny cup coral (fig. 5). There are two species of large oysters, as well as an ark shell and others that typically cement themselves to or wedge themselves among the rocks *(Cardita affinis* and *Chama mexicana).* Many additional mollusks found elsewhere on the old seabed also occur within the deposit overlying the abandoned sea cliff. Gastropods indicative of an intertidal setting *(Turbo fluctuosus* and *Cerithium maculosum)* are quite abundant. Although the fossils are bleached white, the condition of this specialized rocky-shore biota is amazingly fresh, as if the sea had retreated only yesterday.

Connected to the old sea cliff is a tidal platform that extends from the top of the cliff more than 200 feet (60 m) inland to the northwest atop the west bank of the arroyo. Clusters of oysters encrust parts of the platform. Elsewhere, dense populations of a pholad bivalve, each about the size of a person's thumb, bore the surface in profusion. This is the same species encountered earlier, at the end of the arroyo leading inland from the oyster bank. The red rock into which these bivalves bored is extremely dense. Laboratory analysis of a sample collected from the platform proves that the hard rock is dolomite, a variety of limestone enriched with the element magnesium. This particular dolomite is locally confined, however, and shows no traces of broken shells. I suspect it represents chemical precipitation from a hydrothermal source. Traces of the

Figure 5. Fossil shells, coral, and algae encrusting an ancient cliff face (Pleistocene).
Photo by author.

blue-green mineral malachite, a copper ore, also occur just here. Hot springs are found in many parts of the Baja California peninsula, and mineral precipitation is a related feature. This former spring was somewhat unusual in that it issued adjacent to the old shoreline and was drowned by a rising sea level. Although the red dolomite is quite hard, the boring bivalves thrived here because they were able to penetrate the surface using biochemical means.

We have continued inland along the present arroyo, where a narrowing streambed is deeply incised in andesite bedrock and the cover of unconsolidated carbonate sands gradually shrinks to less than 3 feet (1 m) thick. This is the apogee of today's circuit. From here, we turn back toward the dirt road that diverges from the arroyo on a northwest bearing, away from the coast, to intersect the main road to Hotel Punta Chivato.

Artificial or otherwise, a road is not merely a conveyance from one point to another on a map; rather, it reveals the landscape it traverses. It is a valuable source of information every step of the way. Some 820 feet (250 m) farther inland on this road, there is a subtle rise, less than 5 feet (1.5 m) in elevation. Precisely at the toe of the rise, the dirt on the road surface changes from white to pink. Leaving the old seabed of Bahía Santa Inés, we literally step over a former shoreline onto land. The distance inland from the present shore on the bay is about 2,000 feet (600 m), and the base of the rise is approximately 36 feet (11 m) above present sea level. If, as we know, worldwide sea level reached only 20 feet (6 m) above present sea level 125,000 years ago, and we have explored the same ancient seabed most of the day, then why should this landfall reach so much higher than the global average? The top of the abandoned sea cliff behind us is situated near the predicted level for the last interglacial epoch—a little more than 20 feet (6 m) above present sea level. Here, we stand nearly twice as high in elevation as the old sea cliff. This new mystery is one that must be pondered a while longer.

The challenge right now is to quit the road and follow the modest change in elevation and associated colors along the old shoreline. The broken trail of evidence completes an elliptical path and returns to the same place on the road (map 2). Our encounter is with a small abandoned island of deeply weathered andesite volcanics measuring 1,300 feet (400 m) long and 250 feet (75 m) wide on an east-west orientation. It is so obscure in profile that the students who first walked its shores with me insisted on giving it the name Isla Fantasma (Phantom Island). As at the old sea cliff, the paleobiological relationships found along the margins of this island exude the odd but exciting feeling of a place only recently left by the sea. A few steps away from the first rise in the road, numerous great conchs *(Strombus galeatus)* lie strewn over the landscape. It is a species we have not found before now. This is the largest surviving gastropod in the Gulf of California, with an adult shell length of 10 inches (25 cm). Its present habitat throughout the gulf is characterized by intertidal to subtidal sand flats, rocky rubble, and water depths of less than 150 feet (45 m). These old fellows clearly shuffled along near the shoreline.

At the eastern terminus of the old island, a narrow arroyo is entrenched in soft sediments bordering on igneous rocks. The streambed exposes a margin of the former, rocky shoreline, complete with an apron of cemented cobbles. There, peering through the thorny underbrush, we may find whole shells of the bivalves *Codakia distinguenda* and *Periglypta multicostata* wedged among andesite cobbles, as in life. I have not seen these large species before, either on Shell Beach or elsewhere on the old seabed of Bahía Santa Inés. A member of the lucinid family with its distinctively elongated muscle scar on the rear inside of the shell, this species of *Codakia* exhibits a fine external pattern of closely etched, semicircular growth lines intersected by equally spaced radial lines emanating from its small but well-defined beak. The largest adult specimens I have found as fossils commonly reach 5.5 inches (14 cm) in diameter. The living species has a preference for flats at the extreme low tide level. *Periglypta* is a member of the venerid family of Venus shells, the most robust of its kind in the Gulf of California. More obese but smaller than *Codakia,* with an adult shell length of 4.75 inches (12 cm), this species of *Periglypta* shows deeply incised growth lines superimposed by radial lines that are faint by comparison. The overall effect of the exterior shell is that of a finely checkered pattern that trips a wave of shadows in the strong sunlight. The living species inhabits rocks at the extreme low tide level. Preserved in growth position on the fringe of Phantom Island, these fossil bivalves are caught in time in full character. Photograph them, but leave them for others to marvel at.

I wonder how many people have raced back and forth on this access road without realizing that the hollow they feel in the pit of their stomach is the result of their sudden lift across the neck of a small, forgotten island, now choked with dust. This is the secret this strange place hides, ironically, in the open landscape. Leaving the Pleistocene island behind, the road intersects with the trunk road to Punta Chivato after a short distance. The sun beats down on our shoulders as we trek northwest on the main road beneath the early shadows cast by Mesa El Coloradito. The shoreline of the former seabed runs sometimes at our feet but otherwise parallel to our path on the right. There is a vantage point no more than 0.8 mile (1.3 km) down the road where cream-colored rocks appear to rest against the slopes of the Little Red Table on the left. It requires only a brief side excursion from the main road and a gentle climb to reach the perch. For most of the ascent, reddish soil eroded from andesite bedrock covers the slope. The cream-colored layers sit atop a thin rock ledge, separated from the higher crest of the mesa. To the southeast, the exposed, white Pleistocene seabed is framed in reflected sunlight against the pale aquamarine of Bahía Santa Inés.

The cream-colored beds at our feet are limestone, which I confirm by placing a single drop of dilute hydrochloric acid (from the small acid bottle I carry for just this purpose) on a freshly broken surface of the rock. The acid reacts with the limestone to produce a brief but furious stream of bubbles. The limestone represents the traces of another marine basin that adheres stubbornly against the side of the volcanic mesa. There are no obvious fossils to pick over, but here and there are fragments of oyster shells. I strike a detached slab of the rock with my geology hammer, and it rings like a bell. The layers are well packed and firmly cemented. I am cautious, because cavities eroded in the limestone, as well as the shelter of broken slabs that slump off the outcrop, make ideal homes for rattlesnakes. Had they been here, they almost surely heard our noisy approach from a distance and retreated.

The airstrip and the south shore's edging of brown Pliocene sandstone are below us to the east. On the lower slopes of the Punta Chivato promontory appear similar traces of creamy stratified rocks at about the same elevation as our present perch. The visual effect is something like peering over the edge of a giant bathtub and surveying the curve of a persistent ring left behind after dirty bathwater drained away. If you allow your eyes to follow the flank of Mesa El Coloradito at approximately the 130-foot (40-m) contour line, you will see clearly that the limestone is discontinuous. The dirty ring has been partially scrubbed away in places. What is the relative age of these more elevated limestone layers? How do they relate to the brown sandstone—with its abundant Lower Pliocene sand dollars and sea biscuits—which formed a corner of the basin and predated the Late Pleistocene seabed of Bahía Santa Inés?

FEATURE / Benoît de Maillet and the Diminution of the Sea

The laws of stratigraphy promulgated by Nicolaus Steno during the later half of the seventeenth century are a starting point in interpreting rock layers that are older or younger than others. Those simple laws explain how to recognize natural breaks in the rock record, like those seen in Steno's tilted strata. Subsequent innovations on this theme, however, brought additional clarity to the search for profound chapter breaks in the geological history of our planet. Such divisions in the rock record are associated with what geologists call "unconformities." Rock layers said to "conform" to one another are those that follow one after the other in a continuous sequence unbroken in time. An unconformity is a boundary separating two groups of rocks that fail to conform. That boundary invariably represents a lapse of time, during which part of the succession was reduced by erosion. The Frenchman Benoît de Maillet (1656–1738) was the earliest person to conceive and articulate a model of this rock cycle based on changes in global sea level.

De Maillet's book, entitled *Telliamed, or Conversations between an Indian Philosopher and a French Missionary on the Diminution of the Sea,* was published posthumously in 1748.[14] Although the book was meant to be anonymous, the astute reader will recognize that Telliamed is de Maillet's name spelled backward. Only 25 years younger than Nicholaus Steno, Benoît de Maillet apparently wrote and refined his manuscript on the global retreat of the sea during the years shortly before and after 1700. Private manuscript copies circulated in Europe during the author's lifetime. The earliest printed edition of the book appeared in Amsterdam, 79 years after Steno's *Prodromus.* Steno submitted his manuscript for formal censorship by the authorities in Florence and won certification that its contents represented nothing contrary to the Christian faith. De Maillet's manuscript underwent no such scrutiny in Amsterdam. Its contents, in fact, scandalized the orthodox establishment with bold pronouncements on a world reckoned to be at least 2 billion years in age. De Maillet attempted to protect himself through the ruse that the ideas expressed in his manuscript were not his own but those communicated by an Indian thinker outside the pale of Christian doctrine.

Not much is known about the early life of Benoît de Maillet. He belonged to an aristocratic family and was well educated. From 1692 until 1708, he served as the general consul of France in Egypt. He held other official posts representing France in the Near East and North Africa from 1708 to 1720. His 28 years of government service abroad allowed him ample opportunity for travel and geological observations along the shores of the Mediterranean Sea, including southern Europe. De Maillet also traveled in Tuscany, where he saw and interpreted the same landscape experienced by Steno. There is no evidence, however, that he was aware of Steno's *Prodromus*. De Maillet eventually retired in Marseilles, where he died at the respectable old age of 82.[15]

It was important to de Maillet to advance his theory on the global retreat of sea level as if it were the result of direct observations made by three generations of natural philosophers. Thus, the fictional Telliamed shares not only his own experience but also those going back to experiments begun by his inventive and equally fictional grandfather. De Maillet contended that the ongoing fall in global sea level amounted to less than 3 inches (7 cm) per century and that the rate was sufficient to be observed against known markers over a span of years represented by a few generations. The following description is for a sea-level gauging station purportedly designed and built by Telliamed's grandfather. It consisted of four wells excavated on a small island:

> In the middle of each well's bottom, a small horizontal tunnel was opened which communicated with the sea in order to admit water to the wells every time it was necessary. These wells were paved and lined with the hardest and best cemented stones. Then columns were erected in the middle of the wells, and after having introduced for eighteen months, several times the waters of the sea during the periods of greatest calm, it was easy to determine the present-day sea level, which during the interval of time, was almost always at the same elevation. Then my grandfather had not only the columns but also the walls of the wells divided into engraved lines from present-day sea level downward, and took care that the year of this observation, relative to the calendars of all known nations, was also engraved with deep letters on both columns and walls of the wells.[16]

In this realistic fabrication, de Maillet was inspired by the famous Nilometer on the island of Roda in Cairo, Egypt, which still survives and was used to gauge the rise and fall of the Nile River.[17]

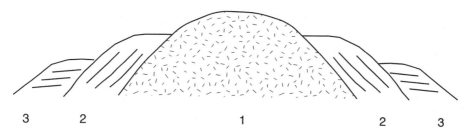

Figure 6. De Maillet's concept of the rock cycle (1748),
modified from Johnson (1992).

According to de Maillet's theory, the world's oldest mountains were sub-marine mounds hardened from sediments heaped together by ocean currents. The author employed a uniformitarian approach in describing this process through an account of deep-ocean exploration. Telliamed's grandfather designs, builds, and operates an elaborate "aquatic lantern," the description of which bears more than a passing resemblance to the early-twentieth-century bathy-sphere of Beebe and Barton. A significant part of the dialog, however, is devoted to the concept of cannibalization of older mountains to form progressively newer mountains, all in the context of coastal erosion. At the heart of de Maillet's theory is the following passage:

> The summits of the first mountains, having appeared above water, were immediately attacked by the combined forces of winds and waves typical of the surface of the sea. Their substance, still soft, was broken up and ground by them in different places. Heat and cold helped the waves, which were also assisted by the rivers and torrents formed by the rains. Everything which was broken loose by the agents from the first rocks began to contribute to the new works of the sea. Of these new deposits, the closest to the summits of the first mountains were themselves in turn attacked and broken up as soon as they appeared above the surface of the waves, and their debris were used in the same manner in the formation of similar deposits which the sea was building below them. The debris of the latter afterward served the same end, and new deposits were generated from them at a lower level.[18]

This early version of the rock cycle can be represented, cartoon fashion, as secondary and tertiary mountains symmetrically arrayed about the core of a primary (or primitive) mountain (fig. 6). Secondary mountains occur adjacent to, but below, the summit of the primary mountain. Likewise, tertiary mountains adjoin secondary mountains, but at a lower level. Essentially, the boundaries between rock layers in the primary and secondary mountains or between those in the secondary and tertiary mountains are geological unconformities.

De Maillet had no technical term for it, but he implicitly understood how such unconformities could be formed in the context of coastal erosion. He noted:

> At the foot of steep shores, new deposits were formed, consisting sometimes of large and sometimes of small stones, according to the nature of the rocks which were loosened by weathering and fell from the upper part of the cliffs into the sea. Among these large and small stones some were often of a different kind and color and had been brought by accident from far away; all those stones were cemented together by the mud or sand into which they had fallen or which had been deposited between them by the waters of the sea.[19]

That de Maillet must have witnessed authentic unconformities indicating ancient rocky shorelines somewhere during his travels is strongly implied by the following passage:

> The marks of the attacks of stormy seas on them after their formation were deeply imprinted in a hundred steep places of these mountains; amphitheaters eroded by the sea step by step on their slopes according to the stages of its diminution which in such a manner was clearly displayed; corals which the sea had left attached there after having given birth to them and nourished them in the same places where they were petrified; and the borings of sea-worms that live only in marine water, which occurred in many rocks. All these features were to him [Telliamed's grandfather] further convincing proofs of the real origin of mountains and of their ancient state.[20]

It is difficult to know whether all de Maillet's amphitheaters are valid examples of wave-eroded rocky shorelines, but his mention of fossils attached to abandoned sea cliffs is unequivocal. The borings of "sea-worms" were undoubtedly the cavities left by pholad bivalves of the kind seen on the abrasion platform near the south end of Playa La Palmita. Similar borings are found on the limestone ramparts of the Giza Plateau on which the great pyramids were built. De Maillet certainly visited the pyramids, and he might well have observed the borings on the north side of the plateau. They are still there today, marking a genuine example of an ancient rocky shoreline.[21] De Maillet would approve of our exploration of the former seabed of Bahía Santa Inés, especially the abandoned sea cliff and Phantom Island. Moreover, I think he would be ecstatic to sit exactly here, on the east side of Mesa El Coloradito. Were he able to join us now, I feel certain he would exclaim something like this: "Look around you and see the evidence of perhaps three different marine basins, one below the margin of another like a set of nested mixing bowls. Look around you and believe in the diminution of the sea!"

———————

The sun is lower in the west, and shadows cast by the Little Red Table stretch farther out toward the bay. I move a short distance to the north where the limestone has been eroded to expose the underlying andesite of the thin ridge. When first extruded, the volcanics formed flat layers. The clinometer on my compass indicates that the layers dip steeply at an angle of 53° to the northwest. The limestone ledge sits more or less level on the tilted andesite beds. Geologists refer to this arrangement as an angular unconformity. Here is one of those clear chapter breaks in a landscape's history. I have stood at this spot before with two students who tramped back and forth across the countryside of Punta Chivato with me in 1995. One of them, Laura Libbey, chose to study the Late Pleistocene seabed that extends out to Playa La Palmita far below us.[22] The other, Max Simian, was intrigued by older basins that hug the higher mesa margins.[23] I usually alternated between them, spending two days with one and then two days with the other in their respective study areas. Some days, all three of us went into the field together to puzzle over something special one of us had discovered. Cooperating as a team, we were able to gradually deduce the story told by the rocks of Punta Chivato. That January was one of the most contented months in my life.

Something in me wants to linger here and relish the contrasting tastes of before-and-after knowledge. But we must descend back to the trunk road and press homeward on our march toward Punta Mezquitito. A short distance along the main road, there is an abrupt jog to the northwest (map 2). A faded stop sign stands straight ahead on an old extension of the road that once crossed the airfield. The rerouted road makes a considerable detour around the airfield perimeter. I like to call the new bypass Johanson's Swing. When Jim Johanson decided to build the first proper hangar on the airfield, federal inspectors descended on Punta Chivato to ensure that all the necessary permits were in force. It was soon discovered that the Punta Chivato airfield had never been properly registered, fuel permits were in abeyance, and safety features such as a perimeter fence had never been erected. Needless to say, a road that so casually crosses an unprotected airfield violates necessary safety standards. Without a bypass, the airfield would be shut down. We follow the old road as far as it allows and turn to the southwest along the new perimeter fence. It consists of three strands of barbed wire strung on whitewashed fence posts. On its nightly patrols, the local coyote pack pays no heed to the new fence, but another modicum of progress has reached Punta Chivato. The line of houses that clings to the south shore faces the airfield across an access road. Beyond stands the green oasis of Hotel Punta Chivato, crowning the basaltic rise on the outer arm of Bahía Santa Inés. Our first day's hike is completed.

East Shore: Puntas Cacarizo and Cerotito

*Every day a new picture is painted and framed, held up for half an hour
in such lights as the Great Artist chooses, and then withdrawn and the
curtain falls. And then the sun goes down, and long the afterglow gives
light. And then the damask curtains glow along the western window.*
—Henry David Thoreau, *Journal*

The sea beyond Bahía Santa Inés is becalmed. When I rise, I find that the
shrimp trawlers sheltered in the bay yesterday have departed. Only the
lone sailboat remains. The pennant on its masthead hangs limp. At seven my
students and I meet on the terrace near the hotel kitchen to settle a bet. All eyes
train due east into the predawn grayness to the left of the northernmost Islas
Santa Inés, a few miles offshore. Tattered bits of clouds drift darkly over the
Concepción Peninsula, but the eastern sky is clear. The minutes pass unevent-
fully. Suddenly, a point of green light shines as clearly as the starboard running
light of a sea-going vessel. Could one of the trawlers have turned to make its
way back to Bahía Santa Inés? Just as quickly, the blood-red edge of the sun rises
at precisely the same spot and floods the seascape with warm light. The wager is
settled: the fabled green flash is a genuine atmospheric phenomenon.

It is 7:18 A.M.: day's start. Just offshore, a small fish leaps into the air and
splashes back down, sending out ripples in the water. A troop of brown pelicans
(Pelecanus occidentalis) descends from the southwest, like so many pterodactyls
from the Jurassic past. I never tire of watching them. They glide in single file,
effortlessly skimming the sea surface. Then the lead bird begins its wing stroke,
and one by one the whole troop powers up for sustained flight.

It is a fine morning to hike along the east shore north to Punta Cacarizo and
beyond to the rocky ribs of Punta Cerotito (map 3). Later, a climb onto the goat's
head will offer a clear view over the Gulf of California from the east face of the
Punta Chivato promontory. After breakfast, we reassemble on the kitchen terrace and descend the stairs to the beach, which leads northeast along basaltic
cliffs slightly more than half a mile (1 km) to the neck of sand that connects the
mainland with Punta Cacarizo. Because of its distinctive shape, American residents know the place as Hammerhead Point. The most important geological
observation along this stretch of the coast has to do with what is absent. Nowhere
to be found is the brown to tan silty sandstone that forms the principal edge of
the south shore.

Only a short distance along the beach the dark basaltic rocks give way to
reddish-colored tuffaceous rocks, though soon the basalt reasserts itself. The

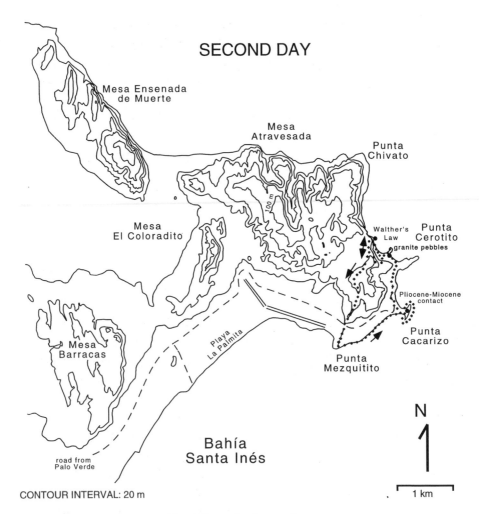

SECOND DAY

Mesa Ensenada
de Muerte

Mesa
Atravesada

Punta
Chivato

Mesa
El Coloradito

100 m

Walther's
Law

Punta
Cerotito

granite pebbles

Pliocene-Miocene
contact

Mesa
Barracas

Playa
La Palmita

Punta
Cacarizo

Punta
Mezquitito

Bahía
Santa Inés

road from
Palo Verde

N

CONTOUR INTERVAL: 20 m

1 km

Map 3. Route for the east shore.

tuff originated as volcanic ash that accumulated horizontally. Sharp contacts between the rock types make it easy to measure how much these layers were later tilted. The beds dip 40° due west. The orientation and dip angle hold constant as more measurements are collected at other places along the cliffs where the tuff beds reappear. Although the cliff line is recessed here and there and sometimes disappears altogether, the overall cliff height persists.

On the basaltic shelf above the beach are homes belonging to expatriate Americans. The first is a large compound modeled after a colonial mainland hacienda; its tiled domes sparkle in the bright morning sunshine, and a great wooden cross stands back from the shore. This is the largest private dwelling on Punta Chivato, known locally as Fort Campbell. I watched the building rise from nothing on a vacant lot during two of my successive January visits to Punta Chivato. Baja California has always been a hardscrabble place, reluctant to give up its native riches to colonists, past or present. No such dwelling was raised by the Spaniards who arrived here after the first explorations of Hernán Cortés and his lieutenants in 1535. Wealth eventually came from mining operations and from pearls, but the profits went to imposing edifices elsewhere. Next comes Casa Grande, the original dwelling built by the hotel developers, followed by more than a half dozen other homes, reaching to the spit of sand arcing from the east shore to Punta Cacarizo.

Cacarizo means "pockmarked," alluding to the deeply pitted surface of the limestone on the north end of the headland. The hammer-headed snout of the point is more than 1,000 feet (about 320 m) in length (map 3). To reach it, one must cross a spit connecting the rocky point with the mainland. The same sort of spit occurs at Isla Requesón to the south, in Bahía Concepción, although it is much larger. Geomorphologists use the technical term *tombolo,* from the Italian, to designate an impermanent sandbar linking what would otherwise be a permanent island to a solid coastline. At Isla Requesón, where the sandbar is made entirely from crushed rhodolith debris, the midsection of the tombolo is flooded at high tide. Although the tombolo at Punta Cacarizo is dry at high tide and the crossing may be made safely at any time, day or night, tombolos are nonetheless inherently unstable, existing at the whim of the winds and coastal currents. Ideally, a tombolo forms where two currents converge from opposite directions along the shore and deposit their sandy loads. What the winds and currents bring at one time, they may take away at another. A subtle difference between the tombolos at Isla Requesón and Punta Cacarizo is that thickets of mangle dulce *(Maytenus phyllanthoides)* have stabilized the sands leading to Punta Cacarizo, whereas the longer approach to Isla Requesón is completely bare. Aware of a deeper cycle of time, I cross all tombolos as if I were skating on thin ice. It is good to rejoin the rock-solid world of Punta Cacarizo at the far end.

Unlike the creamy limestone that clings to the slopes of Mesa El Colora-dito, this limestone is full of fossil molds. The external and internal impressions of a shell in its surrounding sediments are all that remain after the original calcareous shell is dissolved from a rock deposit. Particularly abundant here are the molds of pecten shells and other bivalves, such as the bittersweet shell in the glycymerid family. In the middle of the headland looking seaward, I can see how the limestone beds of Punta Cacarizo dip gently east to the edge of the water. The layering is crude, so I always march my students toward the north end of the point, turn them around, and have them hold a compass at arm's length to level the built-in clinometer against the general profile of the dipping beds. The dip angle is 6°. No piece of the puzzle is trivial, and this number soon will take on greater significance.

Near the north end of the point, the limestone is deeply pitted as a result of karst erosion. The rocks are continually wetted by the waves and dried by the sun. Seawater flushed through the limestone has dissolved circular pits 10 inches (about 25 cm) in diameter and nearly as deep. Small pools of saltwater remain standing in some of the pits, although the surface stands 13 feet (4 m) above mean sea level. The trapped water is subject to intense evaporation; indeed, we can see salt (NaCl) being actively precipitated as the solution passes the point of supersaturation (fig. 7). Generally, salt crystallizes from seawater when nine-tenths of the original water volume in a lagoon or other vessel, such as these pits, is reduced by evaporation. The greatest salt pan in the world is farmed at Guerrero Negro on the low Pacific shores of Baja California Sur, where saltwater is pumped behind levees to sit for days and months beneath the baking sun.

On the whole, the seawater in the Gulf of California is slightly more saline than that in the Pacific Ocean, on the other side of the peninsula. Directly offshore in the Guaymas Basin, for example, gulf salinity grades upward from 34.6 parts per thousand at a depth of 6,560 feet (2,000 m) to 35.3 parts per thousand at the surface.[1] Deep currents entering the Gulf of California in the south are relatively cold and bear water from the Pacific that is normal in salinity. Water that flows out of the gulf to the Pacific Ocean at or near the surface is elevated in salinity due to the subtropical temperatures and natural aridity of the place. This sort of natural exchange between the gulf and the open ocean is called thermohaline circulation. On average, the rate of evaporation in the gulf amounts to 3 feet (slightly less than 1 m) of seawater per year.[2] Water is steadily removed from an almost enclosed system but is just as steadily replaced through the narrow access to the limitless Pacific Ocean. Most of the year, circulation patterns are counterclockwise; normal-salinity waters flow in along the Mexican mainland as more highly saline waters exit the gulf along the peninsular shores. The pattern reverses to clockwise circulation during the summer, when the salinity gradient reaches its peak.[3] The influx of deep, nutrient-laden waters from the Pacific Ocean is what makes the isolated Gulf of California such a bountiful sea.

Thermohaline circulation not only affects fisheries in the gulf but also stimulates the biodiversity of marine invertebrates. The 86 species of shelled invertebrates recorded as Late Pleistocene fossils in Playa La Palmita's deposits indicate that the system has been healthy for a long time. The rocky ledge that slopes into the water at Punta Cacarizo is worlds apart from the shallow embayment of Bahía Santa Inés. Specialized organisms dominate this environment. In

Figure 7. Salt precipitation on Punta Cacarizo. Photo by author.

the mid-intertidal zone, a profusion of the purple sea urchin *(Echinometra vanbrunti)*, the most common sea urchin in the Gulf of California, reveals itself. The adults' tests reach a size less than 3 inches (7 cm) in diameter, but the spines are almost twice as long. It is very difficult to retrieve a complete specimen, for each is securely fitted into a cuplike depression worn in the limestone. Elsewhere on the shallow rocks are large colonies of an olive-green anemone species *(Palythoa ignota)*. The anemone bears stinging cells in its tentacles, which it uses to subdue tiny prey. The toxin is potent, but it would take a larger dose than this small anemone can inflict to endanger a person. Also, the callused skin of our thumb is too thick to be penetrated by the anemone's nematocysts. If you hold your thumb against the waving tentacles of the colony, you will feel a Velcro sensation against your skin. Alexander Agassiz, who succeeded his father as a naturalist and geologist at Harvard, once experimented by placing the tip of his tongue against an anemone: his tongue was painfully swollen for several days.[4]

With the tide out, we can explore other important geological relationships. Turn and follow across the dip slope of the limestone beds back to the tombolo's terminus. Here, we are crossing the gentle *cuesta* of Punta Cacarizo. *Cuesta* is a Spanish topographic term commonly used by geologists to refer to a long sloping plane terminated by a steep drop. In shape, this is reminiscent of a wooden wedge used as a doorstop. The long, low-angled side forced under the door is the cuesta. For the geomorphologist interested in the shape of the land, the cuesta often conforms to the dip slope of tilted sedimentary rocks. The thick end of the wedge is the escarpment where the truncated edges of tilted strata are exposed. Indeed, the landward margin of Punta Cacarizo, adjacent to the sand tombolo, reveals limestone layers in the stubby cliff line. Along the bottom of the cliff, however, the basal layers of the limestone are loaded with dark igneous cobbles and pebbles eroded from a basaltic or andesitic source. At low tide, it becomes apparent that the bottommost limestone sits directly on igneous rocks similar to those we followed along the beach from Punta Mezquito. The main difference is that these igneous rocks were once part of a blocky surface flow welded into a rubblelike consistency. These blocky rocks form the floor of the lagoons on either side of the tombolo.

Here we find another unconformity, or natural break, between two kinds of rocks, the igneous below and the sedimentary above. In this case, it is not hard to imagine how it was shaped. The scenario is much as Benoît de Maillet described for the action of the sea on a rocky shoreline, but with a twist. The parent rocks of the igneous sea cliff shed debris into the sea, and offshore carbonate sediments cemented around and over the conglomeration of volcanic rocks. The greatest concentration of black and red igneous cobbles is deposited in the basal layer of the sloping limestone beds that rise 16.5 feet (nearly 5 m) above the surface of this unconformity. The upper limestone layers feature fewer cobbles but more pebbles derived from the same igneous source. In addition, the cobbles in the lowest bed tend to be closely packed, whereas the pebbles in the upper beds are dispersed throughout the limestone. Fossils are most abundant in the top layers at Punta Cacarizo, where the limestone includes only scattered granules of igneous material. The basal conglomerate was in direct contact with a former rocky shoreline, so it received the largest amount of eroded material. The succeeding layers of limestone received fewer and smaller clasts or particles of the igneous parent rock, because the shoreline was in retreat. All the evidence suggests that sea level was on the rise while the limestone layers were formed.

This scenario is corroborated by the slopes that rise inland above the east shore to a height of about 195 feet (60 m), well behind the shelf on which the American houses sit. Binoculars are helpful in picking out the details near the skyline. On this stretch of the east shore, the Punta Chivato promontory is crowned by red cliffs overlain by tan-colored layers. What we see is the same unconformity as at Punta Cacarizo, but approximately one-third mile (about half a kilometer) away and elevated perhaps 148 feet (45 m) above sea level.

With my back to the little escarpment on the Hammerhead, I aim the clinometer in my compass at the unconformity high on the slope beyond the tombolo. Using the mirror on the compass lid, I can see the clinometer with one eye and adjust it until it is level. My line of sight extends directly from the unconformity behind me to the analogous unconformity near the top of the hill. The clinometer registers an angle of about 6°, meaning that the dip slope of the cuesta on Punta Cacarizo is well aligned with the unconformity on the hill.

Sea level, in short, advanced along a gentle slope with an inclination of 6°, owing to local subsidence of the land, a global rise in sea level, or some combination of the two. This relationship reveals a minor variation in Nicolaus Steno's law of original horizontality. The limestone beds on the east shore of the Punta Chivato promontory were not deposited on a perfectly flat surface. Instead, they compose what is called a carbonate (limestone) ramp that extended landward with a rise in sea level; Benoît de Maillet's concept of a global sea-level fall thus does not apply locally. The dirty rings along the edge of the giant washbasin tell a more complicated story, as does the ledge of basaltic rock that runs from Punta Mezquitito most of the way to the tombolo. This ledge is an erosional feature much younger in age than the carbonate ramp. In fact, the Punta Cacarizo carbonates are a remnant that barely survived removal by erosion long after their deposition. The entire east flank of the Punta Chivato promontory was formerly sheathed in limestone, most of which is now gone. The coastal step on which the American homes are built has a completely different origin.

The remains of the unconformity on the east side of Punta Chivato mark a clear chapter break between igneous rocks assigned to the Comondú Group, which includes basalt, andesite, and tuff beds, and the overlying fossiliferous limestone, named the San Marcos Formation. Comondú is a name that comes from a small village high in the Sierra de la Giganta, well to the south. Perhaps more than 13,000 feet (4,000 m) in total thickness, the Comondú volcanics are crudely bedded, forming much of the eastern escarpment of the Baja California peninsula.[5] The beds making up this enormous group formed at the earth's surface, layer after layer, throughout Miocene time, roughly 25 million to 5 million years ago. San Marcos is a designation that comes from Isla San Marcos, 8.5 miles (about 14 km) northwest of Punta Chivato. There, the geologist Charles Anderson first recognized during his 1940 visit the same kinds of limestone and fossils as those found here at Punta Cacarizo.[6] The San Marcos Formation was deposited between 5 million and 3 million years ago, during the early Pliocene. Taken from representative localities, such formal names help categorize all the rocks that regionally fit the same description. Why, however, does Lower Pliocene limestone occur at Punta Cacarizo, whereas Lower

Pliocene sandstone forms the south shore we explored yesterday? The answer awaits our discovery farther along the coast.

The land heats up quickly under a cloudless sky, and it is refreshing to wade through the shallows behind Punta Cacarizo. On the south side of the tombolo, where there is less rock rubble, a closer look at some of the marine invertebrate life is possible. Attached to the rocky floor of the tidal pools on the Miocene-Pliocene unconformity are stumpy growths of the emerald coral *(Porites californica)*. This stony coral is a colonial animal. The tiny polyps that extrude from small pits on the surface of the colony look much like miniature anemones, each with its ring of tentacles. Corals exposed to the air during low tide withdraw their tentacles. The fat, fingerlike colony may reach 3–4 inches (7–10 cm) in height, with a diameter nearly wrist size. The fleshy tissue of the polyps hosts algal cells called zooxanthellae, which bear chlorophyll and give the colony its green coloration. Skeletons of dead corals, whether still in the water or washed onshore, are bleached white. This species ranges from the intertidal zone to a depth of more than 65 feet (20 m).[7]

Inspired by the corals and the calmness of the day, we strip to our swimsuits, don masks and snorkels, and begin to explore the waist-deep waters around the southern end of Punta Cacarizo. The corals are more plentiful immediately offshore. Some 10 square feet (a single square meter) of seabed support 20 to 25 of the coral colonies. The density of the colonies is much too low, however, to resemble anything like a coral reef. The nearest living coral reefs (built by another species) are located far to the south near La Paz, where the water temperature is slightly warmer year round.

Becoming accustomed to the temperature, I venture into the open waters that front Punta Cacarizo. While diving a short distance out from the limestone shore with its prominent sea urchin zone, I notice how the emerald corals maintain their highest density along almost the full length of the Hammerhead. Other colors and shapes vie for my attention. With its deep coloration, the red velvet sponge *(Acarnus erithacus)* beckons. Though not as common as the corals, they tend to be larger. I feel guided by beacons as I move from one bright sponge to another. Here and there lurks a pyramid sea star *(Pharia pyramidata)*, which reaches a size between 5 and 12 inches (13–30 cm). The large sea star has a distinctive mottled brown and yellow color. Punta Cacarizo is a rock reef, and many reef fish are present, including the bright orange or yellow angelfish with its electric blue racing stripes. The ghostly translucence and odd shape of the California needlefish *(Strongylura exilis)* are also striking. Around the north end of the point, the water deepens and the seabed is covered by rocky rubble. The corals have vanished. Here the point takes the brunt of the waves when the weather is windy, and the upper north end exhibits the namesake pockmarks, splashed by unruly waves.

I've now looped around the Hammerhead to emerge from the north lagoon, and the sun quickly warms my chilled body. The water's saltiness leaves my mouth parched; it is good to rinse with fresh water. Across the tombolo, the main road runs farther north through the campground. From the road, ribs of tilted Comondú andesite protrude from the water in the lagoon, extending in a north-south direction. The pelicans take their late morning leisure there, sitting on the rocks at a safe distance from meddlesome children and nosy dogs. At the end of the campground, near the last *palapa,* or palm-thatch shelter, the beach abuts reddish andesite cliffs interbedded with soft white tuff. Like the rocky ribs that protrude from the lagoon, the tilted layers exposed in the cliff strike north-south, and like the igneous rocks at Punta Mezquitito, they dip steeply about 40° to the west. Thus far, the structure of the east shore beneath the Lower Pliocene limestone is consistent.

At extreme low tide, it is possible to circumnavigate the next point to the north by walking along the shore. There is really no need for the long detour around Punta Cerotito (Little Horn Point). The sand dunes that festoon the rocky topography ahead make an enticing landscape to explore. We set out for a low saddle between the higher conical hill to our right and the neighboring pinnacle of Punta Cerotito, marked by a cross, to the left (map 3). The vertical climb is less than 65 feet (20 m), but the sand underfoot makes the going cumbersome. At the crest in the saddle, Isla Tortuga—Turtle Island—becomes visible on the skyline 25 miles (40 km) due north. The island is a dormant volcano that rose 3,280 feet (more than 1,000 m) from the floor of the Guaymas Basin about 1.7 million years ago. I have flown over the island in a small plane with Jim Johanson and peered into the yawning crater at the summit of its broad shield. From sea level, however, the island reveals nothing of its volcanic origin, and its low-arched profile indeed resembles that of a great turtle.

There is an automated weather station on Isla Tortuga. Wind amplitude and vector data from the station confirm that winds blow intermittently out of the north from October through April.[8] Wind speeds of 30–45 feet per second (10–15 m/sec), or 20–27 miles per hour, are not uncommon on the island during the winter, and Punta Chivato is exposed directly downwind. Below us is the uninhabited Playa El Cerotito, beautifully strung between a robust spur of rock from Little Horn Point's main part, on the right, and a more slender projection of naked rock to the left. The unspoiled white beach sands extend for more than 650 feet (200 m) between the dark, bull-like horns of rock that point guardingly to the northeast into the open Gulf of California. At this spot, I have leaned into wind blowing from Isla Tortuga with sustained gusts up to 12 feet per second (8 m/sec), as measured by a hand-held anemometer. At around this velocity, sea salt is able to enter the air from white-capped waves whipped by the prevailing wind and the popping of air bubbles at the water's surface. The salt transforms into an aerosol that blasts the north-facing shores of Punta Chivato. Modestly elevated salinity on the western side of the gulf during the winter variation in thermohaline circulation lends itself to the formation of such aerosols. For anyone who wears eyeglasses, as I do, the evidence for salt aerosols on a windy day is unmistakable. After only a few minutes, my glasses are blurred by a white film; a tentative lick of the tongue confirms that the blur is more than water vapor. Fieldwork is impossible on days like these. Happily, today is tranquil, and the scene below us on Playa El Cerotito is idyllic.

We move to an overlook directly below the larger of the two conical hills on Punta Cerotito. Behind us on the northern slope of the hill are shrub-size leatherplants *(Jatropha cuneata),* which bow to the ground like supplicants. They point south, away from the wind. These and other plants on north-facing slopes are pruned by the salt aerosols. The branches extend close to the ground in the lee of their own trunk, where the leaves are more sheltered from salt poisoning, and no leaves survive on the windward side. Without the munificence of a washing rain, salt accumulation on its leaves will kill the plant. This kind of misshapen tree is known as a krummholz, from the German for twisted wood. Another of my former students, Patrick Russell, spent weeks here and elsewhere around Punta Chivato carefully mapping the location and growth direction of scores of shrubs and trees.[9] The plants on these shores function as living wind socks that plot with uncanny accuracy not only the prevailing wind direction but also the subtle details of small eddies that swirl around the contours of the land.

Beneath the ledge on which we stand are the scant remains of a Pleistocene deposit dating from the same time as the vast seabed behind Playa La Palmita on Bahía Santa Inés. Here, on the windward north side of Punta Cerotito, more than 6 feet (2 m) of densely packed shell beds are arrayed in layers only 1–2 inches (2.5–5 cm) thick. The thinner layers contain dark basaltic pebbles thoroughly mixed with broken and worn mollusk shells. Sandwiched among them are thicker layers of finely comminuted shell material and basaltic granules mixed together as coarse sand. Because the basaltic pebbles give the thinner layers a darker tone, the overall effect of the outcrop is that of black and white stripes.

Some of the gastropods in the deposit are familiar, such as the turban shell *(Turbo fluctuosus).* Bivalves are represented by small Venus shells such as *Chione californiensis* and the similar but more coarsely pleated *Chione tumens.* Everything here is broken and worn. The contrast with the old seabed of Bahía Santa Inés could not be more pronounced. This banded deposit represents an abandoned Pleistocene beach that sits high above Playa El Cerotito. The coarser layers with recognizable shells are storm beds. Basaltic pebbles incorporated into these layers came from the eroded igneous horns that frame the beach. The horns were even more prominent 125,000 years ago. The finer shell material and basaltic granules in the thicker layers represent beach sand that accumulated through the normal cycle of tides and lesser storms. There is no trace of rhodolith debris in these old beach deposits.

Descending to the present-day shore on our northerly progress, the next point of interest is the small rocky spur that defines the west margin of the beach (map 3). Where the rocks are well washed, there are pebble- to cobble-size pieces of "salt-and-pepper" granite. Yesterday we saw rare granite pebbles strewn among basaltic and andesitic clasts that washed onto the old seabed of Bahía Santa Inés during unusually heavy rains. In contrast, here on Punta Cerotito the granite bits are fixed within the surrounding matrix of Miocene andesite, having been brought to the surface from deep basement rocks via dikes that fed into the thick pile of Comondú volcanics. Comparable spots must occur on Mesa El Coloradito, and it was from them that the granite weathered free of its surrounding matrix and was swept away by floods to the Bahía Santa Inés foreshore.

Geologists have a good term for igneous rocks contained within other igneous rocks. The odd bits are called xenoliths, from the Greek root word for foreign or stranger. A xenolith is a piece of igneous rock that is a stranger to its igneous surroundings. Such fragments are brought upward through the crust of the earth by the flow of magma under pressure. The magma is forced through conduits in the basement rock and tears off pieces of the rock by sheer pressure. The nearest outcrops of the same salt-and-pepper granite are large up-faulted blocks of basement rock on Peninsula Concepción, 25 miles (more than 40 km) to the southeast. The same granite is found inland at a depth of more than 5,500 feet (1,700 m), judging from exploration drilling at Las Tres Vírgenes near Santa Rosalia to the northwest.[10] The granite basement rocks in this part of Baja California Sur are dated to 84 million years ago and formed during the Cretaceous Period. Similar granite is found at the tip of Baja California in the famous sea arches of Cabo San Lucas. More significantly, much the same granite forms the exposed backbone of the Baja California peninsula to the north through the Central Desert and the Sierra San Pedro Mártir.

The basic geological history of Baja California can be visualized as the architecture of an immense building. Most of the basement level is constructed on Cretaceous granite. The granite cooled from magma in enormous subterranean chambers originally overlain by massive roof rocks that have long since been eroded away around much of the peninsula. The first floor of the structure, particularly on the gulf coast, is dominated by the thick layers of Comondú volcanics. These were piped and vented through the basement rocks, to spill out on the surface as stratified layers of basalt and andesite, or they rained down on the surface as volcanic ash throughout most of Miocene time. The second story is formed by marine sedimentary rocks that represent the development of the protogulf. The muddy sandstone on the south shore and the limestone of Punta Cacarizo on the east shore are characteristic of this stage. The fossils from these strata typically date from the start of the Pliocene. Almost as if a decorative afterthought, the attic of our edifice is festooned by very young deposits not yet properly lithified. The Late Pleistocene seabed of Bahía Santa Inés and the abandoned beach deposits of Punta Cerotito manifest the recent past. Here and there, the great building has slumped, so that the floors are mismatched or missing. All other architectural features are embellishments on this simple outline.

The most prized adornment nearby reveals important constructional de-tails about the second story of this colossal edifice. From the tip of the little horn, the view to the northwest across the water to the east cliff face of the Punta Chivato promontory shows a spectacular cross section through strata above a south-dipping unconformity with a maximum slope of about 9° (fig. 8). The rocks below the unconformity belong to the Comondú volcanics. The rocks above are part of the San Macros Formation. The key relationship fea-tures interfingered Pliocene conglomerate and limestone beds that are best seen at a distance, from this spot, with the sun behind us in the early light of the day. I recall the excitement with which Max Simian reported to me the discovery he made here, and my own astonishment when I first stood here and realized that the east cliff face is a textbook example of a pair of important stratigraphic concepts—the concepts of facies and of their correlation across time and space. These form the cornerstone of my geological philosophy and practice, and I had taught those ideas to Max scarcely a few years before. Nowhere else in my worldly travels had I seen anything to rival this extraordinary view.

Earlier in the day, Punta Cacarizo offered us a practical perspective on the Miocene-Pliocene unconformity, which portrays an ancient coastal relation-ship. The disadvantage of that locality, however, is that most of the limestone belonging to the San Marcos Formation has been eroded away, together with part of the underlying unconformity surface. By drawing a connection between the unconformity at sea level and the identical unconformity at a higher eleva-tion on the hill slope, we are able to make certain assumptions about how the land-sea relationship changed in early Pliocene time. The sea slowly rose, or the

Figure 8. East cliff face, Punta Chivato promontory. Photo by author.

land slowly sank, or both. There was no choice but to fill in the blank places between the two unconformities and assume a continuous connection between them. In contrast, the stratigraphic profile on the east cliff face before us is complete. Here, the land-sea relationship is viewed from another perspective: obliquely from the side. It is helpful to use binoculars, because rock identification from such a distance is not easy. Most notable is a thin, dark line that crosses the middle of the cliff face from the right and terminates at a point toward the left. This line is formed by conglomerate. In fact, the conglomerate layer is 180 feet (55 m) long and about 3.3 feet (1 m) thick. Following the line to its origin on the right, it appears to grow thicker and eventually merges with the landscape in a very steep slope. Other, shorter spikes also terminate as points on the left. All the spikes are joined on one side like a ragged comb with teeth of different lengths and thicknesses.

The steep slope in our right field of view represents land composed almost totally of dark Comondú andesite. Our left field of view is occupied by light-colored rocks that consist of San Marcos limestone. They represent marine deposits immediately offshore. The intervening conglomerate highlights the merger of these two rock types on a shifting shoreline. Boulders and cobbles now encased in the conglomerate are composed of andesite eroded by the waves from the adjacent land. The distinctive zigzag pattern traced by the conglomerate shows sharp invasions against the neighboring limestone. Over-all, the cross section indicates that changes in the Pliocene coastline were not the result of a single, continuous marine inundation. The drowning of the ancient coastline experienced abrupt halts, during which a coarse beach of andesite boulders and cobbles advanced sharply seaward. Resumption in the rise of sea level resulted in the retreat of the beach and its burial by carbonate sediments that eventually became consolidated as limestone. This view reveals that the land area on the right once extended toward us and is now truncated by the high cliffs. In short, the east cliff face portrays a discontinuous, 164-foot (50-m) rise in relative sea level over a distance of less than 650 feet (200 m) across a former south-facing coastline.

FEATURE / Amanz Gressly and the Facies Concept

The profound idea advanced by Benoît de Maillet at the turn of the eighteenth century—that the world's sea level is not static—carries with it certain assumptions. Those assumptions apply not only to shifts in the boundary between land and sea but also to the conditions under which sediments, deposited side by side at the same time, differ from one another. Through his direct observations of coastlines around the Mediterranean Sea and through his somewhat more fanciful discussion of submarine explorations off those shores, de Maillet came to understand a system of interrelated marine environments. He appreciated that conglomerate is the sort of rock that develops from deposition of coarse material below the wave-washed cliffs of rocky shores. He recognized that boulders and cobbles wrestled by the sea from their parent rocks ashore might be encased below the sea cliffs in sandy sediment from farther offshore. He understood that parts of the adjacent seafloor were muddier in their constitution. De Maillet also realized that certain marine organisms are specialized to live in the intertidal zone on rocky shores, that they dwell nowhere else, and that they might well be fossilized in place. All these factors are implicit in what is called the facies concept—the notion that organisms and the sediments around them become, respectively, fossils and strata that vary from one location to the next as reflections of different but contemporaneous environments. Amanz Gressly (1814–1865) was the young Swiss geologist who in 1838 coined the word "facies" and explicitly spelled out its meaning in terms of different life zones associated with specific environments of sedimentary deposition.[11] Thus, 90 years after publication of *Telliamed,* key ideas were refined with respect to ecological patterns and the pathways by which they enter the rock record.

Amanz Gressly grew up in the Swiss canton of Solothurn, the son of a well-to-do family of artisans who operated the glassworks at Bärschwyl.[12] After matriculating as a medical student in Strasbourg in 1834, Gressly attended his first course in geology and was inspired to undertake independent fieldwork in the mountain landscape of the Jura Alps in his native canton of northwestern Switzerland. There, he skillfully mapped and interpreted sedimentary rock layers of Late Jurassic age that revealed the organization of ancient seas long ago drained and thrust skyward. His Strasbourg mentors urged Gressly to prepare his preliminary results for formal presentation at a conference in 1836, where the 22-year-old medical student was awed by the geological savants of the day. One of the influential persons who immediately recognized Gressly's talents was Louis Agassiz, who, as editor of the journal of the Swiss Society of Natural Sciences, was in a position to help him publish his studies on the Jura Alps. Gressly attended Agassiz's lectures in Neuchâtel and was eventually hired as an assistant by Agassiz.

The first of four installments of Gressly's seminal paper, "Geological observations on the Solothurn Jura," appeared in 1838, two years after he met Agassiz. The original definition of facies reads:

Above all, there are two major facts which define everywhere the sum of the variables which I call facies or the aspects of a stratigraphic unit: one is that within a stratigraphic unit the occurrence of a specific lithology necessarily also requires the occurrence of a specific paleontological association; and the other is that a given paleontological association rigorously excludes those genera and species of fossils which are frequent in other facies.[13]

Gressly went on to explain more precisely, in clear uniformitarian terms, what he meant by this new concept:

I think that the petrographic or paleontological changes of a stratigraphic unit in the horizontal are caused by the changes in environment and other circumstances, which still so powerfully influence today the different genera and species which inhabit the ocean and the seas. At least, I often have been astonished to find in the distribution of our fossils the laws of living communities and in the corresponding assemblages of petrographic characteristics which correspond to the living communities, the environmental conditions which rule in the submarine world.[14]

There could hardly be a more straightforward vision than the facies concept. Life is divided and partitioned around the planet for maximum success in different environments. Certain kinds of plants and animals form a natural and often interdependent association adjusted to the rigors of life on mountaintops, in deserts, in freshwater lakes, in swamps, on river deltas, on coastal mud flats, along rocky shores, in shallow seas, and in the deep ocean. In these settings, the remains of plants and animals collect and are buried in sediments that are locally derived and specific to the host environment. At this very moment in countless parts of the world, the organic and sedimentological by-products of each ecosystem combine to make contemporaneous deposits. They do so now and have done so through long periods of geological time.

In the marine realm, the geological evidence is most readily seen for a range of different facies lined up one astride the other. Gressly's descriptive study of the Jura Alps surpassed de Maillet's earlier observations on Mediterranean shores in detailing the nature of more sheltered and offshore zones. In his 1838 report, Gressly contributed the following description of the "muddy facies," which clearly received less wave energy than exposed rocky shorelines:

A general trait, which is constant for all paleontological assemblages of the muddy facies, is that the dominant genera and species have tests less apt to resist destructive effects of reworking. The shells, among others, are normally very thin, very much smoother, less ornate, less ornamented with different protuberances than in the preceding [coral] facies where they have a very pronounced massive resistant character.[15]

In this light, it is possible to understand how the basaltic conglomerate and associated limestone with its fossil bivalves on the east shore of Punta Chivato relates to the dirty brown sandstone with its fossil sand dollars and echinoids along the south shore on Bahía Santa Inés. The two deposits formed simultaneously during the early Pliocene. They are adjoining facies of the San Marcos Formation, and both consist of lithified sediments and the incorporated remains of marine organisms. But one formed in more turbulent water at the side of a rocky shoreline open to the Gulf of California, while the other accumulated along a low plain bordering Bahía Santa Inés.

In Gressly's original colored map and cross section of the Jura Alps, published in 1840, his geographic reconstruction of Mesozoic facies comes alive.[16] He reconstituted ancient coastal highlands, intervening gulfs, and islands, all with their associated deposits derived from the mixture of organic and inorganic matter in adjacent nearshore and offshore settings. Gressly's labor in differentiating the ancient facies of the Jura Alps is revealed by his extensive fossil collection, said to have numbered 25,000 specimens. His accomplishment is astonishing, because the young Swiss inlander waited 19 years before he first visited the Mediterranean Sea. It was in 1859, at Sète on the French

Riviera, that Gressly found much the same ecological zones in the living sea-scape as he had previously deduced from his studies of geological facies in Switzerland.

Throughout his adult life, Gressly experienced attacks of melancholia. He suffered a grave blow in 1846 when Louis Agassiz departed Switzerland for the United States and a new academic post at Harvard, taking with him a substantial part of Gressly's fossil collection.[17] During later years, Agassiz's former apprentice was employed as a consultant on the construction of tunnels for the expanding system of alpine railroads.

The concept of facies and the closely related notion of how facies shift through geologic time were not immediately integrated into the education and practice of stratigraphers and paleontologists. With the Darwinian emphasis on evolution in fossil groups as a means of dating rocks, the valuable environmental information represented by fossils was commonly overlooked. The authoritative textbook by Johannes Walther, published under the title *Introduction to Geology as Historical Science* (from the German) in 1893–1894, brought Gressly's ideas into the mainstream of European thought.[18] It took longer yet for the facies concept to be exported farther abroad and routinely adopted by North America geologists. Walther's law of the correlation of facies reiterates that in concert with their diagnostic fossils, facies migrate through time and space along an environmental track that results in the same vertical succession of strata as that expressed by the arrangement of adjacent facies.[19] In marine environments, the shifting of the facies track is caused by changes in sea level. Facies are said to move landward during a marine transgression and seaward during a marine regression. All the while, the distance from shore and the water depth characteristic of any given marine facies remains constant.

The zigzag pattern of shifting facies exhibited before us on the east cliff face of the Punta Chivato promontory is precisely what Walther's law predicts. The conglomerate beds trace the shifting position of the shoreline through time. Packing away the binoculars and quitting the horn of rock, we retrace our steps landward and follow the curve in the next beach to the base of the bluff, 650 feet (200 m) to the northwest (map 3). At the far corner of the beach, the walls rise above 160 feet (some 50 m) and mercifully block the glare of the noontime sun. The air is cool from the damp sand at the water's edge, making this a pleasant spot for lunch. Great blocks of limestone that have fallen from the bluff are readily accessible for study. Many are fractured along their original bedding plains, revealing a rich trove of fossil pectens densely packed in silty limestone. The absence of fossils other than pectens and the lack of reworked igneous clasts indicate that the strata piled high above us were deposited off-shore, beyond the Pliocene shoreline. Pliocene land is situated directly to the north. A narrow trail crosses the bluff at the end of the beach to an enormous talus field. Max and I once picked our way over precariously toppled blocks to within an arm's length of the dark conglomerate bed high in the cliff face. The going was slow and risked a fall onto sharp and unforgiving rocks. That is how we determined that the principal conglomerate bed is 3.3 feet (1 m) thick. Sometimes a calculated risk is necessary in order to retrieve a vital piece of information. But I will not interrupt my midday repast to make the climb today. The size of the talus pile and the freshness of the exposed rock tell us this is a dangerous place that has witnessed catastrophic cliff failure.

———————

We are at the halfway point in today's circuit, and the plateau on the east edge of the goat's head promises a diversionary return route to Punta Mezquitito. We retreat from the towering Pliocene cliff face and retrace our steps along the arc of a white sand beach. A shallow trough cuts into the dune field on the west side of the great conical hill overlooking Playa El Cerotito, which offers the opportunity to study the sand that sweeps almost uninterrupted from the small embayment to the top of the hill. Although the climb through the hollow to the first ledge of solid rock is not far, the going is laborious. I take three steps forward and slide back one. The beach is derived from the embayment below, and the sand in the dunes here on this slope is the windblown chaff that has been separated from the beach sand.

We pause near an acacia tree, but not for shade. There are more than 50 species of the genus *Acacia* in the Sonoran Desert and southward. I can't say which species this is, but the plant looks more like a creeping hedge than a tree. Like the more abundant leatherplants on the slope, the acacia has been disfigured by the salt-laden winds that blow out of the north. Its exposed trunk is 18 inches (45 cm) in diameter, but this and a cluster of smaller trunks behind it bend sharply through 90° and send branches sprawling south for 16 feet (5 m).

The smallest details in this place are astounding. Low on the slope above the beach, there are spots where tiny, translucent bivalve shells, each three-eighths of an inch (only 5 mm) across, litter the surface. The shells probably belong to one of the many species of lucinid bivalves that dwell buried in the shallow sand flats. These are disarticulated, meaning that the two shells that comprise one animal are separated from one another. Most of the shells lie with their concave side facing down and are stable in this position. Those that come to rest concave side up, like the turned-up margin of a paper plate, may easily catch the wind and be transported farther inland. A wind blowing 30 feet per second (10 m/sec) is capable of picking up bits of material like these small shells. Generic sand is also transported by wind through a process called saltation. The word literally refers to jumping. A single grain of sand is lifted by the wind and flies through the air for a short distance before crashing down on the surface. Its landing jostles neighbor grains, which may now be picked up by the wind. In this fashion, windblown sand travels, or saltates, along a dune. Near the acacia, I bend to examine a row of closely spaced ripples sculpted in the sand by the wind. The ripple crests are white, but the intervening swales trap a thin cover of sand that is green in color. Where do the different fractions of beach and dune sand come from? This was the question I sent my student Patrick Russell out to answer in 1996 and 1997.

Once Patrick had characterized the wind field over Punta Cerotito by plotting most of the twisted trees growing on its northern flank, he turned to the origin of the sand in the bays, beaches, and dunes.[20] This he did in a way peculiar to geologists accustomed to identifying rocks from thin sections. A petrographic thin section is a paper-thin slice of rock mounted on a glass slide under a cover slip. The thin section allows examination of individual grains under a microscope. Identification of minerals is based on properties of each grain as determined by their optical characteristics. The obvious source for the dark sand was the weathering of the igneous rock spurs that protrude from Punta Cerotito. Working on the assumption that the white sand was organic in origin, Patrick collected samples of various bivalves, sea urchins, barnacles, and rock-encrusting red algae living in the bays. These he segregated and crushed into sand-size particles that he artificially bound together using epoxy. Broken bits of bivalve shells, for example, show parallel bands in various shades of brown related to the microscopic lamination of shell layers. Barnacles tend to break into elongate pieces, most of which show diagnostic perforations related to their shell structure. With such telltale information, Patrick could examine thin sections from sand samples likewise aggregated by epoxy and draw conclusions about their inorganic and organic components.

Patrick collected sand samples starting from the shallows off Playa El Cerotito and extending in a line across the beach and over the dunes to the crest of the conical hill 160 feet (49 m) above sea level. He subjected thin sections from each location to a random census of 400 grains per slide, which allowed him to estimate the composition of each sample. Pie diagrams (fig. 9) summarize the compositional range of three samples from different elevations. The top tier shows that the rock and mineral component composes more than half of each sample. This is surprising, because the sand has an overall buff coloration that suggests a major carbonate contribution. The middle tier of pies indicates that grains derived from mollusk shells account overwhelmingly for the organic

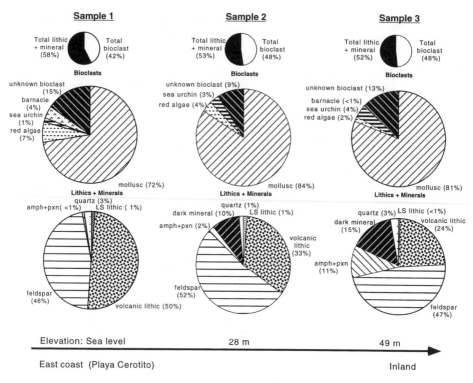

Figure 9. Pie charts for beach and dune sand composition.

sand fraction, ranging from 72 percent on the beach to 84 percent in the dunes on the slope. In contrast, coralline red algae accounts for a small amount of organic sand, from 7 percent on the beach to 2 percent at the top of the hill. This result stands in marked contrast to the carbonate sands of Bahía Santa Inés visited yesterday. There, the coarse, pustular texture of broken rhodoliths is easily distinguished with the naked eye, and the abandoned Pleistocene seabed behind Playa La Palmita is thoroughly dominated in volume by sediments derived from coralline red algae. Wind and wave energy is so diffused on the south side of the Punta Chivato promontory that the materials were not further reduced to beach or dune sand.

In the inorganic fraction of sand, represented by the bottom tier of pies in figure 9, volcanic grains of eroded andesite account for 50 percent of the beach sample by bulk but decrease to 24 percent upslope in the dunes. Dark grains, which include the green mineral olivine, are not found on the beach but occur preferentially on the slope. This is unexpected, but it may be explained by the fact that the sand cover on the hill slope is thin in places, and the dark minerals may be weathered directly from exposed igneous bedrock. In any case, the entrapment of green mineral grains in the low troughs of migrating dune ripples is accounted for by the higher specific gravity of minerals such as olivine, in contrast to sand grains derived from seashells.

How absurd it must seem that anyone would spend hours in a laboratory—much less sitting on a beach or dune—to count out sand grains and determine where they came from. In *Gulliver's Travels,* Jonathan Swift pokes fun at science by having his character visit professors who toil at their research in the Grand Academy of Lagado. The first academic Gulliver meets is a bearded, raggedly dressed man who has devoted eight years of his life to extracting sunbeams from cucumbers. What difference does it make where the sand on Playa El Cerotito comes from, or how it is winnowed by the wind? In defense, I can only reply that just as it is rational for an accountant to sort out financial entanglements in the human world, it is entirely rational for a geologist, fascinated by the natural world, to sort out the sand budget for Punta Chivato. In their own way, the transactions of the sand budget are just as important. What emerges from such study is a deeper insight into a complex ecosystem that infuses wind and wave energy through the fabric of biological associations of astonishing fertility.

It is a struggle to climb the sand dunes between the great hill of Punta Cerotito and the main escarpment of the east shore. The footing improves near the 130-foot (40-m) contour of elevation, where the path crosses onto solid volcanic rock. A little higher is the Miocene-Pliocene unconformity at the juncture between andesite rocks and the tan limestone beds that cap the plateau. The view due east across Punta Cerotito looks over open water. Guaymas, on the Mexican mainland, is only 80 miles (130 km) away, yet on the clearest of days, I swear that I can barely make out the farther shore. Between these shores sits the deep Gulf of California. In concert with the winds and waves that sweep along its axis, this great body of water is a dynamo that brings renewed energy and life to the shores it touches. The gulf has its own entrenched rhythms that long predate the first humans to reach this land.

A brief stroll to the north along the edge of the plateau takes us across the thickest accumulation of silty limestone that formed the pecten facies and filled an east-west indentation on the former Pliocene shoreline. A convenient stopping point overlooks our lunch stop on the beach below. Well ahead, the plateau meets a sudden rise of some 65 feet (20 m) that represents part of the old, resistant shoreline. We will not go so far today. The way through the sparse desert brush is easy to navigate. Deep fractures in the rocks parallel the margin of the plateau. Six to ten feet (2–3 m) of the cliff edge are separated from us by a yawning chasm. This is where the next catastrophic collapse of poorly cemented limestone will occur on the east shore. The drop below is precipitous. A concrete boundary post is planted toward the edge of the plateau nearby.

Figure 10. Punta Cacarizo (Hammerhead), view to east. Photo by author.

Eventually, it will tumble into the sea below. Ongoing changes in the landscape under the hand of nature are predictable and certain. The post marker reminds me of the practical world of bankers, lawyers, and business people.

A short distance inland is a well-defined jeep track (map 3) that will bring us back to Punta Mezquitito. The track bypasses the spot where we climbed onto the plateau from the beach but takes us south to another overlook of the distinctive hammerhead of Punta Cacarizo (fig. 10). From this fresh perspective, the truncated plane of limestone rises to meet us on its 6° ramp. In the distance beyond, but parallel to the strike of Punta Cacarizo, is the thin profile of the largest of the Santa Inés islands. The jeep track negotiates more complicated topography to the south. Yesterday's lesson about changes in road coloration comes to mind. Now the track is tan at an elevation of almost 200 feet (60 m) above sea level, and an occasional slab of limestone reveals traces of a fossil pecten. Farther along, the track abruptly turns red as it crosses an unconformity onto the former Pliocene land surface. From the road alone, it is difficult to know whether the advance of the Pliocene sea halted permanently at about this level or whether the limestone was eroded away. In either case, the boundary line represents a former shoreline. Only a more thorough survey of the surrounding area can provide the answer. The hotel is slightly more than a half mile (1 km) away. At the hillcrest, Punta Mezquitito and Bahía Santa Inés come into view. I feel a strong attachment to this section of the road, partly because I have tramped here so often, but also because the road flows so graciously with the contours of the country. The descent toward Punta Mezquitito follows a narrow nose of land with declivities that fall away steeply on either side.

Below, the road crosses a bench on which the water reservoir for the hotel and the rest of the Punta Chivato community resides. The pipes leading to and from the concrete basin are leaky, and the vegetation surrounding the covered reservoir is luxurious, even during the most drought-ridden years. A pair of palm trees provides shade. The ubiquitous brittlebush *(Encelia farinoso)* is constantly in bloom here, its bright yellow flowers on bushy branches with silver-gray leaves. The plant belongs to the sunflower tribe, but the flowers remind me of black-eyed Susans. During wet years, brittlebush covers the landscape like a yellow carpet. During dry years, the plant fails to bloom, the leaves and branches dry out, and the plant dies back. Some of my students have been startled by the noise the dead plant makes when brushed against—a sound similar to a rattlesnake's warning. The leaves are aromatic; the local name for this plant is *incienso,* because gum derived from the plant may be used as incense. A profusion of plants is usually in bloom here; another one is the malva rosa *(Melochina tomentosa)* with its purple flower.

Two roads diverge from the water reservoir. One follows a pair of gentle switchbacks to reach the narrow plain on the eastern side of the Punta Chivato promontory and the homes perched on the east shore. The other makes a precipitous dive of 50 feet (about 15 m) to rejoin the same broad shelf that wraps around the promontory's southeastern terminus. We take the latter, south toward the hotel and the conclusion of the day's circuit.

The winter sun sets early over Bahía Santa Inés and sinks behind a line of jagged mountains southeast of Punta Chivato, typically around 6:00 P.M. I like to sit on the veranda above the sea cliffs outside the hotel restaurant and watch the day come to its colorful close. There is rarely a day without a beautiful sunset, and I am never too busy to catch it. When the cloud cover is scant, the setting sun creates an orb of rosy colors. Tonight, a formation of cirrus clouds, or mare's tails, crowns the western horizon. The last rays of sunlight diffuse through the wispy clouds to spread a thin, warm glow across the sky. Then the sun is gone and the rosy colors briefly intensify. The air over the desert country immediately chills. I linger for the long afterglow. The landscape is briefly trapped in a vacuum that is neither day nor night. The backdrop of the Sierra Guadalupe sets up a succession of silhouettes bathed in ethereal shades of blue and purple. If you look carefully, you might count five or six distinct ridgelines against the horizon, each with its own uniquely delicate color. The blue tones slowly change to purple, and the purple tones imperceptibly fade to gray. The night curtain comes down, but the bright light of this now-finished day has framed for us a more intricate picture than the one experienced yesterday. We are getting to know the place and how it has greeted the varied days over 5,000 millennia since the dawning of the first Pliocene day.

Near North Shore: Punta Chivato

Every species lives a life unique to itself, and every species dies
a different way.—E. O. Wilson, *The Diversity of Life*

W hy do certain plants and animals live where they do, and not somewhere else? Biogeographic boundaries encircle the globe in bold swaths,
often related to gradients of temperature and moisture on an all-encompassing
north-south axis.[1] At Punta Chivato, the opposite sides of the high-shouldered
promontory are less than 2 miles (more than 3 km) apart but host strikingly
different biological domains. How do new organisms appear, and why are some
susceptible to extinction? Great upheavals in the history of life have occurred
and doubtless will continue to occur periodically on a global scale. But lesser
coups take place sometimes only on a regional scale, when life is trapped at a
dead end without safe egress to survival. The Gulf of California and its adjacent peninsula are two outposts where marine and terrestrial life experiment
side by side in splendid isolation. It has never been easy for foreign plants and
animals—like other travelers—to reach these shores. Once here, however, life
adapted to a biological paradise from which it subsequently became difficult, if
not impossible, to flee during hardships imposed by climatic change or other
catastrophes.

On this third day, our trek takes us from Punta Mezquitito across the
promontory's roof to the corner of land at Punta Chivato that lends its name to
the entire region. From there, our circuit follows the rugged near north shore,
then turns inland to recross the promontory through one of the several long
valleys that carve deep incisions in the land (map 4). The land near the promontory's center rises about 330 feet (more than 100 m) above sea level and
affords a grand, panoramic view. Descent from the crest of the mesa to the main
road will be via a shorter, steeper valley, back to Punta Mezquitito by the end of
the day. Much of the way follows coyote tracks or natural trails through dry
streambeds. The distance for today's hike is 5.3 miles (8.5 km) with relatively
steep climbs through rough country. It is wise to pack plenty of water and some
quick-energy foods.

The main road from the hotel leads between the *tienda* on one side and the
electrical generating plant on the other, then swings west below the base of the
ridge on which the water reservoir is notched. We leave the main road at the
auto mechanic's shop, soon after making the turn and reaching the bottom of a
hill. A short walk north 100 feet (about 30 m) brings us to the pigpens on the
embankment of an arroyo. The pigs raised here are destined for the Christmas

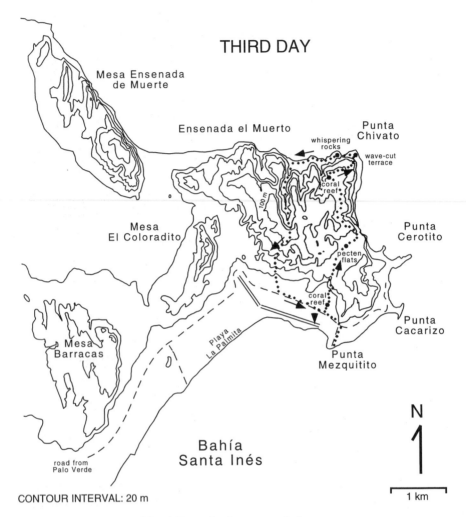

THIRD DAY

Mesa Ensenada
de Muerte

Ensenada el Muerto

Punta
Chivato

whispering
rocks

wave-cut
terrace

coral
reef

Mesa
El Coloradito

100 m

Punta
Cerotito

pecten
flats

coral
reef

Mesa
Barracas

Playa
La Palmita

Punta
Cacarizo

Punta
Mezquitito

Bahía
Santa Inés

N

road from
Palo Verde

CONTOUR INTERVAL: 20 m

1 km

Map 4. Route for the near north shore.

and Easter feasts held annually at the hotel. The pungent smell of swine excrement reminds me of childhood travels across the prairie states. It is impossible to lose your way here. Just follow your nose. A sow and several piglets are usually in residence. Before the pigs are visible, however, four or five turkey vultures *(Cathartes aura)* may be seen loitering on the fence railings. Torpid examples of their race, they wait to steal the pig's swill rather than scout for their own food. In 1940, John Steinbeck witnessed a similar standoff between domestic pigs and vultures at Cabo San Lucas.[2] These birds are not much perturbed by our presence. Their featherless, leathery red hoods permit them to thrust their heads into the bodies of dead animals without becoming matted by

Figure 11. Coral reef (Pleistocene) in arroyo embankment. Photo by author.

gore. Wheeling in clumsy circles high in the desert sky, their more energetic cousins search for carrion.

The immediate surroundings suggest an inauspicious start to the day's journey. Two colloquial expressions cross my mind. "You can't make a silk purse out of a pig's ear" is one, and the other relates to "pearls cast before swine." Ahead, the landscape is degraded by a junkyard littered with rusted cars and old refrigerators. Where is the silk purse? What pearl of nature could possibly be hidden here? Our immediate destination is the west embankment of the wide arroyo, which exposes the most complete Pleistocene coral reef I have ever encountered. The smell and the refuse disappear from my consciousness, and I am transported to a ghostly wonder world. The place features colonies of emerald coral *(Porites californica)* exquisitely arrayed in growth position (fig. 11) along a cross section that extends through the center of the ancient reef for a distance of 230 feet (70 m). This is the same coral species observed yesterday in its natural element around Punta Cacarizo's perimeter. The fossil colonies are larger and more densely packed. The base of the reef rests, variably, on Pleistocene river gravel or older Pliocene limestone. The unconformity between these beds and the overlying coral reef rises in elevation from 25 to 33 feet (7.5 m to 10 m) above present sea level, forming a gentle ramp to the north. The reef itself averages about 3.3 feet (1 m) in thickness, capped in places by as much as 12 inches (30 cm) of shell and rhodolith debris similar to the thick Pleistocene deposits previously visited behind Playa La Palmita.

The multibranched coral colonies are bouquet shaped. They stand upright as high as 6 inches (15 cm) and attain a diameter of about the same. Each colony expands from the point where the initial growth of the coral occurred. At least three generations of successive reef growth supplant one another and may be traced laterally along the embankment in distinct layers. An odd sensation prevails here, like that of wandering along a vegetable stall in a deserted food market where bunches of broccoli are stacked in neat clumps, row upon row—but the emerald color of the plant-shaped corals has long since faded away to a skeletal whiteness. Scattered here and there in the sandy streambed are entire colonies that have weathered free from the outcrop.

Moving up the arroyo to the center of the structure, we reach a large block of reef limestone broken off from the lip of the embankment and now on the floor of the streambed. When the block came to rest on its side, the overlying protective layer of shell and rhodolith debris split away to reveal the upper surface of the reef. Essentially, the view is what a swimmer would see looking down on the last generation of reef growth from above. Ten square feet (1 m²) of this surface includes roughly 40–45 coral colonies packed together as they grew in life. The density of these larger corals is nearly twice that of the *Porites californica* observed on the seafloor around Punta Cacarizo. The remaining part of the overhang at the top of the outcrop affords the opportunity to examine the size and packing of *Porites* colonies from below and to see how cavities in the crowded colonies are occupied by other reef-dwelling species.

Diving to see a modern reef is an exhilarating adventure full of vivid colors and the opportunity to witness the interaction of the living reef fauna. Yet the exposed growing mantle of a live reef represents only a facade that conceals its internal architecture. Geologists and paleontologists have an uncontrollable urge to see inside a reef in order to trace its pattern of growth. In this arroyo, below a junkyard, with a whiff of pig manure in the air, it is possible to accomplish just that with respect to a 125,000-year-old coral reef. Another dedicated student, Cordelia Ransom, spent untold hours taking the pulse of this old reef and deciphering its serial demise. She looked into all the reef's nooks and crannies from above, from below, and in cross section, carefully mapping relationships on an intricate system of grids.[3] She found that in addition to *Porites californica* and various morphotypes of coralline red algae, more than 50 species of marine invertebrates are preserved within the matrix of the fossil reef. One of the more abundant species is a small, rotund bivalve with a distinctive checkered pattern etched on its shell. The species, which has no common name, is *Divalinga eburnea*. Today, it dwells in intertidal waters to a depth of 180 feet (55 m) and ranges from the Gulf of California to Peru.[4] Its closest relative lives on the opposite side of the Americas in the Caribbean Sea.

Less common is the noble sundial shell *(Architectonica nobilis),* in the order Archaeogastropoda; it represents a living holdover from an ancient tribe of marine snails. This small, delicately sculptured gastropod exhibits a primitive coiling pattern in which each turn of the shell rises slightly above the periphery of the previous whorl. Today, the species typically inhabits tidal flats or shallow waters that range to a depth of 120 feet (37 m) from the Gulf of California to Peru.[5] The same species also occurs on both sides of the Atlantic Ocean. Other mollusks commonly found nestled within the branches of the coral colonies include an ark shell *(Barbatia reeveana)* and the turban shell *(Turbo fluctuosus),* both of which typically thrive today on rocky intertidal shores. Most of the marine invertebrates within the fossil reef were capable of living elsewhere, but the reef structure provided a maze of interstices that nurtured biodiversity.

For the most part, the Pleistocene reef is exposed only in the arroyo wall. If the streambed were to change its path, a different part of the reef would be revealed in cross section. During the spring of 1999, I helped Cordelia dig a series of sample pits beyond the banks of the arroyo in order to establish the overall dimensions of the reef. Based on some 50 pits excavated through the overlying soil and gravel, we determined that the reef extends across a small, south-facing cove that occupies an area of approximately 25 acres (10 hectares). The superb reef preservation is due to the prevailing seasonal winds, which were strongest from the north during all but the summer months. The Punta Chivato promontory shielded the reef from direct assault by wind-driven waves out of the north. A south-facing cove, however, provided no protection from storm runoff. Coral die-off due to smothering by terrestrial sediments explains the colonies' relatively small size and repetitive colonization cycles. I have seen fossil *Porites* colonies at other places in Baja California Sur that are four to five times the size of these. A growth estimate of three-eighths of an inch (1 cm) per year for this species, based on a radiograph image of internal banding, suggests that the largest colonies in the junkyard reef had a maximum life span of about 15 years. A thin cover of pebbles and shells separates the successive generations of coral colonies from one another. The overall impression is similar to that of the repetitive aprons of outwashed volcanic cobbles and pebbles on the old seabed of Bahía Santa Inés, as seen in the arroyos above Playa La Palmita two days ago.

According to residents, an intense cell of tropical storm Nora crossed directly over the Punta Chivato promontory in September 1997 and dumped 20 inches (just under a half meter) of water in 24 hours. Under such unusual conditions, it does not take long for the ground to become saturated, after which the water flows away in surface sheets. On the east shore, Marge and Jere Summers broke a hole through the cinder-block wall in the lower level of their home in order to relieve pressure after water began to sprout from the electrical outlets. They opened the back door on the same level, leading to the beach below, allowing the water to flow freely through the house. The previous January, I had started with another student on the survey of the *Porites* reef, but thickets of vegetation and debris slumps that draped the arroyo wall hampered our observations. The September flood cleared out the streambed and washed the arroyo embankment free of obstructions. Afterward, the reef and the entire stream course never looked better, and Cordelia's project was assured success.

Crossing the reef along the streambed, it is easy to pinpoint where the *Porites* corals ceased to grow in shoal water. The top of the embankment is littered with pebbles and cobbles encrusted by coralline red algae. Here the arroyo wall is formed by San Marcos limestone footed on basement rocks belonging to the Comondú andesite. Farther along, a shallow lagoon formed behind the reef, marked by beige Pleistocene limestone entrenched below the former surface of the older, Pliocene limestone. The back-reef environment was enclosed and placid, with the result that mostly fine-grained carbonate sediments accumulated there. It is possible to explore the faunal contents of the lagoon to the east or west. In places, individuals of the large conch *(Strombus galeatus)* are weathered out from the lagoonal beds and lie partially embedded in loose stream sediments on the arroyo bottom.

To the north, the cove in which the Pleistocene reef and lagoon reside ends in an amphitheater surrounded by cliffs of San Marcos limestone towering almost 100 feet (30 m) above the rear of the cove. The streambed that cuts across the coral reef traces back and upward to a notch in the cliff face, from which a 50-foot (15-m) waterfall cascades during heavy rainfall. A pile of rock rubble has accumulated below this notch, flushed through the canyon above. The cliff face at the waterfall is too abrupt to climb, but the streambed in the upper canyon is accessible by a zigzag traverse up the talus slope and over benchlike cliffs to the east (map 4). The object is to reach the waterfall's edge and proceed north through the canyon. Surprisingly, near the top of the slope are large bivalve shells, many of them broken, lying scattered among the rocks. Although bleached white, these shells belonged to contemporary, living mollusks flown here by birds such as the yellow-footed seagull *(Larus livens)* and dropped on the rocks from a height in order to break the shells and expose the meat. The cluster of broken shells represents a bird midden, so the nesting sites cannot be very far away.

We scamper up low benches of limestone in the Pliocene escarpment in order to reach the flats overlooking the coral cove to the west. The detour north is through open level ground, but the dry waterfall's lip can be reached only by a short descent through strata exposed at the mouth of the canyon. The limestone in these parts has a rather different local appearance: it is full of large cavities where the calcium carbonate was dissolved away sometime after lithification. Back at the hotel, some boulders from this area are arranged along one of the parking areas with flowers potted in the sizable cavities. Here in the canyon, the largest cavities are the size of small caves. A former hotel manager kept a pair of bobcats on the premises. On a previous visit to this canyon, I caught a fleeting glimpse of one as it disappeared into the mouth of a large cavity on the west flank above the coral cove. I was never certain whether it was one of the semitame animals or a wild cousin. Nonetheless, the larger openings in the canyon walls make excellent dens. The abundance of scat suggests the place is frequented by coyotes, and I would not be surprised if they rear their families in this vicinity. Somewhere to the west on higher ground, Max Simian discovered a pair of bore tusks during his field mapping. The locals don't seem to know anything about javelinas here; perhaps there are feral pigs.

The 1997 flood flushed out the streambed, which previously was choked with small boulders and a tangle of brambles. The path through this scenic small canyon is now wide and clear. Clumps of vegetation still survive, such as the legumes known as palo blanco *(Lysiloma candida)* with its smooth, white bark and palo verde *(Cercidium microphyllum)* with its smooth green bark. These small trees are conspicuous members of the desert plant community at lower elevations throughout Baja California Sur, but at Punta Chivato they are found only in the protected draws and canyons on the promontory's south side, where shade and water are reliable. Both trees bear the seed pods distinct to legumes, but the palo blanco is a thornless plant, which makes it all the more attractive and graceful. Except for the infrequent flash flood, the canyon is a peaceful refuge well protected from sun and wind. The overall diversity of plant and animal life is higher here than elsewhere on the promontory. Standing near the lip of the dry streambed, it is possible to look back over the Pleistocene coral reef below and then up the draw toward the inviting clusters of trees. I can't help thinking that vastly different kinds of marine and plant life have conformed to the same basic game plan in seeking shelter from the elements on the south side of the promontory. What slight perturbations to the environment would restore the *Porites* reef at Punta Cacarizo? What changes would banish the local legumes from their tenuous foothold in the southern draws? Species come and go—sometimes permanently.

On the northward march, we gain elevation slowly against the modest incline of the arroyo. The steep ramparts of the enclosing canyon gradually begin to lose their stature and recede. The landscape opens out onto a broad flat, across which streambeds converge from all directions in a dendritic drainage pattern. Our natural footpath reaches fork after fork and constantly narrows at each branch. From an elevation of about 165 feet (50 m) above sea level, the vistas to the east and west take in another 33 feet (10 m) or more of relief at the lip of a panlike landscape. Here, vegetation grows sparse. An invisible boundary has been crossed that separates coarser limestone with its weathered cavities from more compact layers of silty limestone with a thin soil cover. It is useless to follow miniscule branches of the streambed any farther. The way forward is northeast toward the low basin rim. Although hard to distinguish, the jeep track that brought us home at the end of the day yesterday is only a short distance east.

I call this place the pecten flats (map 4) because of the numbers of fossil shells that have weathered out of the silty limestone. This is the same offshore facies exposed in the cliffs of the east shore. In fact, we are at the top of the same pile of Pliocene strata that we visited at sea level during the lunch break yesterday. It is barely more than a third of a mile (a half kilometer) to the great fracture where the next catastrophic failure of the east cliff face is expected. The ground is littered with fossil pectens and a few oysters. Whereas the rocks on the shore below retain only the molds of these shells (empty space where the original shell was dissolved away), the surface layer on the pecten flats yields complete but disarticulated shells.

You may know you hold a pecten shell in your hands, but not which species you've found. The semitropical to tropical west coast of the Americas supports some 29 pecten species, and it takes a specialist to tell them apart.[6] When one adds fossil pectens to the mix, the situation is even more taxing. I am not a pecten expert, but I know someone who can help identify the shells from the pecten flats. As it turns out, there are four different species of fossil pectens here, all of which are extinct. All are restricted to the Pliocene strata. However, an earlier visitor to these flats considered the shells and topography to be consistent with those of a Pleistocene terrace, similar to but older than the shelf on which the east-shore houses now sit.[7] There might be other, more elevated Pleistocene terraces on the Punta Chivato promontory, but not here. This is the outer part of a carbonate ramp. If time travel made it possible to be here during Pliocene time, 3 million years ago or more, we would be in water well over our heads. Very little of the Punta Chivato promontory remained above sea level at that time.

The ancient Pliocene shoreline rises from the low hills to the north. We rejoin the worn jeep track and meet a protruding topographic nose near the east edge of the promontory. The steep track divides into two lanes. Gaining the top of the hill, we find ourselves on the Pliocene conglomerate that makes such a prominent zigzag pattern in the great sea cliff below. We have exceeded the northern limit of yesterday's circuit and are halfway north to Punta Chivato (map 4). The tan roadbed swings wide to the northwest to circumvent a short, deep ravine eroded far back from the margin of the east shore. At the huge cleft, the road abruptly changes to red, and we are back on Pliocene land represented by andesitic Comondú rocks. Now the track straightens out to the north, parallel to the east shore for about a third of a mile (a half kilometer).

To the west, it soon becomes apparent that a north-south valley demarcates a deep divide in the promontory. The track descends a mere hint of a slope, and the roadbed is tan once again. Here, I want to abandon the track and cut northwest across country to reach the edge of the gorge. The valley's side drops precipitously some 250 feet (about 75 m), then flattens out, joining the sea on the near north shore. On the edge of the precipice is an outcrop of Pliocene conglomerate and limestone scarcely more than 10 feet (3 m) thick. The beds make up part of another carbonate ramp that dips 5° in a northerly direction, parallel to the axis of the gorge. The conglomerate includes black boulders and cobbles eroded from the Miocene andesite bedrock immediately below the lip of the gorge. Blended with the limestone matrix in the conglomerate are dome-shaped coral colonies (fig. 12) that attain a maximum diameter of nearly 9 inches (22 cm).

In both shape and fabric, this Pliocene species is radically different from the delicately branching Pleistocene corals in the reef traversed at the day's start. These display larger openings for the fleshy coral polyps, which long ago rotted away from their stony embrasures. The domed colonies' surfaces vaguely resemble curved wasp nests in that individual receptacles are packed together in a polygonal pattern. Tiny star-shaped ridges stamp the floor of each cell. The Pliocene corals here seem not to be linked together in a rigid reef structure. Judging from the associated conglomerate and the proximity of the Miocene-Pliocene unconformity, however, it is certain that these corals on the north shore of the Punta Chivato promontory thrived under vigorous waves hitting the shore. The coral heads are sufficiently large and stable that bivalves related to the *Thracia curta* in the dolomite platform off the south end of Playa La Palmita bored into the relative safety of some colonies.

Tracing the identity of the Pliocene coral yielded intriguing information. The coral is *Solenastrea fairbanksi,* an extinct species endemic to the Gulf of California. It is known from few localities other than Carrizo Creek in southern California, where it occurs in strata belonging to the Imperial Formation, which is regarded as late Miocene to early Pliocene in age.[8] That part of southern California, 470 miles (760 km) northwest of Punta Chivato on the

Figure 12. *Solenastrea* coral (Pliocene). Photo by author.

edge of the Salton Sea, was once the northernmost extent of the Gulf of California when global sea level stood higher than it is today. The closest surviving relatives of this particular coral species are found in the Caribbean. The species' progenitor is believed to have reached the nascent Gulf of California from the Caribbean before the Isthmus of Panama formed a geographic barrier between the Atlantic and Pacific Oceans. Likewise, extant species such as *Architectonica nobilis* and *Divalinga eburnea,* found as Pleistocene fossils in the junkyard reef, reached the Pacific via the Atlantic and Caribbean prior to 3.5 million years ago, when the Isthmus of Panama became a permanent barrier. Other species, such as the geoduck *(Panopea globosa)* found buried in the Pleistocene seabed of Bahía Santa Inés, clearly reached the Gulf of California from the north Pacific.

Although easy to overlook, the thin Pliocene deposit here at the edge of the gorge is a significant geological hangnail, on the verge of being separated from the slender finger of land that juts northward. Max's indefatigable inspection drew my attention to it. The dark andesite below the crust of conglomerate has a startlingly fresh look about it, although it cooled from a surface flow earlier than the marine conglomerate cannibalized from it. The igneous rock looks fresh because the exposure at the lip of the gorge is relatively recent. In time, the gorge's margin will be enlarged through continued erosion, and the tenuous bit of physical evidence that incorporates the odd story of *Solenastrea fairbanksi* will disappear without a trace.

We have reached the near north shore, but the shortest path to the water's edge from this spot is straight down. It's best to make a jog east and rejoin the jeep track that leads to Punta Chivato; it follows a red path across the terrain, although a more substantial cover of limestone borders the road to the north (with no trace of *Solenastrea fairbanksi*). In the distance to the northwest, nearly 9 miles (14 km) away, looms the large island of San Marcos. The southern end of the island hosts a large strip-mining operation for gypsum. Sometimes I've seen a tiny puff of dust rise from the island; a few seconds later, I would hear the report of an explosion from the mining operation. Farther away, almost due north, is Isla Tortuga.

The trail brings us to the northeast corner of the peninsula and plunges over the edge to the automated light tower at Punta Chivato, some 115 feet (35 m) below. The jeep track that crosses this end of the promontory was built to service the tower. I can't imagine driving a vehicle down this slope or, worse yet, attempting to come back up again. Clearly it has been done, although the track is now deeply rutted by the runoff from the 1997 rainstorm. The next driver to attempt the descent will take a parallel path, and the scars in the landscape will not fade easily. It's difficult to walk straight down, so I zigzag back and forth until I reach the foot of the slope. The light tower stands on a magnificent marine terrace that curves around the corner of the promontory like the wide brim of a hat, the steep crown of which we have just descended. The seaward edge of the terrace sits 40 feet (12 m) above the waves. The surface is strewn with loose fossil shells, mainly the ubiquitous turban shell, a species of the horse-hoof limpet (in the genus *Hipponix*), and the large ark shell *(Arca pacifica)*. All strongly imply that intertidal conditions once prevailed here and that waves formerly beat against the toe of the steep hill. At the base of the high sea cliffs, the waves are actively eroding another rock platform.

A wave-cut terrace is a nearly flat platform eroded in solid rock that usually adjoins coastal bluffs. Depending on tidal range, the shelflike structure may be entirely exposed at low tide. During high tide, it is awash with waves that beat against the adjacent sea cliffs and enlarge the structure in a landward direction. Abrasion occurs when sand and gravel grind over the platform and against the associated sea cliffs. During storms, the intensity of the erosion is heightened, and waves that force their way into cracks and crevices at the bottom of the cliff line loosen and pry out rock fragments. This in turn creates overhangs that weaken the cliff face above. An abandoned marine terrace often entails a deposit containing the fossil remains of marine invertebrates left behind when sea level retreated. The terrace deposit in the vicinity of the light tower is exceedingly thin, although a Pleistocene beach deposit of coarse carbonate sand drapes the platform some 650 feet (200 m) to the south.

The terrace height here at Punta Chivato matches well with the shoreline elevation of the abandoned Phantom Island behind Bahía Santa Inés and with the top of the junkyard reef stranded above the south shore, suggesting that the maximum advance in sea level during the last interglacial epoch, about 125,000 years ago, left a consistent line of evidence chiseled on the landscape's perimeter. The Punta Chivato platform, however, is more than twice as high at its seaward edge than the analogous shelf on the southeastern shore where many of the American homes we passed yesterday are situated. A glance at our topographic map (map 4) shows that a line of sea cliffs once existed at about the same elevation as that found here, well behind the line of homes. Using the 65-foot (20 m) contour line as a reference, the wave-cut platform on the southeast shore is seen to be twice as wide as the platform at this locality. The marine terraces are thus variable in their dimensions and may entail a slight seaward angle. The wider any given marine terrace, the less energy is expended by waves that reach the back sea cliffs. The bench here at Punta Chivato is comparatively narrow and was certainly subject to more aggressive erosion than the bench southward past Punta Cacarizo.

Give or take a bit, a persistent terrace 40 feet (12 m) high is widely regarded as the handiwork of the maximum rise in sea level throughout the midriff region of the gulf during the last interglacial epoch. A small volcanic neck, fittingly named El Sombrerito, is a well-known landmark located not far away to the south in the Mulegé harbor. Indeed, the "little sombrero" looks like a wide-brimmed hat scored by a wave-cut terrace incised around its towerlike base. The Mulegé platform has an elevation 40 feet (12 m) above sea level; its dating is based on isotopes from fossil corals formed before the advance of the last major ice age in the Northern Hemisphere.[9] A comparable terrace is indented almost as a continuous coastal roadbed along the outer shores of the massive Concepción Peninsula to the southeast.[10] As discussed in chapter 2, however, the average global rise in sea level was only about 20 feet (6 m) above its present level 125,000 years ago, when the overall climate was somewhat warmer than today's. Why, then, are these marine terraces about twice as high for their reputed age than those found in many other parts of the world?

The answer is that the peninsular coast of Baja California has not remained static in elevation since the terraces were cut but has undergone a slow and continuous process of uplift. The process of coastal uplift is imperceptible to us: it is calculated in the range of 2 inches (5 cm) per millennium. Why the gulf coast of Baja California should be affected in this way is another question that requires our further exploration to resolve. The concept of multiple terraces and their bearing on local or global changes in sea level became known to science through the work of Robert Chambers.

FEATURE / Robert Chambers and the Discovery of Stepped Terraces

In expanding on Amanz Gressly's facies concept, the law of the correlation of facies advanced by Johannes Walther necessarily invokes various mechanisms through which sea level may gradually advance and retreat over geologic time. The zigzag pattern of shifting facies observed yesterday in the east cliff face of the Punta Chivato promontory speaks empirically to this concept. But what if relative sea level remained fixed over some intervals of time and underwent rapid changes during other intervals? In contrast to the long Pliocene ramps now familiar to us, such as that anchored to Punta Cacarizo, static sea level on a stable shoreline results in just the sort of Pleistocene marine terrace found at Punta Chivato. If sea level remains static over a prolonged interval of time, but the rocky shoreline against which it washes is subjected to episodic uplift or subsidence, then a succession of stepped terraces will form. The same will occur if the land remains stable over a prolonged interval of time but sea level undergoes a series of rapid, episodic advances or retreats. Robert Chambers (1802–1871) was the first to recognize the regularity imposed on landscapes by stepped terraces. He collected systematic measurements on a vast interregional scale in order to correlate different terrace levels throughout the British Isles, and he related those data to information from elsewhere around the world.

Raised in the family of a Scottish cotton manufacturer, Robert Chambers developed a life-long passion for books.[11] After gaining experience running his own bookstore, he became at the age of 30 a partner in a successful publishing firm based in Edinburgh. He was also a writer, publishing his own books. His greatest claim to notoriety is as the anonymous author of a book titled *Vestiges of the Natural History of Creation,* published by his firm in 1844. Better known simply as the *Vestiges,* the book was a hotly debated item in mid-nineteenth-century British society. It went through 10 editions before Charles Darwin got around to publishing his groundbreaking book *On the Origin of Species* in 1859. Even in his own time, Chambers rightfully was regarded as a dilettante. His research for the *Vestiges* on progressive trends in the geological history of life was conducted strictly in the library. In marked contrast, Darwin's great effort entailed a substantial component of field experience as well as library research. Chambers wrote and published another book in 1848, less well known than the *Vestiges,* under the title *Ancient Sea-Margins as Memorials of Changes in the Relative Level of Sea and Land*. In this instance, the author brought a substantial amount of original fieldwork to bear on the topic and freely lent his name to the book.

Wasting no time in setting the tone of his treatise on ancient British shorelines, Chambers wrote:

> Taking observed facts for our data, we know that there was a time subsequent to the completion of the rock formations, when this island (not to speak of other parts of the earth) was submerged to the height of at least 1700 feet. The proofs lie plain and palpable before our eyes, in the soft detrital masses, mixed in many places with marine shells, which overlie the hardened formations, reaching in some places to that height above the present sea-level.[12]

So introduced, the premise of the book invokes the important features that define a marine terrace. Thereafter, the author clearly poses the object of his extensive labors as a succession of questions:

> Has the change of the relative level of land and sea been accomplished by an upward movement of the land, or by the recession of the sea? Has the shift been slow and equable with regard to time, or by fits and starts with long pauses between, or by a slow movement interrupted by pauses? Has the time embraced by the whole series of phenomena been long or short, geologically speaking?[13]

What follows is a long exposition on stepped terraces at specific localities, mostly in proximity to the shores of the British Isles. Early on, Chambers introduces the first of 24 scaled cross sections for a set of terraces situated on the south shore of Loch Linnhe in the Scottish shire of Inverness:

> The open space at the mouth of Glen Rie, about half a mile wide, is filled with gravelly flats presenting peat bogs and corn patches. Amongst the confusion of objects, it is easy to trace a succession of terraces falling back from the sea-shore,—first, one about 32 feet, then one at 43. It is of no consequence at the present moment, but will be so by-and-by, that these are followed by others at 56, and from 65 to 70 [feet].[14]

In addition to cross sections with recorded elevations, Chambers illustrated his book with many sketches of terraced landscapes. The frontispiece is a lithograph from the famous golf links of St. Andrews, and the text includes a description of terraces associated with the "chief ground for playing the game of golf in Scotland." Noting that the lowest tract at St. Andrews is composed of a sandy deposit full of white shells, the author complains that it is difficult to retrieve a golf ball which errantly falls that way.

Another impressive feature of *Ancient Sea-Margins* is the accompanying foldout map of the Lochaber region in Scotland, which traces the terraces or shelves surrounding Glen Roy. Not everything Chambers originally regarded as a marine terrace has stood the test of time, and the three tiers or "parallel roads" of Glen Roy were later found conclusively to be related to changing levels in a glacial lake unrelated to the sea. Likewise, the parallel features Chambers described and illustrated on the River Tweed are certainly river terraces and not marine terraces. Other localities with bedrock and associated shell deposits, as defined at the book's outset, qualify as genuine marine terraces. At Covesea on the Moray Firth northeast of Inverness, for example, Chambers describes sea caves eroded in the Devonian Old Red Sandstone that are well above the present shoreline but are floored with deposits of mixed sand, pebbles, and fossil shells.

Appendices and tables at the back of the book summarize data on terrace levels accumulated from Scotland, England, Ireland, France, Norway, Canada, and the United States. In this regard, Chambers was the first to try to assemble a global database on Pleistocene sea-level changes. With few refinements, the working approach to this kind of inquiry has remained much the same during the last century and a half. The French geologist Luc Ortlieb, for example, extensively surveyed territories surrounding the Gulf of California.[15] His measured profiles are strikingly analogous to those pioneered by Robert Chambers. The goal is essentially the same: to correlate trends in stepped terraces from one locality to another.

Ortlieb's studies have drawn attention because the trends in terrace elevations on the gulf coast of Baja California are internally consistent, for the most part, but do not correspond to trends on the opposite coast of mainland Mexico. Chambers concluded his 1848 book with vague references to abrupt uplift along the Chilean coast of South America (caused by earthquakes) and to gradual uplift around the Baltic Sea (caused by glacial rebound after the recession of the Scandinavian ice sheets). Although he did not appreciate the mechanics of these processes, both involve changes in land elevation in opposition to static global sea level. Chambers also suggested that changes in the subsidence of the ocean floor, known from Charles Darwin's research on the formation of coral atolls, could cause episodic drops in sea level.

Landscapes of the Punta Chivato promontory confront us with two different lines of physical evidence for relative changes in sea level in the Gulf of

Figure 13. North shore, Punta Chivato promontory. Photo by author.

California. One concerns Pleistocene unconformities associated with marine terraces, for which the example underfoot here at the light tower is exceptionally clear. The other is related to Miocene-Pliocene unconformities that conform to inclined ramps. Due south from the light tower, a level marine terrace stretches out before us for more than half a mile (1 km) along the eastern shore. Rotating 90° due west, however, we see a superb example of a carbonate ramp sloping off the north escarpment of the Punta Chivato promontory (fig. 13). The ramp structure is approximately 820 feet (250 m) away. The only way to reach it is to leave the safety of the wide marine terrace and cling to a narrow coyote trail that negotiates the north shore on a steep slope above sea cliffs at a slightly higher elevation than the footing of the light tower. I wonder about the wild animals that regularly patrol this path at night, and I have no doubt that four legs are more stable than two anytime.

The path spans an indenture in the shoreline caused by erosion and cliff failure. No hint of the marine terrace is left intact below the coyote trail, but the deep bite taken out of the coast at this place gives us a wonderful opportunity to examine the exposed Miocene-Pliocene unconformity where the land swings out again. It is soon midday, and relief from the sun is found in the shade of the northeast-facing cliff face, where dark Miocene andesite and orange tuffaceous

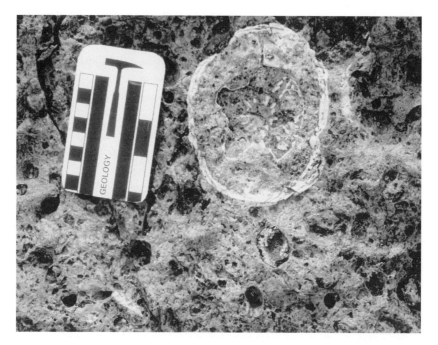

Figure 14. Outline of large echinoid test (Pliocene). Photo by author.

rocks are overlain by Pliocene conglomerate and limestone. A bench eroded in the rocks gives access to the unconformity. The ramp angle, measured directly against the cliff face, is 8°, dipping due north. Cobbles and small boulders of andesite form a diffuse conglomerate held firmly together by a limestone matrix. The internal molds of marine fossils are plentiful. Fossils are not easy to identify at the species level from internal molds, but the tightly coiled, flat top of the cone shell (gastropod genus *Conus*) and the bold crease of finlike projections along the anterior and posterior margins of the bittersweet shell (bivalve genus *Glycymeris*) are distinctive. Many species belonging to these genera are known today to inhabit intertidal rocky shorelines or sand flats.

A visit to the crumbling limestone that tops the carbonate ramp is guaranteed to yield fossil molds that have weathered free from the surface. A half dozen kinds of fossil mollusks are plentiful. Previously unmet and particularly arresting is an outline of white rings commonly embossed in these rocks (fig. 14). Almost 5 inches (12 cm) in diameter, the rings trace the outline of a large sea biscuit *(Clypeaster bowersi)*. If you look carefully, a spot may be found where a perfectly preserved corner of the calcite test pokes through the limestone. This heavy echinoderm, known only from the San Marcos Formation, is extinct. The rocky shoreline and associated carbonate ramp here, near the water's edge, as well as the ramp fragment high on the hill crest with the *Solenastrea* corals, date from the early Pliocene. Unlike the fossil sand dollars found in large numbers in the muddy sandstone on the promontory's south shore on day one, the related sea biscuit is built like a heavily armored tank, capable of living in shallow waters around the north side's windswept and wave-tossed rocky shores. No sand dollars are to be found here.

Except once, I have never encountered anyone else on this shore, other than my research colleagues or students. One afternoon, Laura Libbey agreed to assist on Max's project at the close of the 1995 field season. We had left our gear here while we searched for more fossils and made measurements upland farther along the coast. Suddenly, I spotted a lone figure coming our way from the west across the north shore on the edge of the coastal cliff. I rubbed my eyes and looked again to make sure it was a person. The only access to the west is the remote beach at Ensenada El Muerto, almost 2 miles (3 km) away as the crow flies. We returned to stand guard over our possessions.

I introduced myself using rusty Spanish. "Cómo está," I said. He shook my hand firmly and gave me his name, Juan, I believe. "Mucho gusto," I said and he returned the favor. "¿Tú hija?" he asked, pointing to Laura. I was not sure what he meant. Gesturing to me, he inquired "¿Papá?" I laughed and replied "Estudiante," with a nod to Laura. "Estudiamos geología," I continued. This drew a blank. "Tenemos fósiles," I tried, handing him one of the fossil molds. "¡Ah, maestro!" he exclaimed, pointing again to me with a smile on his face. "¿Cuántos años?" he asked, holding a clam mold in the palm of his hand. "Cinco millón, más o menos," I replied. "Es muy interesante," he said, turning the fossil over in his hands. He paused for a moment, wondering how to explain his business here. He must have realized that our limited knowledge of Spanish was going to make the job difficult.

Then our new friend sighed and swung the small pack he carried off his shoulders. From within he withdrew a single fat photo album. We sat down, side by side on the rough limestone, and he began to turn the pages. Page after page unfolded a collection of color prints showing the coastal rock formations with the spray of waves dashed against rugged shores. Some photos captured the wonderful blue of the sea against the muted colors of the shore cliffs; others caught the shifting moods of the setting sun on the land. Not a single photo showed a human figure—only the land and the sea. Laura and I were astonished.

"La costa rocosa es muy bonito," I managed to stammer. "Sí, claro," he replied, closing the album and packing it away. There was nothing more to be said. We shook hands again, and he went on his way toward the Punta Chivato light tower. For a fleeting moment, I wanted to run after him and explain where the coyote trail would bring him. I wanted to tell him how the present and ancient geographies of the shoreline meld into one another. He should know more about "las líneas de costas rocosas antiguas." But somehow I think he understood. "Maestro," he had called me. After he disappeared, Laura and I wondered if the encounter had actually occurred. "There was nothing else in his backpack," she observed. Indeed, there was no sign of any camera equipment.

Sally lightfoot crabs *(Graspus graspus)* restlessly scurry over the wet rocks in the shade below. Occasionally, a large wave smacks against the shore and sends up a restrained shower of spray. During the early afternoon on a calm day, a few whitecaps typically begin to kick up on the waters between the Punta Chivato promontory and Isla San Marcos. I recall only one visit to the north shore when the sea remained dead flat. That was during March 1996, when my student Patrick Russell joined me for a swim directly off these shores. Here the lime-stone layers of the San Marcos Formation form sea cliffs rising about 13 feet (4 m) out of the water. These same limestone strata also project underwater as evenly spaced ramparts, similar to the "groove and spur" morphology on the windward side of some reefs. Protruding spurs dissipate the impact of waves against the reef, and the return flow of the waves is channeled away by the grooves. Under a moderate northerly wind, the attack of waves on this coast-line is intense. On that becalmed day, however, it was possible to stand upright in waist-deep water on the shallow spurs and then dive down into the interven-ing grooves, where tropical fish darted to and fro. In this case, the parallel ramparts and retreats had developed not through coral growth but through wave erosion. The same joints in the limestone that permit waves to remove material along zones of weakness extend far back into the cliffs. With each advance of a wave, water may be forced under considerable pressure through crevices and small caverns.

Equipped only with swim masks and snorkels, Patrick and I didn't try to explore such openings underwater. But while warming ourselves in the sun on the sea cliffs afterward, we heard a peculiar sound issuing from the rocks nearby, as if the land itself were breathing like a giant in slumber. The noise had a gentle, even cadence to it. The shore rocks paused to breathe in, and then let out a soft hiss. We got to our feet and crawled over the rocks, back and forth in different directions, in order to find precisely from where it issued. As we listened, the sighing led to a small, innocuous crack in the limestone. Today, as I search, the waves are more active and the hiss is a bit more emphatic.

Rediscovering the spot, I drop a half fistful of sand into the crack during a lull in the noise. With the next exhalation, some of the sand flies out the crack and into the air like a tiny geyser. Each pause is accompanied by a rollback in the waves from shore below us, and each exhalation is perfectly timed to occur after the arrival of the next wave. Air is driven by the waves into the rocks and compressed, so it must escape upward though this crack during the maximum collision of each wave. Whispering Rocks is what I call this place (map 4). Someday, the fracture below the crack will widen into a cavern, and the chamber will become a blowhole where water will erupt like a fountain when fed by the largest waves.

Up slope approximately about 100 feet (30 m) inland from the whispering rocks is an unexpected world of karst pinnacles. This feature is part of the Pleistocene marine terrace where a small pocket beach of carbonate sand was trapped between two prongs of San Marcos limestone that formerly projected into the sea. On a smaller scale, the setting is similar to the rock ribs that embrace the beach at Playa Cerotito, visited yesterday. The elevation is 36 feet (11 m) above sea level, nearly even with the light tower at Punta Chivato. The pinnacles are small, closely spaced towers of coarse beach limestone that stand individually about 20–30 inches (50–70 cm) high and cover an area less than about one acre (a half hectare). In cross section traceable from one small tower to the next, the cemented beach deposit is lined by laminations that dip gently seaward at an angle of between 4° and 10°, indicating that the Pleistocene beach angle was fairly high. Partial dissolution of the beach deposit and development of the karst pinnacles occurred well after sea level fell and the carbonate sands turned to stone. Whereas karst erosion requires repetitious dousing by water, the environment here is very arid. Seawater does not reach these rocks— unlike those pocked with karst pits on exposed Punta Cacarizo—and probably has not for thousands of years. It is more likely that the pinnacles were formed long ago under a wetter climate, when the temperate climatic zone extended farther south.

We think of the American Southwest, which includes the Sonoran Desert on both sides of the border between Arizona and the Mexican state of Sonora, as a vast arid land. During a series of repeated glacial advances and retreats in the Northern Hemisphere during the last 2 million years, however, the region south of the Colorado Plateau was periodically dotted by a constellation of pluvial, or freshwater, lakes.[16] One of the larger Arizona lakes was Lake Cochise, east of Tucson. To the west, in southern California, and to the northwest, in Utah and Nevada, even larger lakes came and went as climatic conditions oscillated. They developed under conditions of extensive rainfall that caused the region's water table to rise significantly. The largest pluvial lake in the

American Southwest was Lake Bonneville, of which the Great Salt Lake is a holdover. During its maximum expansion, between 17,000 and 15,000 years ago, Lake Bonneville covered an area of nearly 20,000 square miles (about 51,700 km²), seven times the size of the Great Salt Lake.[17] Lake Bonneville and others like it left behind a succession of lake terraces that would have impressed Robert Chambers. A dry chain of small pluvial lakes that crosses Mexican Highway 1 north at Laguna Chapala attests to changes in climate that brought cooler summer temperatures and wetter conditions to Baja California. During one of those earlier glacial episodes, the geoduck first made its way from northern Pacific latitudes to the Gulf of California, and wetter conditions at Punta Chivato stimulated erosion of the karst pinnacles.

I can envisage an Asian garden planted within the recesses of the karst topography, complete with graceful footbridges to bring us to various overlooks on the acreage. In China or Japan, such a spot would be walled off and protected. The spires are delicate, and it would be a travesty to attempt to cross the intricate maze on foot. These are not the only karst pinnacles on the north coast of the Punta Chivato promontory. The coastal trail passes below another abandoned beach 820 feet (250 m) farther west along the shore but at a higher elevation, some 90 feet (27 m) above sea level. Pinnacles sprout there like a bed of portly white asparagus on a rib of land that thrusts seaward from the escarpment. The place may correspond to an older marine terrace of the kind widely interpreted by Luc Ortlieb at higher elevations along the gulf coast of Baja California Sur.

The coastal cliffs on this part of the north shore rise abruptly from the water's edge to stand more than 30 feet (9 m) above sea level. Near the entrance to the first deep valley that dissects the Punta Chivato promontory (viewed earlier from above), our path crosses to Miocene andesite from the basal conglomerate and limestone typical of the San Marcos Formation. Tilted volcanic layers exposed here conform to a north-south orientation, but their dip is only 20° to 23° to the west, about half as steep as that observed yesterday along the east shore. Descending to the arroyo's mouth near the cobble beach yields a look upstream into the valley. Save for the thin wedge of coral-rich limestone at the top of the east valley wall, no trace of buff to tan limestone is in sight. Also, the coastal terrace fails to penetrate inland along the lower valley walls. The valley is a recent feature, eroded after the changes in sea level that left behind Pliocene carbonate ramps and the much younger Pleistocene terrace. We must climb the far wall of the arroyo to regain the other side of the 30-foot (9-m) terrace. Farther west, the slope in Comondú volcanics rising from the terrace on our left is dotted with leatherplants *(Jatropha cuneata),* all of which bend at ground level and flare out to the south as stunted krummholz. The coastal plain is barren, save for the perennial *Hofmeisteria fasciculata.* With sufficient rainfall, this plant sprouts a long dandelion-like stem bearing a frizzy, lavender-colored flower. During a drought, only the ground-hugging leaves persist. The leaf blades are oval in shape and feel like felt.

Soon, we arrive at the mouth of another north-south arroyo. Here, at the third major valley, some 1,600 feet (500 m) from the first, we remain in the streambed and start to follow its course inland (map 4). This is the longest continuous valley on the Punta Chivato promontory. The gently ascending path of its dry streambed leads due south for eight-tenths of a mile (1.3 km). Over the first 1,600 feet (500 m), the most abundant plants are the lavender *Hofmeisteria,* the saltbush *(Atriplex barclayana),* known locally as *saladillo,* and the desert hollyhock *(Sphaeralcea ambigua).* All are halophytes, salt-tolerant plants. Their leaves feature tiny hairs that project above the leaf blade to keep wind-laden salt mists off the delicate plant tissues. Small pink to orange flowers distinguish the desert hollyhock, one of the *plantas muy malas,* or "very bad plants," on account of the allergic reaction it provokes.[18] I recall a visit when I asked a group of students hiking with me, "Do you see that orange flower over there?" Before I could say another word, one of them impulsively plucked a flower. The resulting rash was vaguely like poison ivy.

Halfway through the valley, clusters of copal trees *(Bursera hindsiana)* festoon the opposing slopes as spectacular examples of krummholz deformation. They prostrate themselves from the trunk and send their branches over the ground like long streamers (fig. 15). The trees bear mute testimony to the seasonal north wind from Isla Tortuga that blows boldly through the valley and carries its salt aerosol well inland. Henry Art, one of my teaching colleagues and a botanist, accompanied me to Punta Chivato in January 1997 and brought with him a coring device that allowed the retrieval of slender, pencil-shaped samples from the trunks of some copals. Analysis of the growth rings revealed that the largest trees were about 45 years old.[19] At least on a human time scale, the winter winds have blown south down the axis of the Gulf of California season after season.

Another prominent feature is the tuff beds exposed from place to place in the walls on either side of the arroyo. The beds are mostly white, sometimes pale orange. Composed of pressed volcanic ash, they remain comparatively soft and easy to erode. Their placement is strategic in the entrenchment of arroyos. The winds blow north-south, but by coincidence, the Miocene rocks of the Comondú Group are also tilted on a north-south axis, with interbedded layers of basalt, andesite, and softer tuff dipping consistently to the west. This orientation reflects the prevailing structure observed on the flanks of Mesa El Coloradito on day one and at Punta Mezquitito yesterday. During a downpour, sheets

Figure 15. Wind-pruned copal trees *(Bursera hindsiana)*. Photo by author.

of water flow naturally downhill and erode softer rocks, where exposed. Thus, the surface occurrence of Miocene tuff layers, tilted on end, controls the locations of the main north-south valleys. Flash floods, probably more frequent 10,000 to 20,000 years ago, are responsible for the down-cutting of the valleys. Judging from what we have seen so far, local valley erosion is something that postdates the Pliocene-Pleistocene fossil record on the promontory. If the valleys had existed during Pliocene time, for example, we might expect fingers of limestone with marine fossils to extend inland from the coast along the valley floors.

At the abrupt termination of the valley, a steep climb of at least 150 feet (45 m) awaits us. I track sideways, back and forth up the northeast face of a slope. The going is slow, and there is no cooling breeze from the sea. Small boulders of andesite are easily dislodged from the hillside; it is important to make sure no one is immediately below as you climb the slope. I pause often to catch my breath. Looking back down the valley to the north, my line of sight is arrested by the cobalt blue color of the gulf waters that fill the sharp V-shape profile of the valley. Mercifully, the slope begins to flatten out. The roof of the Punta Chivato promontory is joined slightly more than 330 feet (100 m) above sea level. Here, the Comondú volcanic sequence still forms the top of the mesa.

The views from these heights under a slanting afternoon sun are entrancing.

To the north, with the sun behind us, the dark blue of the open gulf spills out over the deep notch of our valley to form an imposing backdrop behind the rusty red tones of the mesa. If you turn 180°, with the sun shining askance, you can see short valleys that quickly drop to the coastal plain and beyond to the sparkling, pale blue waters of Bahía Santa Inés. The valleys on the south differ from those on the north because they mainly cut down through the limestone cover that skirts the igneous core of the promontory. We have come three-quarters of the way through the day's long circuit. The passage home is down-hill from here, but I linger a while, turning around to view first one side of the promontory and then the other. The two sides differ in mood. The names bestowed on the opposing bodies of water by early explorers capture the sense of drama in the landscape.

To the north, the expanse between Punta Chivato and Isla San Marcos carries the dark and forbidding designation "Ensenada El Muerto." An *en-senada* is something on a grander scale than an ordinary bay. This is the Embay-ment of the Dead. To the south is the now familiar Santa Inés Bay. Spanish mariners customarily employed the celebratory calendar of saints' days to name their discoveries. On the holiday of January 21 sometime during the mid-1600s, the lieutenants of Cortés must have anchored in the bay that now bears Santa Inés's name. Who was she? The standard book on the lives of the saints informs us that she was a beautiful young girl who lived during the second century and was martyred at the age of 12 for refusing to renounce her Chris-tian faith.[20] Because she was so small and lithe, the manacles meant to restrain her body were too loose to hold her. It was said that she could have slipped away from her jailers, who were sympathetic. She chose, instead, to remain incarcer-ated and face her execution with calm resolve. The calendar dictated that Santa Inés's name, and not that of some other saint, would grace this peaceful bay. Yet I am struck by the symbolism. The Embayment of the Dead conjures images of a risky passage under peril of the elements. Santa Inés Bay invokes a tranquillity of the mind.

The sun is slipping lower in the west; reluctantly, I pull myself away from the most commanding overlook on the mesa. The landscape ahead has yet more secrets to share. Below the brow of the promontory to the south are fossil-rich outcrops of the San Marcos limestone that mantle the western shoulders of Mesa Atravesada, as the Punta Chivato promontory is more formally known. Loose fossil molds weathered from the Pliocene outcrop lie scattered on the ground. A swirl of stone the size and shape of a fat cinnamon bun protrudes from the thin soil; I stoop to pick it up. The kernel of a conch with a slotted aperture is revealed. The mold of a tun shell *(Malea ringens),* this gastropod is still found in gulf waters on rocky ledges at extreme low tide and in shallow sand flats. Here, its fossil remains are about 300 feet (90 m) above present sea level. A few steps away, I spy quite another fossil fragment, a piece of bone distinguished by the filigree of porous bone marrow that is unmistakably mammalian. It is hard to say which marine mammal this bone fragment represents, but seals and whales come to mind. On the flanks of neighboring Mesa Ensenada de Muerte, Max discovered what were undoubtedly the long rib bones of a fossil whale.

This is the highest elevation on the promontory where Pliocene fossils occur. Not much of the Atravesada rises above us. At other parts of the Punta Chivato promontory where Miocene andesite reaches the surface, it does so only because overlying Pliocene strata have been stripped away. The overall distribution of rocks and fossils must be pieced together like a puzzle. Bits of information about the promontory come from the pecten flats, the *Solenastrea* complex, the low fringe of limestone at Punta Cacarizo, and here near the crown of the promontory. All contribute to tell us that the entire Miocene core of the Punta Chivato promontory was once sheathed in Lower Pliocene strata. The relationships show that the promontory slowly foundered through the early Pliocene and was converted into a great shoal on the margin of the young Gulf of California. The Late Pleistocene marine terrace circumscribed around the shores of Punta Chivato and the hint of older terraces notched above the north coast testify that the promontory was haltingly restored to its present prominence during the last 2 million years.

From here, descent of the south flank passes through a bushy glen lined by San Marcos conglomerate and limestone. The palo verde reappears, and the copal trees are fully upright. Before long, we reach the bottom of the short arroyo and emerge onto the open *bajada,* or low apron of alluvial outwash, above the main road (map 4). East of us is a low lobe of andesite protruding onto the plain from beneath the limestone hills above. The Pleistocene *Porites* reef visited this morning fills the cove on the other side of the barrier. The elevation on this side of the dividing lobe is slightly higher than the top of the coral beds on the opposite side. Perhaps the outwash of sediments from the arroyos above buried a sister reef, but I suspect this is the original bajada surface that fringed the Late Pleistocene shoreline. On the low side of the road are bits of shells that were left behind on the Pleistocene terrace. Near the lobe marking the west boundary of the junkyard reef is a sign announcing the small, grassless golf course called Desert Lynx, maintained by the American community. For Robert Chambers, the Scottish term "links" implied a marine terrace.[21] He would not be disappointed that golf here is played on a genuine marine terrace deposit that thinly blankets the brown, silty sandstone facies of the San Marcos Formation. Here, too, stray golf balls among the bleached shells of Late Pleistocene mollusks are devilishly hard to retrieve.

Two distinct complexions cast by opposing environments of the Punta Chivato promontory—windward and leeward—have profoundly affected its plant life and marine animals. The exposed northern flank sits weather-beaten, in sharp contrast to the sheltered southern side. This contrast reverberates through geologic time from the beginning of the Pliocene, 5 million years ago, to today. The shadowy past and the brilliantly illuminated present are linked by a long history of persistent winds, lapping waves, changing relative sea level, and intermittent rainstorms. Each of these dynamics may have influenced the landscape more intensely at some times than at others. Each species is unique, be it a coral, an echinoid, or a land plant. Each finds its place and its equilibrium amid the confluence of defining environments. Some species arrive from far away but eventually go extinct. Some change and prosper, while some remain the same. The entire promontory of Punta Chivato fell away, rose again, and yet remained much the same across a respectable span of geological time.

The mechanic's shed is just ahead. Our sanctuary on Punta Mezquitito welcomes us around the next bend. We have reached the end of the third day, midway through our visit to a beguiling desert country on the sea.

Far North Shore: Ensenada El Muerto

The wind comes out of the north and whips the water like a beater
pulling up egg whites. I can feel the bite of winter on this wind.
—Jonathan Waterman at Punta Los Muertos, *Kayaking the Vermilion Sea*

The stiff *viento norte* spills out from a clockwise spiral of transitory high-pressure systems that dance across the American southwestern desert during the winter months. Dense with cold air, armlike blasts break off from the cartwheeling highs to be funneled along the topographic spine of the Baja peninsula and down the axis of the Gulf of California. The heavy air behaves like water flowing in a trough. Far south beyond the mouth of the gulf, the blasts are eventually warmed and drawn into the trade winds that feed the buoyant equatorial low-pressure systems. During the North American summer, however, the southwest desert heats up and generates its own low-pressure systems. Strong columns of rising air take in replacement ground air from surrounding regions, including light winds that are pulled up the axis of the gulf from the south. Seasonal wind changes over the Gulf of California are sometimes described as semi-monsoonal. The torrential monsoon rains of South Asia are driven by a similar seasonal pattern on a much grander scale, because the summer warming of the vast Tibetan Plateau feeds into a low-pressure system much stronger than the one above the American southwestern desert during its summer. Nothing remotely like the rains of the Indian monsoon wet the desert soils of Baja California. Nearly half the annual precipitation over the southern gulf region comes during September, when many of the coastal desert plants burst into bloom.[1] While the rugged uplands in the central part of the peninsula average 4 inches (10 cm) of rain annually, the adjacent plains of the gulf coast tend to receive only half that amount.

I am not the first visitor impressed by the commanding ecological and geological roles played by seasonal winds over the Gulf of California. The geologist Charles Anderson, who briefly visited Punta Mezquitito in 1940, spent considerably more time exploring Isla del Carmen about 80 miles (130 km) to the southeast. There, at Bahía Oto on the north end of the island, he found an ancient dune field that he described as consisting of nonfossiliferous, cross-bedded calcareous sandstone. "Considering the strong northwest winds that blow down the gulf in winter and spring, sand dunes are not out of place," he wrote, "and similar winds were undoubtedly important in the past."[2] Likewise, the geologist Ronald L. Ives contributed a 1959 study of the contemporary sand dunes near Punta Peñasco on the Sonoran coast at the top of the gulf.

He, too, recognized the overwhelming calcareous composition of the coastal dunes as being derived from the bountiful shell life of the gulf. Ives attributed the transfer and reworking of shell material from beaches to upland dunes to the muscular labor of the winter viento norte.[3] On day two, we saw for ourselves evidence of the same linkage at Punta Cerotito.

It is still cool in the early morning, and the sun shines low on our shoulders. We pass the Pleistocene cove with its junkyard reef and continue west by northwest on the main road beyond the Desert Lynx golf course. Today's circuit takes us to the far north shore of the Punta Chivato promontory and the remote stretch of beach on the Ensenada El Muerto (map 5). My swim gear is packed, and I hope the day remains relatively calm, although the north shore often fights a northerly breeze that brings strong swells across the Embayment of the Dead. From the end of the beach there, we will climb over coastal bluffs and drop down into a valley that cuts partly through the promontory on a north-south axis. The day's hike covers a distance of 6.2 miles (about 10 km), mostly on level ground.

Just ahead, the landscape reveals a narrow passage between Mesa El Coloradito, to our left, and the Punta Chivato promontory, on our right. The pipeline for the community's water system is routed through this defile. A jeep trail runs along the aqueduct most of the way. The airfield's main runway points in that direction; not far beyond the end of the airstrip sits a small, perfectly shaped, flat-topped mesa at the entrance to the passage. It is indicated on the topographic map as a tiny circle (map 5). The contour lines inland from the shore reveal that the top of this structure is slightly more than 130 feet (40 m) above sea level. The cream-colored limestone capping the mesa is a geological outlier, a body of rock isolated from similar rocks by the denudation of the surrounding landscape. Comparable limestone occurs at about the same level on the east side of the Little Red Table, visited at the end of day one, and it also clad the south flank of the Punta Chivato promontory.

The tiny mesa's location at the entrance to the cleft between the larger landforms indicates that the passage is an imperfectly exhumed valley. The defile existed in the past and it exists now because soft, easily eroded Pliocene limestone filled a narrow corridor between massive structures composed of more resistant Comondú andesite. The level surface of the mesa top implies that the limestone eroded from the central part of the passageway was also flat. Seen up close, the limestone cap sits atop a pedestal of softer, silty limestone known as marl. Great blocks of the caprock have broken free from the fractured perimeter of the small mesa and tumbled down the steep sides, because the softer rock beneath was eroded away, leaving weak overhangs. The limestone debris lies scattered in angular disarray on the mesa slopes, accumulating at

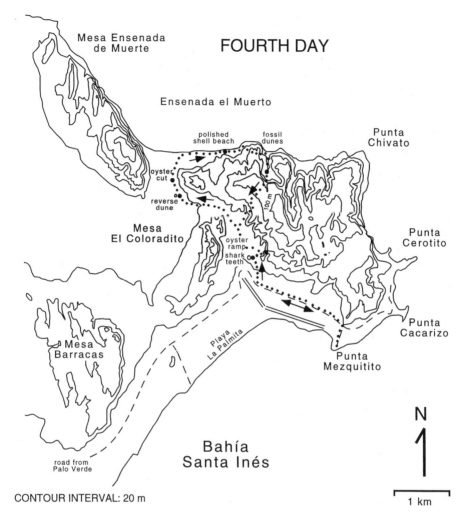

Mesa Ensenada
de Muerte

Ensenada el Muerto

polished
shell beach

fossil
dunes

Punta
Chivato

oyster
cut

reverse
dune

100 m

Mesa
El Coloradito

oyster
ramp

shark
teeth

Punta
Cerotito

Mesa
Barracas

Playa
La Palmita

Punta
Mezquitito

Punta
Cacarizo

N

road from
Palo Verde

Bahía
Santa Inés

CONTOUR INTERVAL: 20 m

1 km

Map 5. Route for the far north shore.

its base like so many wooden blocks tossed on the floor by the hand of a giant child at play.

Nearing the mesa, I am happily reminded of Saylin Elming, a then 10-year-old boy whom I met in January 1996. Saylin's father operated the hotel's concession for wind surfers. When I told Saylin that I was a paleontologist, he asked me to visit his father's shop, where he kept some fossils he wanted to show me. There, he produced an egg carton filled with fossil shark teeth. While exploring on his bicycle, Saylin had been attracted to the fortlike mesa as an enticing natural playground. Once on foot, his attentive eyes detected the teeth, which had been washed out of the hillside. Soon Saylin was a veteran collector.

On the order of 1.5 inches (4 cm) in length, the largest teeth in his collection displayed the broad triangular shape with serrated cutting edges typical of a great white shark *(Carcharodon carcharias)*. The smaller, more pointed teeth lacking serrated edges belonged most likely to a species of sand shark.

When I asked where the fossils came from, Saylin ushered me here, where I had often passed without thinking to check for fossils. You are welcome to try your luck finding some. You must "get your eye in," as it is sometimes said, while scouring the hillside on hands and knees. Some people have a natural ability for fossil hunting. Once they have in mind what they are looking for, they sing out, repeatedly, as they pick out the small specimens from the ground, "I have one," and, "Here's another." Others search on in gloomy silence, unrewarded. My young friend knew what he was doing and put me to shame. My eye for shark teeth was not properly "in" that day. It might have had something to do with my new bifocals.

The great white shark enjoys a cosmopolitan distribution.[4] Both adults and young are known to visit the Gulf of California during summer. The same species was present here during the Pliocene. Only a few would be needed to provide a bumper crop of fossil teeth, because each animal has a prodigious number of exposed teeth, as well as reserve ones, packed away in its cartilaginous jaws. Back at Williams College, I have a mounted head of the much smaller mackerel shark *(Isamna dekayi)* that long ago was acquired by Ward's Natural Science Establishment in Provincetown, Massachusetts. Once a year, I take the head out of storage and carefully bring it down two flights of stairs to the large lecture room in Clark Hall, where I introduce the students in my historical geology class to the classification of living and fossil fish. The lacquered cartilage of the shark skull balances on a brass rod that runs from the small brain case through the open roof of the mouth and the lower jaw to a wooden stand. To carry the skull, I must reach into the gaping mouth, carefully grasping the brass rod in my fist. A slip on the stairs and my hand would be shredded. The inch-long teeth (2.5 cm) are set in rows four to five deep and three-eighths inch (1 cm) apart. It's a small shark, but each jaw bears approximately 80 teeth. Cartilage provides the shark with a light and flexible framework but is not readily fossilized like bone. Upon death, the decayed body releases a wealth of durable teeth into the seabed's sediments. All the teeth buried in this mesa probably came from a few individuals of no more than two or three species.

The little mesa recalls two intersecting themes. I think about Nicolaus Steno in Tuscany and his learned dissection of a shark's head. His shark was reported to be a great white with 13 rows of teeth in its jaws.[5] I try to imagine the number of unbroken generations since Steno who never again confused tongue stones, or glossoptra, with anything other than the fossilized teeth of ancient sharks. Saylin is the latest in a long line of enthusiastic naturalists to be enthralled by the discovery and classification of organic relics from prehistoric times. I smile to myself when I remember him because I recognize a glimmer of myself. I, too, often rode my bicycle out of town to pick through the dirt for hours on end in search of small fossils. My eyes may no longer be what they once were, but deep inside me exists a child's unblemished excitement for the natural world. Geologists and paleontologists, malacologists and algologists, and most other naturalists are people who navigate the adult world but remain children at heart. You need not grow up, entirely, if you don't wish to do so. I wonder sometimes about the business-minded parents of Amanz Gressly in the Swiss Alps. Were they disappointed in their boy, who never took his place in Swiss society as a medical doctor with a successful practice but who changed forever the way geologists visualize ancient landscapes?

The other theme I am impressed by connects the fossil sharks with the dual landscapes at our feet. One is a watery echo from the past and the other is the landscape of the present. When the sharks patrolled this part of the coastline some 4 million years ago, they entered the far corner of Bahía Santa Inés and a restricted channel of water between two adjacent pieces of land. That former topography is now inverted as the small mesa rising above the surrounding plain. More can be learned by taking a short detour to explore this ancient landscape on the adjacent slope of Mesa Atravesada. As at the junkyard reef visited yesterday, a dump blights the immediate area. Heaps of trash are oddly sorted into orderly piles: glass liquor bottles without their paper labels here, and over there a heap of rusty cans. A little farther along is a mound of broken tiles from a renovation project. I curse the person who invented plastic bags, which festoon the scattered mesquite bushes. Punta Chivato, like most other communities on the Baja California peninsula, is badly in need of a more regulated system of trash disposal.

The road forks ahead where a side track leads northeast toward the mouth of a short canyon eroded in the Punta Chivato promontory (map 5). The narrow ridge on our right flank extends well out onto the plain. It is composed of the reddish rocks of Miocene andesite from the Comondú Group. In contrast, the ridge on our left is much abbreviated. Heading into the arroyo's mouth, we soon abandon the streambed and ascend the northwest slope of the longer ridge. I want to reach the 197-foot (60-m) contour level. There, almost on the neck of the ridge, it is possible to sight through the canyon out to the little mesa on the plain.

Our vantage also affords an excellent view to the opposite side of the canyon, revealing another superb exposure of the Miocene-Pliocene unconformity.

Sitting on the unconformity surface above the Comondú andesite is a beige-colored carbonate ramp. According to my compass clinometer, the dip is 6°, which agrees well with that of other ramps on the east and near north sides of the Punta Chivato promontory. The only difference is in the dip direction, to the south. A cover of Pliocene limestone previously draped this place, but the entire igneous ridge was later exhumed by erosion. On yesterday's hike, we found Pliocene limestone below the crest of Mesa Atravesada. From here, we can see that the toe of the carbonate ramp near the base of the opposite ridge reaches out at the same elevation as the caprock on the little mesa. The depositional phase that resulted in marls with fossil shark teeth gave way to another interval of time during which purer limestone floored the passage between mesas El Coloradito and Atravesada. As sea level slowly rose, the limestone climbed the flanks of the surrounding hills and came into direct contact with the exposed Comondú andesite. The relationship implies that the limestone-clad unconformity that we visited on the east side of Mesa El Coloradito during our first day probably lay adjacent to but slightly above a similar marl deposit that was entirely eroded away prior to the expansion of the Pleistocene seabed from Bahía Santa Inés.

There are several such canyons on the southwest flank of the Punta Chivato promontory, most of which feature ramps with comparable dip angles. My student Max Simian's assignment was to explore the region's arroyos to discover and measure the exposed Pliocene structures. His map (fig. 16), with small arrows denoting the locations and orientations of carbonate ramps, outlines the roughly triangular shape of what was formerly an early Pliocene island. As the island foundered and sea level rose, one or two smaller islands were isolated from the main igneous core. The pecten flats visited yesterday morning testify to the rise of waters over a high saddle on the main island. Mesa El Coloradito was another island, although very little of the limestone skirt that formerly encircled it is left in place.

With Max's island map in hand, I cross the arroyo for a closer look at the unconformity and its associated carbonate ramp exposed on the opposite canyon slope. At Punta Cacarizo, and even more so at the ramp structure near Punta Chivato on the north end, the basal conglomerate of the San Marcos Formation features a diverse fossil association, including molds of various cone and bittersweet shells. Near the unconformity on the slope opposite us, the texture of the local limestone looks different from anything previously related to the San Marcos Formation. It is more evenly bedded, and andesite fragments in the basal layers are less common. The associated fossils also differ, consisting of oysters 12 inches (30 cm) long with thickly laminated shells, now fractured open to the elements. Like the colonies on the Pleistocene seabed of Bahía

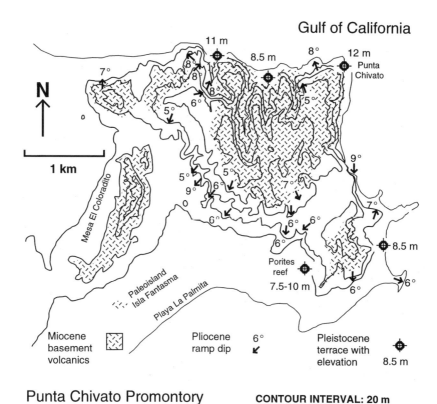

Gulf of California

Punta Chivato Promontory   **CONTOUR INTERVAL: 20 m**

Figure 16. The Pliocene islands of Punta Chivato and El Coloradito.

Santa Inés, these huge Pliocene oysters lived in the quiet leeward shelter of the Punta Chivato promontory. But this colony formed an organic carpet ramped over andesite rocks. The oyster limestone is merely another variation, or facies, of the Lower Pliocene San Marcos Formation.

We retrace our steps to the bottom of the ravine, exiting the arroyo to rejoin the main track that leads northwest (map 5). The defile narrows after passing another branch in the road that snakes up the southwest face of the Punta Chivato promontory. This afternoon our return will be by the same road from the far side of the promontory.

Each time I visit, I find new roads that chew up the local landscape. This particular side road did not exist until 1998. The Ejido San Bruno has sub-divided its former communal property, and the expanded road system makes additional land available for sale for houses. The path that continues ahead is reduced to a single jeep track. I don't relish roads much, but this track is not terribly intrusive. Now and then, part of the water pipeline is exposed along the side of the track. Leaks allow patches of native plants to remain in perpetual bloom, like islands in a desert sea. Here are met again the familiar yellow blooms of the brittlebush *(Encelia farinoso)* and the purple morning glory *(Jacquemontia abutiloides).*

Larger plants are also in bloom. Adam's tree, or the palo Adán *(Fouquieria diguetii),* bears small, bright red flowers on the tips of its long thorny limbs. The strangest plant I have encountered anywhere is the slipper plant, or *Candelilla (Pedilanthus macrocarpus).* It stands erect, about 3 feet (1 m) tall, with long, gray-green, naked stalks. The thick stems feel like rubber. I open my pocket-knife to cut off one of the turgid branches just above a jointed stem. Imme-diately, a milky sap begins to ooze, and I find the sticky fluid difficult to clean from my knife. Unlike common milkweed, these plants are boldly statuesque. But beware: do not taste the sap; it may provoke severe diarrhea.[6] Today I have the fortune to find a slipper plant growing near a leaky joint in the water pipe in bright red bloom. A single female and several male flowers form a composite, slipperlike structure that gives the plant its common name.

The air in the little valley is still. As the day has warmed, I remove my long-sleeved shirt to expose a red T-shirt. Suddenly, I hear an impossibly mechanical whirring noise, faint at first, but which becomes more and more audible. No more than a single hand span from my chest hovers a Costa's hummingbird *(Calypte costae),* its dark wings nearly invisible through furious motion. The bird's green head and body are fixed in midair. I hold my ground and the bird studies me for some moments. Looking down at my chest and back at the little bird suspended below my chin, I realize that I am being contemplated as an attractive, nectar-filled flower of colossal size. An instant later, I am rejected and the Costa zooms away over the desert. Small, unexpected moments like these accumulate one by one like precious jewels.

At the maximum constriction of the passage between the Atravesada and El Coloradito mesas, the jeep track swings from a northwesterly to a more westerly direction. Less than half a mile (1 km) away on the plain sits a small rocky knoll bearing the unmistakable reddish hues of Comondú andesite. Close up, it is possible to view a ring of white sand around the dark outcrop (fig. 17). The halo is asymmetrical, because the sand forms a distinct apron that blankets much of the knoll's south face. The north face, exposed to the open gulf through the sandy lowland between Mesa Ensenada de Muerte and the west end of the Punta Chivato promontory, is completely barren. By itself, the knoll is unre-markable. As a topographic remnant, it reveals the erosional deflation of the landscape. Over time, 33 feet (10 m) or more of surface rocks have been stripped away from the plain behind Mesa El Coloradito. The knoll's geology, nonetheless, is monolithic, displaying no obvious chapter breaks. Instead, it is

Figure 17. Dune-draped knoll of Miocene andesite. Photo by author.

the influence of the wind that grabs my attention. If the prevailing wind direction is from north to south, why does the sand adhere to the south side of the knoll? In fact, a reverse sand dune has accumulated in the lee of the knoll. Eddies in the airflow around and over the knoll drop sand grains into dead air space on the sheltered side, where they stay put.

On our immediate right are more substantial dunes that cling at the angle of repose against ravines on the southwest slope of the Punta Chivato promontory. Fling a stone at the dunes and you may trigger a tiny sand avalanche that slumps thickly down the slope. The white sand is 50-percent ground mollusk shell in origin, as found by my student Patrick Russell. This is a much higher percentage than is found in the dunes at Playa Cerotito, visited two days ago. Sand samples from the valley floor in this vicinity and halfway up the dune face have a mean grain size of 0.013 inch (a third of a millimeter), coarse in comparison with those from the seaside dunes on Punta Cerotito.[7] This peculiarity bears further thought, but the explanation is not immediately apparent. What can be said with certainty is that we stand within the wind shadow of the main promontory, well protected from the winter frenzy of the Ensenada El Muerto. The comminuted mollusk shells comprising the bulk of these valley dunes were blasted off the exposed beach on the other side of the ridge. Wind gusts capable of carrying the grains by stages up and over the nearly 200-foot-high (60-m) ridge clearly must be powerful; the clean north face of the small rocky knoll to our west is mute evidence of this condition.

Exiting through the west end of the valley, the jeep track leads directly to the rocky knoll. Immediately beyond is an arroyo that drains north across the plain between mesas Atravesada and Ensenada de Muerte. The great beach on the Ensenada El Muerto is little more than a half mile (1 km) away. Adjacent to the rocky knoll, the arroyo's embankment is littered with the abundant loose valves of another oyster, Fischer's *(Ostrea fischeri)*. Marine waters once lapped this spot. Runoff from the September 1997 storm cleared the arroyo of brush, and our path is relatively free. Andesite boulders and cobbles eroded from the Comondú Group line the embankments. At waist level, along one stretch of the east wall, a line of fossil oysters is attached directly to the rocky substrate. These are small compared with Fischer's oyster. Given the low elevation, proximity to the shoreline, and excellent preservation of the shells, the oysters must be Pleistocene in age.

This place gives us a remarkable sense of geographic closure. At the maximum rise in sea level during the last interglacial epoch, seawater shallowly flooded the 1,640-foot-wide (half-kilometer) strip of land between mesas Atravesada and Ensenada de Muerte. At that time, the rocky knoll was almost an islet, and the two neighboring mesas had much the same topographic dimensions as today. The Pleistocene rise in sea level was insufficient, however, to flood the valley we traversed earlier, between mesas Atravesada and El Coloradito.

Dense thickets of mangle dulce *(Maytenus phyllanthoides)* line the sides of the arroyo closer to the coast. This plant's leaves are thick and rubbery; it does well in saline soil. Finally, we leave behind the arroyo's confines, and the wide coastal shore of the Ensenada El Muerto emerges (map 5). Here, we may take in more than three-quarters of a mile (1.25 km) of pristine beach. Less than 500 feet (150 m) of low sandy ground lies between us and the unbroken berm that stretches like a defensive earthwork parallel to the shoreline. The berm crest marks the landward extent of the highest tides whipped by storm winds. Crossing toward the berm, we turn first to the northeast and then due east. A dark cliff line rises above the flats, demarcating the solid north edge of the Punta Chivato promontory. The nearest cliffs reach 50 feet (15 m) in height, but farther east they lose stature and swing out toward the beach. A pleasant landward breeze blows, and the tide is low. It will take some time to see whether the tide is rising or falling. From the berm crest, some 164 feet (50 m) of open beach extends to the edge of the water. Long swells march directly onto the beach out of the north, but no whitecaps are in sight.

Ensenada El Muerto is one of the most spectacular beaches I have seen anywhere, and I have visited many of the top-rated beaches around the world, from the coral sands of St. John in the U.S. Virgin Islands to the black basaltic sands on the big island of Hawaii and the splendor of Muriwai Beach on the North Island of New Zealand. Beaches mean different things to different people. For me, a beach gets a high ranking for solitude and the opportunity it offers to understand how ocean waves and currents craft the shoreline's raw materials. The beach at Ensenada El Muerto is superlative in both categories. El Muerto is composed of a staggering aggregate of polished shell bits. Pebbles of dark andesite and salt-and-pepper granite make only a minor contribution. According to Patrick's analysis, a typical sample from the lower part of the beach has a mean grain size of one-eight inch (2.5 mm), and 80 percent of it consists of ground-up mollusk shells.[8] A sizable fraction includes highly burnished pieces of larger shell fragments. Given this, it is not surprising that the sand dunes trapped in the narrow valley on the other side of the ridge are relatively coarse and superenriched with shelly detritus compared with other local dunes.

The beach aggregate is so thoroughly reduced, in fact, that it is hard to determine which species of mollusks contributed their shells to its tremendous mass. Whole shells scattered about the beach are scarce. Among the bivalves, there is an ark shell *(Anadara grandis)*, the remains of two species of Venus shells *(Chione gnidia* and *Dosinia ponderosa)*, a cockle *(Laevicardium elatum)*, a good many chocolate shells *(Megapitaria squalida)*, and a few pectens *(Pecten sericeus)*. Recognizable gastropod shells are less abundant. There are some cone shells *(Conus regularis)*, a few large fragments of conch shells *(Strombus galeatus)*, and an unknown species of the slipper shell *(Crepidula)*. With the possible exception of the slipper shell, all are characteristic of habitats that range from tidal sand flats to subtidal sandbars with a maximum offshore depth of about 328 feet (100 m).[9] The great expanse of sandy bottom in the Ensenada El Muerto harbors prodigious mollusk populations. Less than 1 percent of the beach's sediments are derived from coralline red algae. The differences in composition between the beach at Playa La Palmita on the protected Bahía Santa Inés and the exposed beach of El Muerto could hardly be more extreme.

In the Gulf of California, various species of the slipper shell are typical of cobble- and boulder-strewn intertidal habitats. Our specimens come from the east end of the beach, where andesite cliffs reach the water's edge and a jumble of large boulders and cobbles spills into the shallows. It is certain now that the tide is still falling. A way around the base of the cliffs over the rocks is exposed. Crossing loose rocks and skirting a few small tidal pools, we find ourselves peering around the corner at a hidden stretch of beach that adds another 1,640 feet (500 m) to the overall length of El Muerto. For me, this is the most inviting spot on the entire north shore. The high cliff at the water's edge provides a shady spot for lunch, and I immediately remove my boots and roll up the legs of my jeans, for I can't resist the sensual pleasure of walking barefoot along this part of the beach. The worn shell bits concentrated at this corner of the beach are the largest I have seen anywhere, usually the size of small coins (fig. 18). Many bear the unmistakable cream and brown color banding of the chocolate shell, the original grand donor of this astonishing wealth.

I stoop to pick up one of the thick shell bits, turning the piece over and over. The polished shell feels utterly smooth and silken, with no rough edges. The unending rhythmic wash of the waves over this part of the lower beach has acted like a vast lapidary barrel, tumbling the shells against one another. Slowly, the shells are ground down and reduced to a burnished remnant of their former architecture. There could hardly be a more profound difference between the beaches at El Muerto and La Palmita. Here, on a relatively quiet day, it is a pleasure to wander barefoot over the entire beach. At Playa la Palmita, it is painful to go shoeless over the twisted tangle of jagged shells that form the berm crest on that sheltered bay.

The coin-shaped pieces of shell are spread over great patches on this segment of El Muerto beach. To check their depth, I retrieve from my pack a photo card with a scale embossed in centimeters and inches. Using the card as a straight-edged blade, I kneel on the beach and carefully press it vertically into the sand to a depth not more than half an inch (1.25 cm). Drawing the card toward me on an even plane, I use it like a toy road grader to push to either side the upper surface of the shell deposit. Exposed to the sun is a different layer with much smaller pieces of shell. I repeat the same operation, grading through the newly revealed level to a similar depth. A third layer emerges, consisting of the same large bits found on the beach surface. Now the archaeologist in me takes over; I painstakingly work down through the thin layers. The next layer below again consists of tiny shell bits. I could continue, except that the trench's sides are beginning to slump.

During various visits, my students have performed this experiment using a proper trenching tool, discovering that the alternation of coarse and fine shell layers continues to a considerable depth until seawater seeps into the excavation, halting further progress. These layers stunningly reveal the ceaseless work of the waves and the tides and their roles in shifting two adjacent microfacies of shell material back and forth, one overlapping the other—something I will return to later when we meet a phenomenon called a standing wave. Working together, the wind and waves bring fresh material to the beach along a great conveyor belt from the offshore sandbars. Wind is the necessary helpmate to the waves and tides on this natural production line. The fickle viento norte sends the sea swells and resulting waves on their collision course with the Punta Chivato promontory. What happens to the smallest of shell bits that are

Figure 18. Worn shell fragments on Ensenada El Muerto beach. Photo by author.

relentlessly shorn from their parental coinage? If the entire biological detritus were left here to accumulate over the millennia, the beach, despite its size, would scarcely have enough space to store it all. In this case, too, the wind plays an important role. When it blows hard out of the north, it deflates the beach by picking up the smallest grains and exporting them inland over the west end of the promontory, where the ridge is narrow. As we saw before, the wind also carries sand through the passage between the mesas Atravesada and Ensenada de Muerte to a spacious plain on Mesa El Coloradito's west side (map 5).

I have engaged in other kinds of instructive play with my students here on the Ensenada El Muerto. If you follow our lead, you will find the water cold but refreshing, and you won't need water socks. The sun heats the beach sand, and you can warm up quickly after a swim. I recall a passage from *The Immense Journey,* by Loren Eiseley. In "The Flow of the River," he describes floating on the Platte River in Nebraska and becoming absorbed by it on its course to the ocean.[10] We can carry out a similar experiment here at El Muerto.

The sea swells that bore their way across the ensenada create something known to coastal oceanographers as standing waves. In a nutshell, these are phenomena that appear where incoming waves meet outgoing waves in such a way that water moves horizontally at some points along them and vertically at other points; these points are called nodes and antinodes, respectively (fig. 19). At regular intervals along the beachfront, sets of crescent-shaped sandbars extend offshore for some 395 feet (120 m). As many as four sandbars, separated from one another by deeper water, are arrayed in each set (fig. 19A). From tip to tip, the outermost crescents cover a linear distance of more than 500 feet (150 m); there is space for as many as 8–10 nested sets of these sandbars along the nearly one-mile (1.5-km) length of the Ensenada El Muerto beachfront. I have seen them well outlined from the air on a fly-over in Jim Johanson's airplane. One such set occurs off this part of the beach. In taking to the water like Eiseley, one may transform one's body into a thinking molecule that senses how the energy in the system gives shape to the sandbars.

The receding tide is at least midway out, and the hidden shore face is steep at this stage in the tidal cycle. Stepping off the sand at the water's edge, I am immediately up to my waist in water. It is tempting to dive headlong into the oncoming waves and cross the moat to the first sandbar, some 33 feet (10 m) offshore. As an incoming wave strikes the wall-like beach straight on, the water is reflected off the shore as an outgoing wave that has nearly the same wavelength (distance from wave crest to crest) as the incoming wave but is much less strong (fig. 19B). Struggling to hold my footing against the waves that pass to crash on the beach and buffet me on their return, I am about one-quarter of the way offshore to the next approaching wave crest. (My students never fail to rise to the challenge and join me here.) Around my ankles I feel the whipsaw movement of coarse shell bits shifting violently back and forth with the energy of the waves. This is the first nodal point—the point where the incoming and outgoing waves are out of phase and cancel each other—of the phenomenon called a standing wave. The sensation is very different from that of a lazy float down a river in Nebraska. Although the wave energy is not overwhelming, it is too intense to lose myself in thought, so I throw myself forward and paddle a few strokes until I feel the edge of the first sandbar rise abruptly under my feet. This sand is smoother than that trapped behind me in the moat. Here, the water barely reaches past my knees. I squat so that water reaches my chest and move forward, crablike. Paying attention to the waves crossing the shoal and those that trail behind, I ascertain that I am at a distance one-half wavelength offshore. As oncoming swells ride up and over the sandbar, I feel my body rhythmically lifted up and down. I have reached what is called an antinode (fig. 19C).

Ever so gradually, the water level rises as I leave the first sandbar and ease into the next moat, some 50 feet (15 m) offshore. Here, the deeper water between adjacent sandbars extends somewhat farther than it does immediately offshore. I paddle out a few strokes and stand. The water reaches my breast-

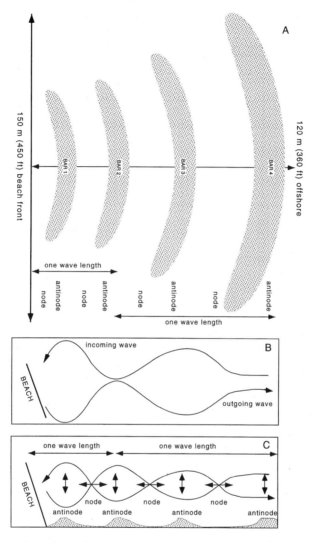

Figure 19. (A) Sandbars of Ensenada El Muerto; (B) incoming and outgoing waves; (C) positions of nodes and antinodes.

bone. I am now almost three-quarters of a wavelength offshore, near the second nodal point of the standing wave (fig. 19). Unending wave crests pass by and mount in amplitude as they crest the sandbar I have just crossed. The experiment begins a few strokes nearer to the center of the moat. I think back to my first swimming lessons as a seven-year-old, when I learned how to do the jellyfish float.

With legs tucked up under my body and knees grasped loosely, I float face down. Eyes closed for concentration, I am turned toward the shore. At this nodal point, I don't feel the same up and down movement I sensed a few moments ago on the sandbar. Incoming waves pass by. Thinking about how those waves are countermanded by outgoing waves reflected off the beach wall is what's required. Gradually, I begin to sense that my body floats evenly in the water. A modification of the jellyfish float is the dead man's float, in which the arms are extended forward and the legs hang down from a prostrate body. Slowly, I let my toes fall to the sandy surface. With eyes still closed, I feel how the body absorbs some of the gentle back-and-forth movement of the water. During a strong wind, the sand in this depression between two bars will be swept away in two directions. Some goes to build up the landward sandbar, and some migrates to increase the next bar seaward. I hold my breath as long as I am able and then open my goggled eyes, dive down, and watch sand particles gently sway to and fro on the seabed.

A standing wave occurs because the nodal and antinodal points are fixed in place, shifting only slightly with the tides.[11] There are two nodal points evenly arranged one-quarter and three-quarters of the way through any given wavelength, sitting astride a central antinode (fig. 19C). The pair of points does not oscillate up and down, but the water column below them shifts back and forth perpendicular to the shoreline. The antinodes are where sandbars accumulate from the sweeping action of the adjacent nodal points. At the antinodes, the incoming and outgoing waves are in phase with each another, and the water column rises and falls, vertically. I cross the second moat and swim onto the second sandbar. It is some 130 feet (40 m) offshore in water waist deep. Repeating the experiment, I turn landward, close my eyes, and do the jellyfish float. The up-and-down oscillation of the standing wave is very apparent. I assume the dead man's float, open my eyes, and stare at the seabed, devoid of sand movement.

Standing waves are a genuine phenomenon, accounting for the more or less regular spacing of the offshore sandbars that pattern scallop-like across the Ensenada El Muerto. The bars accumulate during major storms, when the return waves are intensified, but they migrate shoreward during more normal shoaling conditions, when sand works its way over the bars and down the steep landward fronts. The bars' progressive spacing farther apart offshore occurs because the wavelength of incoming swells is reduced as they reach shallow waters and are slowed by frictional drag against the seabed.

I decide to cross over to the third sandbar, about 230 feet (70 m) offshore. The water is now over my head. Every so often, I dive to find it getting deeper. Eventually, I reach the front of the third sandbar, where I can just barely stand with my nose above water. My head is submerged with every passing oscillation. I've never gone beyond this point, but I know at least one more bar waits farther out. I've reached my limit. I swim with a slow but steady breaststroke to bring me back to the second and first sandbars, where I pause to rest and enjoy the shoaling waves. Getting out takes energy: I am no longer a mere water molecule, or part fish, and my body feels the gravity. I flop belly down onto a concentration of polished shell chips, and my chilled body instantly begins to absorb the stored warmth of the beach. Roasted from the mollusk sand below and the strong sun above, I am soon fully air-dried.

Our hike now brings us to the far east end of the beach (map 5). Never having been here during high tide, I ponder the layering of coarse and fine shell bits below the berm line on this beach. The nearest nodal point at extreme low tide must shift up the beach when the tide turns, bringing with it the distinctive lag deposit of polished shell chips that spill onto higher ground. The alternation of shell bits uncovered in our excavations reflects the spatial shift of the onshore nodal and antinodal points over a relatively short distance. Essentially, each pair of layers represents the fulfillment of a single tidal cycle and the relentless shift and processing of shelly sand from offshore to onshore.

Halfway down the beach, a band of dark water runs perpendicular from the shore out to sea like a narrow corridor. This is a potentially dangerous spot where strong rip currents operate during part of the tidal cycle. The passage of deeper water forms a natural boundary between two cells of crescent-shaped sandbars that occupy the far end of El Muerto. The very name, Embayment of Death, brings dark thoughts. Several such zones occur at regular intervals along the beach. Rip currents are caused by an excessive volume of seawater that spills over the inner sandbar and is not fully accommodated by reflected waves that return seaward to form a standing wave. The surplus water flows parallel to the beach until it finds a low point in the inner sandbar, where it is diverted seaward under pressure. The strongest rip currents are active during high tide. A swimmer taken by surprise may find that the speed with which she is carried seaward through such a passage exceeds the strength with which she is able to return to shore. Under such conditions, the safest course of action is to swim parallel to the shore in either direction. The width of the passage is generally small, and it is always possible to escape the channeled rip current by swimming athwart it.

A shallow grave lies at the far end of the beach near the cliffs. It is marked by a makeshift cross formed by two sticks bound with wire. I can't say for certain, but I suppose a drowning occurred here. The line of cobbles and small boulders heaped on the grave implies that the person buried in it is an adult. Perhaps someone was digging for clams and decided to go for a swim, or the victim might have been a fisherman caught in a violent change of weather on this rugged shoreline. The variety of rocks marking the grave represent a sampling of the promontory's geology. Most of the cobbles are igneous in origin, including black basalt, rusted andesite, and orange tuff. A few blocks of tan limestone are present as well. One includes a specimen of the Pliocene coral *Solenastrea fairbanksi* encountered yesterday high above the cliffs at the opposite end of the north shore. Most likely, the block was not carried far to the gravesite, and so the distinctive coral must be present in this vicinity. Careful searching in the cliffs above the gravesite confirms the presence of an unconformity between the Miocene igneous rocks in the Comondú Group and the basal limestone of the Lower Pliocene San Marcos Formation, with corals intact. Originally, a carbonate ramp extended along much of the north shore. The now extinct coral prospered on this coastline in the face of turbulent waters whipped by the north winds. The cause of its death, too, is unknown—perhaps a change in climate, but surely not the combination of wind, waves, and tides that brought daily sustenance to the immobile corals.

The way farther east is impassible at shore level, and it is necessary to scramble up a ravine to reach the top of the cliffs above. There, the ground assumes a gentle incline covered by a thin sand dune, the contents of which have been blasted high off the beach below. A small, wiry shrub that has taken a beating from the shifting wind arrests my attention. The tips of its branches inscribe a half circle in the surrounding sand through a 20-inch (half-meter) radius from the southeast to the southwest quadrants of the compass (fig. 20). The effect was forceful enough to push pebbles out of the way and to cut a shallow, perfectly arcuate path. Clearly, the bush was laid flat by the lashing wind. On this calm day, only the fragile traces of the concentric half-rings testify to the intransigence of the winter north wind.

We must do some uphill hiking on our detour inland around the coastal cliffs to the next valley, but the views of the merging land and seascape are rewarding. Out to sea, maybe a mile (1.6 km) away, a patch of water swarms with birds. For a few moments the water is animated with black specks moving about on the choppy surface. The next moment, the water is absolutely devoid of life. I retrieve my binoculars to have a better look. A flock of 50 to 75 eared grebes *(Podiceps nigricollis)* is bobbing on the water. All looks peaceful for a while. Then, a sudden commotion spreads through the flock and the birds dive in unison. They are gone for a minute or two and then suddenly reappear at the surface en masse. Another group of similar size is working a different sector. Migrants from the north, the small fishing birds spend their winter months here.

A commanding prospect opens up on the austere but beautiful north shore, terminated by the Mesa Ensenada de Muerte (fig. 21). The near beach sits unoccupied like an alcove below a raised terrace that would bring a smile of

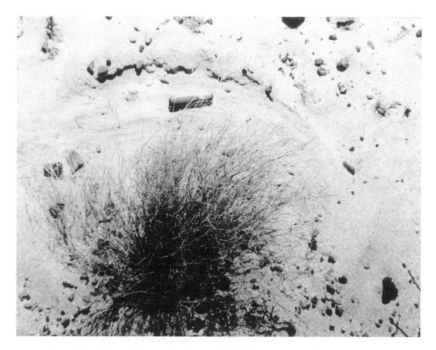

Figure 20. Wind circle on the Ensenada El Muerto coast. Photo by author.

recognition to the lips of Robert Chambers. A small sand dune perches on the neck of land that forms the west arm of the terrace and divides the lesser from the greater beach to the west. There is life here, tenacious on land and prolific beyond measure in the bordering sea. Without exception, however, everything on this exposed shore bows to the combined power of wind, waves, and tides.

It is necessary to make our own path cross-country, keeping to the high ground and skirting gullies that would return us unprofitably to the edge of the sea cliffs with no prospect of a safe descent to the coast. Everywhere, salt-pruned leatherplants hug the ground, pointing mainly south but also conforming to the natural flow of the land. Now and then, a fishhook cactus (*Mammillaria* sp.) is encountered with its telltale, wine-red spines that imitate the shape of a fishhook. They lean unerringly to the southwest like drunken sentinels about to topple over. It is thought that the cacti orient themselves this way to minimize the harmful effects of the sun during the hottest part of the year.[12] A cousin, the barrel cactus *(Ferocactus peninsulae),* performs the same trick and is commonly known as the compass plant.

After a third of a mile (half a kilometer) and a circuitous climb of some 165 feet (50 m), we reach the edge of an entrenched valley. Like others, it crosses the Punta Chivato promontory on a north-south axis, but this valley is different in

Figure 21. View west across Ensenada El Muerto. Photo by author.

that it does not leave a raw, red gash through the rusty Comondú volcanics. The rocks exposed in the dry streambed far below are tan. They bear some crude semblance of stratification. Most alluring of all, they extend from the mouth of the arroyo far inland. Patrick liked to call this place his *cañada grande,* or grand canyon. It is not as long as others that dissect the mesa, but it widens out into an open bowl inland from the coast. The descent from the ridge top to the valley floor is best made slowly and carefully, following a zigzag course down the steep scree to the mouth of the canyon.

The arroyo is constricted at its outlet, where a distinct marine terrace occurs on opposite sides of the valley, about 36 feet (11 m) above sea level. The terrace clearly truncates the tan limestone exposed in the canyon walls and the adjacent bedrock of Comondú andesite. A thin terrace deposit includes cobbles that are encrusted with coralline red algae and some turban shells. This is the same terrace level explored at the Punta Chivato light tower yesterday. It sits at about the same level as the terrace above the alcove beach just visited at Ensenada El Muerto. All three localities represent a wave-cut platform that eroded the rocks of the promontory at sea level about 125,000 years ago, during the last interglacial epoch. Because part of the terrace and its associated deposit sits on limestone exposed in the arroyo, the limestone predates the terrace. Moreover, the limestone embedded in the walls at the mouth of the arroyo trace laterally upstream, showing that those rocks formed more than 125,000 years ago. Firmly cemented, the limestone could be significantly older than the Late Pleistocene.

In comparison with other limestone outcrops in the region, two characteristics of these beds are distinct. The rocks appear to be entirely devoid of fossils, and the internal layering is not consistent with the flat tops and bottoms of each compound bed. The first clue tells us that the environment of deposition was not at the shoreline, where seashells would likely have been incorporated. The second clue, a little harder to decipher, is that the limestone is internally cross-bedded; the smaller, individual layers do not follow the same orientation as the master bed in which they are grouped, but show a curved pattern in cross section. The curves are generally concave in profile, starting off flat but arcing to the top of the bed, where they are beveled by the next overlying unit. Streamers of angular andesite pebbles stand out in bas-relief along some of these curved bedding planes. The pebbles are rough, not rounded in the surf. All evidence implies a stream deposit and related dune materials that choked the mouth of a preexisting valley. The main mass of these deposits was derived from carbonate beach sand transported inland by the wind. The rough pebbles originated as debris that fell from the walls of the enclosing andesite valley. They were only briefly reworked by intermittent stream action.

An ancient arroyo was located here, precisely along the course where the present-day streambed has exhumed these deposits. Our route brings us south along the modern arroyo, where its channel cuts through vertical walls of limestone that rise from 13 to 25 feet (4 to 7.5 m) in height. Much of the way, the limestone is exposed on opposite walls of the canyon, but the massive andesite sides of the valley protrude behind the limestone and are always clearly visible below the skyline. At a few places, where recent erosion has completely removed the slim limestone filling, naked andesite reaches all the way down the valley slopes to the streambed. Upstream, the entire valley opens out dramatically to the southeast and southwest. The more expansive southeastern quadrant of the basin reveals only andesite bedrock. High above the streambed to the west, however, limestone adheres to the side of the valley at a level consistent with the 130-foot (40-m) contour on our topographic map.

Not far from beyond the west embankment are thick, wedgelike slabs of limestone that dip northeast at low angles between 15° and 20°. Unlike the limestone at the mouth of the canyon, this formation displays no curvaceous cross beds, and the amount of coarse andesite material is significantly reduced. Nearby, the same class of limestone dips more steeply, 28° to the southwest. No visible fault line runs through the valley, and tectonic forces did not tilt the layers. The beds do not defy Steno's law of original horizontality, because his precepts relate only to sediment in an aqueous medium. Quite simply, the opposing limestone beds recline at the same dip angles today as when they were first formed long ago. Around us are the remains of a large and imposing sand dune that rises gently on its windward side from the margin of the old arroyo. The incline closest to the arroyo is called a stoss slope. The lee of the dune is the steeper side of the structure, where sand that moves up the stoss face reaches the dune crest and tumbles over the edge. This superb example of a nearly intact fossil dune sits off the main north-south extension of the original paleovalley, because it spilled into the southwest quadrant of the basin at the back of the valley.

Pause for a moment and look around for signs of wind-pruned vegetation in the vicinity. With krummholz plants as a guide, it is apparent that the north wind enters the valley straight on but fans out over the contours of the land once it reaches the inner basin. Thus, the orientation of the fossil dune on this side of the basin is perfectly consistent with the contemporary pattern of airflow in the cañada grande. This old dune is now immobilized in solid stone, but once it turned a topographic corner and pressed its lee slope to the valley wall.

According to Patrick's analysis of petrographic thin sections studied under the microscope, fragmented mollusk shells, echinoderm spines, and coralline red algae account for 56 percent of the dune sand at this locality.[13] The balance is composed of weathered grains of andesite or its component minerals. In this case, however, there is a complicating factor. Many of the original carbonate bits in the dune sand were dissolved away or replaced with substitute material precipitated from mineral-laden groundwater after the beds solidified. Although the vacant pores represented by many ghost grains resemble the outlines of mollusk grains, the original composition of the beach-derived sand is underrepresented. A carbonate beach clearly occupied the north shore at the mouth of the valley, but the igneous composition of the coastline and valley walls also played an important role in the derivation of a large fraction of the dune sand. The beachfront outside the cañada grande was not as expansive as the long strand on the Ensenada El Muerto today. Most likely, the erosion of Comondú bedrock was more extensive here than that presently observed on the margins of the great beach.

The route is steep on the climb out of the basin by way of the west slope (map 5). Weathering of the dune limestone has produced sharp karst surfaces that make the path treacherous. The footing is good, but a fall would end in cuts and abrasions. About two-thirds of the way up, the dune limestone ends, and andesite bedrock is exposed. Not long after reaching the shoulder of the confining ridge, about 260 feet (80 m) above sea level, we discover the remains of a carbonate ramp with marine fossils characteristic of the Lower Pliocene San Marcos Formation. Through binoculars, the ridge on the opposite side of the valley to the east shows no signs of this rock unit. The San Marcos may be traced laterally, however, from our ridge location to the thick layers that cap the cliffs at the head of the valley. What remains of the exposed strata indicates that the basal Pliocene beds once stretched over the entire valley like a sheet and fell to the north shore.

The geological relationships revealed from this vantage allow the history of the paleovalley to be reconstructed. Of the four major valleys that dissect the Punta Chivato promontory, only this one features lithified stream and dune deposits. The valley must postdate the marine San Marcos Formation, because it slices through those rocks in two places. As we have already found, a late Pleistocene marine terrace truncates the stream deposits at the mouth of the paleovalley, indicating that all processes, including uplift of the Punta Chivato promontory, subsequent valley erosion, dune development, lithification, and modification due to flowing groundwater, occurred between the end of the Early Pliocene and the start of the last interglacial epoch. The available window of opportunity spans roughly 3 million to 4 million years, although all the physical events just listed might easily have taken place within a few thousand years of one another.

As we continue up slope to the crest of Mesa Atravesada, the surrounding view expands to Mesa Ensenada de Muerto to the west and Mesa El Coloradito to the southwest. Our circumnavigation of the far north shore will be accomplished when we the cross the divide and pick up the graded road descending to the jeep track along the aqueduct. The Punta Chivato promontory is the largest and most complex of the three Pliocene islands in sight. It would be satisfying to have a better grasp of the likely time of development of the paleovalley on the largest island—the one just explored. To achieve this, however, requires more information about the Pliocene-Pleistocene interval than is available here or elsewhere in the Gulf of California. In short, we need to know more about the history of sea-level changes during Pliocene and early Pleistocene time worldwide. It was not so long ago that geologists began to assemble the vast global network of data necessary for such an ambitious task. The Pliocene island underfoot and the two nearby remind me of the life and career of a geologist who pioneered the study of global sea-level changes as related, in part, to ancient islands. Still far from the end of the today's journey, let us consider the contribution of a brilliant scholar who helped import the facies concept to North America during the early 1900s.

The pivotal facies concept introduced by Amanz Gressly in Switzerland and promulgated by the German geologist Johannes Walther during the mid- to late 1800s had not reached the shores of North America by the turn of the last century. Foremost in his generation, the American geologist Amadeus William Grabau (1870–1946) was responsible for promoting the facies concept in North America and expanding that concept into an elaborate but embryonic format summarizing global sea-level changes deciphered from the geologic record.[14] A prolific writer with an encyclopedic approach to his topics, Grabau's most trenchant summary of his life's work appeared in 1940 as a volume titled *The Rhythm of the Ages.* Published under difficult wartime conditions in the capital of China, then called Peking, Grabau's masterpiece appeared in a single edition of only 800 copies. At first glance, the book appears to be a general textbook on historical geology, but two extraordinary features distinguish it from other, contemporary textbooks.

An attractive set of 21 colored paleogeographic maps is appended to the back of the book. These maps depict changes in continental assemblies through-out the last 500 million years, based on the idea of continental drift. Grabau was inspired by the controversial work of Alfred Wegener, as promoted in the 1924 English-language edition of his *The Origin of Continents and Oceans.* By 1940, however, the theory of continental drift had gone out of favor, and Grabau was one of its few advocates. Not until the mid-1960s was the idea of continental drift revived and incorporated into the larger concept of plate tectonics. Some of Grabau's paleogeographic interpretations are remarkably insightful in light of today's researches.

The real centerpiece of Grabau's book is his entirely original Pulsation Theory, according to which the "pulse beat" of the earth can be measured in terms of distinct imprints in the surviving rock record that relate to the coordi-nated advance and retreat of the world's oceans. The regular pattern of such transgressive advances and regressive retreats in marine facies represented, for him, the most salient aspect of the Earth's history—"the rhythm of the ages." In the preface, Grabau wrote:

> The first [concept of importance] is the rhythmic movement or pulsation of the sea, which unlike tidal phenomena, is of simultaneous occurrence in all the oceans of the earth. This is shown by the record of transgressions and regressions everywhere in the strata of all continents, and I have embodied it in the law of slow pulsatory rise and fall of the sea-level in each

geological period. . . . Each positive pulse-beat sends the marine waters in slow transgression into all the geosynclines as the sea-level rises, and each negative pulse-beat causes their withdrawal as the sea-level sinks.[15]

The term geosyncline refers to rock layers that accumulated as sediments in thick, troughlike packages along the margins of the continents. It is not much used nowadays. Early in his book, Grabau offers a tabulation of "pulsation systems" for the Paleozoic Era that lists 13 global transgressions and 14 regressions over an interval of approximately 250 million years. Fewer such paired systems are attributed to the subsequent 250 million years belonging to the Mesozoic and Cenozoic eras. A chapter-by-chapter treatment of each pulsation and interpulsation cycle forms the main body of the text.

Typically, Grabau provided extensive stratigraphic documentation for his pulsation cycles and their correlation, from North America, Europe, and Asia. Altogether, *The Rhythm of the Ages* constitutes the earliest comprehensive survey of sea-level fluctuations related to geological unconformities to be organized on anything like a global scale for the bulk of the decipherable rock record. There is no mystery about Grabau's inspiration for the beautiful paleogeographic maps; they owe much to the Pangaean master continent envisioned by Alfred Wegener. Less obvious is the stimulus for Grabau's Pulsation Theory. An obscure clue in the 1940 volume is important in tracing Grabau's chain of thought concerning sea-level pulsations. In a chapter on mountain building, a key illustration with an accompanying definition is introduced as a special example of a geological inlier. Not to be confused with an outlier, which we encountered earlier this morning at the little mesa with the shark teeth, an inlier is a similarly circular body of rock that is older than the rocks surrounding it. It stands up in bold relief because softer rocks of the same age that formerly encased it were stripped away by erosion. Marine sediments from a younger time interval that accumulate around the base of an inlier do so in what is an island environment.

Grabau was suitably impressed by the rounded, sugarloaf mountains that characterize parts of China; he used one such coastal example from Shantung Province on the Yellow Sea to illustrate the sedimentary burial of a geological inlier. The coastal peak is comprised of old rocks, but in this case the surrounding sediments are from the outwash plain of the Yellow River. Such an inlier was called a "shantung" by Grabau. Commenting in the text, he wrote: "Such buried *shantungs,* are sometimes met with in older geosynclines, or on their marginal platforms. Barraboo ridge of Wisconsin is an example of a 'shantung' which has now been partly re-exhumed, and Caradoc Mountain of Shropshire appears to represent another."[16]

The Precambrian quartzite of the Barraboo area in Wisconsin and the Cambrian sandstones of Caradoc Mountain in Shropshire, England, are comparatively resistant rocks with substantial topographic relief that are surrounded by younger geological formations. In each case, the contact between the older and younger rocks is an unconformity.

In exactly the same way, the Atravesada, Ensenada de Muerte, and El Coloradito mesas consist of older igneous rocks (Miocene age) that are still partially surrounded by younger sedimentary rocks (Pliocene age). If Amadeus Grabau could join our conversation now, with all three paleoislands in sight, he would surely exclaim over the exceptional quality of the Punta Chivato shantungs. The only difference is that Grabau's example of the type shantung is related to regressive facies associated with the geologically recent fall in global sea level that stimulated the seaward advancement of the Yellow River delta and related coastal plain in China. The Barraboo and Caradoc shantungs are mainly linked with transgressive facies. As we know from our visit to the east cliff face of the Punta Chivato promontory on day two, our shantungs are allied with a major Pliocene transgression superimposed over a series of comparatively minor regressions.

Amadeus W. Grabau was born and grew up in Wisconsin, the son of a family of German heritage.[17] A correspondence course in mineralogy from the Massachusetts Institute of Technology began his formal education in geology, and he graduated from that institution with a bachelor's degree in 1896. His master's and doctoral degrees were earned at Harvard University in 1896 and 1900, respectively. From 1901 until 1920 he worked his way through the professorial ranks at Columbia University in New York City, where he taught paleontology and stratigraphy. It was during the early part of Grabau's career that he focused intently on the facies concept and the defining characteristics of marine transgressions and regressions. Some of his research on unconformities and the relationships of facies to ancient shorelines were incorporated into his massive textbook, *Principles of Stratigraphy*, published in 1913. The 1,185-page treatise is dedicated to none other than Johannes Walther. It became the primary instrument by which American students were introduced to the facies concept. Some of Grabau's peers, however, were not well disposed to accept the new school of thought. Among his most formidable adversaries was another German American, Edward O. Ulrich (1857–1944), who served from 1901 to 1932 as the chief stratigrapher-paleontologist in the United States Geological Survey. Ulrich rejected the facies concept, because he was accustomed to studying rock formations that were unvaried and extremely widespread. Furthermore, Ulrich opposed Grabau by arguing that the changes in sea level implied by the rock record were very rapid, due more to tectonic forces that warped the continents than to any true rise or fall in sea level over time.

Grabau had become disillusioned with the climate of geological research in the United States, and his departure from Columbia was precipitated by an offer for a joint appointment as professor of paleontology at the National University of Peking and chief paleontologist at the Geological Survey of China.[18] The opportunity to start fresh with the unknown geology of an entire subcontinent was surely a great inducement. In China, Grabau's government rank was commensurate with the authority carried by Ulrich in the U.S., and as a professor, he attracted and trained the first generation of Chinese stratigraphers and paleontologists. When the United States declared war on Japan in 1941, after the attack on Pearl Harbor, the Japanese arrested the American expatriate and made him a prisoner of war in occupied Peking. The internment years were hard on him, both physically and mentally. After the war, he was unable to resume his career and was cared for by former students until his death in 1946. Grabau's gravesite resides on the pleasant campus of Beijing University, overlooking a tranquil lotus pond.

Some of the specific correlations Grabau made linking geological events in Europe, North America, and Asia have proven erroneous, although others remain valid.[19] What is important is that a renewed and more sophisticated debate continues over the magnitude of past sea-level changes and the roles played by regional tectonics versus other global absolutes. During the mid-1970s, in particular, a group of geologists working for Exxon proposed that major unconformities in the continental shelves correlate worldwide and are directly related to the history of sea-level changes over the last 500 million years.[20] The findings of the Exxon team are controversial, because much of the hard data on which their sea-level analysis is based remain the property of the oil company. Whether or not the Exxon people considered Grabau's pronouncements, the basic premise in reconstructing ancient sea-level patterns remains the same. Unconformities must be dated as accurately as possible from as many places around the world as possible.

The portion of the "Exxon curve" keyed to the global Pliocene rock record specifies that five distinct "highstands" in sea level occurred over a span of 5 million years (fig. 22). Three highstands are scaled as peaks that exceeded present sea level by about 200 to 300 feet (60 to 90 m). In local conformity with this pattern, distribution of the Lower Pliocene San Marcos Formation around Mesa Atravesada relates to highstands 4 and 5 (using the numeric code of the Exxon curve). The occurrence of San Marcos limestone near the top of the 330-foot-high (100-m) promontory generally agrees with the maximum excursion

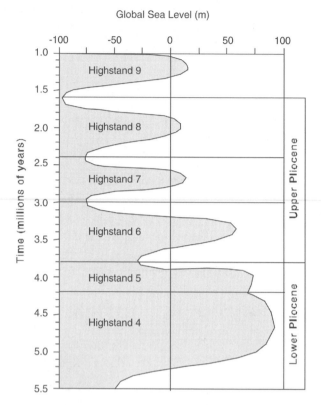

Figure 22. Pliocene sea-level curve (global standard). After Haq et al. (1988).

of Early Pliocene sea level as calculated by the Exxon team. In this case, virtually all of the sea-level change is accounted for by global factors in the absence of local tectonics. Some geologists claim that the Exxon calculations are off by a factor of four while still accepting the basic temporal outline of the curve.[21] If so, it means that close to 250 feet (75 m) of relative sea-level change was due to island subsidence and only about 80 feet (25 m) to a global rise in sea level. Still others assert that the age assignments on the Pliocene curve are askew. Some external evidence suggests that the robust events coupled in highstands 4 and 5 might have been initiated slightly earlier, in the Late Miocene.[22]

More intriguing are ramifications of the Exxon curve for the development of Patrick's cañada grande and its associated fossil sand dune. During later Pliocene time, sea level is shown to have dropped below or substantially below present sea level (fig. 22). If the scale on the Exxon curve is off by a factor of four, then the Late Pliocene highstands in sea level barely met the present datum. Erosion of the paleovalley and its subsequent acquisition of dune sand would have been accelerated at intervals spaced roughly at 3.0 million, 2.5 million, and 1.5 million years ago. It is also possible that little happened until after the first Pleistocene peak in sea level (highstand 9).

The little outlier of Pliocene marl capped by hard limestone, where the day began with a fossil shark hunt, is soon behind us, after we rejoin the jeep track along the water pipeline. We have passed through the south end of the narrow valley that separates the Punta Chivato promontory from Mesa El Coloradito. The main road lies before us, and we are safely returned to the shelter of Bahía Santa Inés. The greater world beyond has had something to tell us about Punta Chivato. Yet Punta Chivato is a mirror through which the entire Gulf of California and all its small islands and peninsulas are reflected. The north wind runs its long, hard course from the dunes of Punta Peñasco at the top of the gulf to Punta Chivato. It blows over the dunes of Isla del Carmen and beyond to the very mouth of the gulf. Rounding Punta Los Muertos near the end of his journey down the length of the Vermilion Sea, kayaker Jonathan Waterman felt behind him the same sting of the viento norte that has seldom failed to make its presence felt for 5 million winters.

6
Mesa Barracas

*Geologists, in their all but closed conversation, inhabit scenes that no one ever
saw, scenes of global sweep, gone and gone again, including seas, mountains,
rivers, forests, and archipelagoes of aching beauty rising in volcanic violence to
settle down quietly and then forever disappear—almost disappear.*
—John McPhee, *Basin and Range*

Our destination, unmarked on the official Mexican topographic map for
Punta Chivato, is Mesa Barracas, the plateau on the southwest perimeter
of the Punta Chivato area, overlooking Bahía Santa Inés (map 6). Members of a
Scripps expedition to the gulf bestowed the name, meaning "barracks," on this
peculiar landscape in 1939.[1] The repetition of several long escarpments over a
territory covering approximately 2.25 square miles (6 km²) resembles an orderly complex with slant-roofed buildings (see fig. 24). Viewed from the sea,
the place's topography apparently stirred memories of military barracks. We are
in luck this morning; a van leaving the hotel on business in Santa Rosalía will
carry us the 3 miles (4.75 km) from Punta Mezquitito to the junction of the
Palo Verde road with a side road between mesas El Coloradito and Las Barracas.
Excluding the ride, today's tour of the mesa covers a rugged circuit of about 4.4
miles (7 km) and involves a good deal of climbing. The highest elevations on
Mesa Barracas stand more than 260 feet (80 m) above sea level, or something
more than 213 feet (65 m) above the Palo Verde road. This afternoon, we'll
cross the Palo Verde road to visit Punta El Coloradito on the bay. A shortcut
back to Punta Mezquitito along Playa La Palmita at day's end adds another 1.8
miles (3 km), making the total distance about the same as that of yesterday's
excursion (6.2 miles, or 10 km).

It is 7:30 A.M. when we alight from the van and offer sleepy thanks to the
driver. The sun has already risen, but its progress is hidden by the profile of the
Punta Chivato promontory. As we hike northwest across the flats on a little used
jeep track, the sun creeps over the Atravesada's wide shoulders, casting a rosy
glow against the beige cliffs on our left. The track continues for more than half a
mile (1 km), then comes to a dead end. Due west is a great cleft in the
escarpment, guarded from above by two small peaks (map 6). If ever there was a
natural gateway to a place, this is surely it. The knobby twins that crown the
ridge stand out like a pair of blunt horns on the horizon. In the sandy draw
leading to the base of the naked gash in the cliff line, I can feel the heat's
shimmer on the ground.

As always, I am absorbed by what I find at my feet as I wind my way through the twists and turns of the little arroyo. The draw is chock full of fossil oysters. Here and there, large blocks of limestone densely packed with the same species litter the narrow wash. Individual valves are nearly 5 inches (12 cm) in length. I am particularly struck by the shells' unusual thickness along their anterior margin (fig. 23). A single valve reaches 4 inches (10 cm) in thickness, through a span of some 35 to 40 strongly etched growth lines. It is unlikely that each line represents a full calendar year, but these bivalves clearly enjoyed long lives. A jumble of rocks packed with the same oysters trails off in opposite directions vaguely parallel to the cliffs rising before us. The sandy wash leads through a break in the loose stones, where the intermittent stream has cleared a passage. Nothing like a solid outcrop is found in the immediate vicinity. I suspect that the fossil oysters did not live and die here.

Due ahead rises a talus slope on which giant blocks of limey siltstone rest askew. These rocks are sparsely fossiliferous but include small pectens *(Argopecten circularis* and *Nodipecten arthriticus);* yet a third species represents another genus *(Flabellipecten).* The pectens weather easily from the relatively soft rocks; their loose shells are concentrated amid the talus debris. All occur as fossils in the Upper Pliocene Marquer and Carmen formations in the gulf region, and the first two species survive today in the gulf waters. This is the first intimation that the strata of Las Barracas are younger than the varied facies that encircle the Punta Chivato promontory. Much of this locality's rock sequence is buried by the talus slope, which allows access to the ridge top. The slope's loose blocks match the lithology of strata above, of which a 20-foot (6-m) thickness is exposed. Some unknown creature made horizontal burrows through the upper layers of the original soft sediment. The sediment that filled the burrows is better cemented than are the surrounding rocks. Coarse, finger-size pieces shaped like the burrows easily weather free from the outcrop and lie loose in the talus.

The climb to the low saddle between the two sentry peaks is steep, but we are fresh and rested. At the saddle, looking north over the flatlands below, an unexpected atmospheric condition takes us by surprise. The rapid warming of the coastal lands under the morning sun has created a thermal high that pulls cooler, dense air laden with moisture down from higher elevations in the foothills of the Sierra de Guadalupe. A low fog bank rolls across the landscape, driven by a gentle westerly breeze. At the west horn's summit, the limestone caprock provides a choice seat from which to watch the drama of the fog.

The advancing fog mimics a marine deluge that spills across the land with the surreal speed of time-lapse photography. Through the fog, the three northern mesas convert to virtual islands before our eyes. On the distant horizon, genuine islands surrounded by gray sea lose perspective and fuse with the

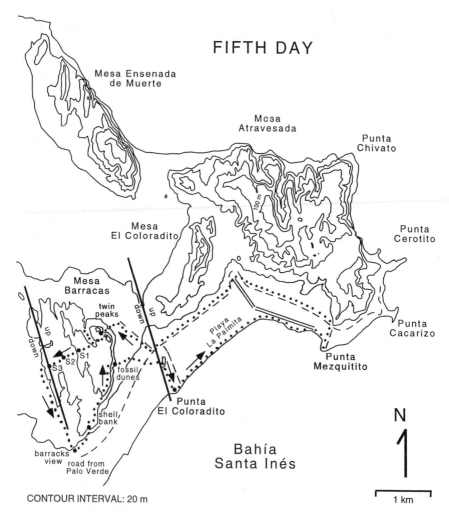

FIFTH DAY

Mesa Ensenada
de Muerte

Mesa
Atravesada

Punta
Chivato

Mesa
El Coloradito

Punta
Cerotito

Mesa
Barracas

twin
peaks

down up

up

Playa
La Palmita

down

S1

S2

S3

fossil
dunes

Punta
Cacarizo

Punta
Mezquitito

shell
bank

Punta
El Coloradito

barracks
view road from
Palo Verde

Bahía
Santa Inés

N

CONTOUR INTERVAL: 20 m

1 km

Map 6. Route for Mesa Barracas.

virtual ones. All now form an archipelago of fleeting beauty. To the west is Isla
San Marcos; next comes Mesa Ensenada de Muerte; and just above the gray
notch between mesas Ensenada de Muerte and Atravesada floats the volcanic
shield of Isla Tortuga. On the far right to the east looms Mesa El Coloradito.

The fog pools on the plain behind the Little Red Table until it sweeps over
its western flank like a tidal wave sweeping across the Palo Verde road. The red
rooftops of houses farthest back from Playa La Palmita rise above the ground-
fog like little boats. These 45 minutes of fog migration reenact events that
occurred in geological time at the start of the Pliocene Epoch, 5 million years
ago. How do Las Barracas fit into this story? I have not visited this place as often

Figure 23. Fossil oysters (Pliocene). Photo by author.

as other parts, and my conception of it is still malleable. The rocks where I sit yield little useful information besides the fact that they are better cemented and more durable than the softer strata below. I decide to visit the neighboring sentry to the southeast.

At its summit, the 2.5-foot-thick (0.75-m) caprock is packed with the same fossil oysters found loose in the arroyo. The chaotic jumble of rocks on the plain represents the natural recession of the principal escarpment of Mesa Barracas. More rapid weathering of the softer underlying siltstone by wind and water continuously undermines the upper ledge of oyster-bearing limestone. The process is similar to the ongoing erosion found at waterfalls, where softer strata underlie a resistant lip. The same oyster bed is sure to form a stratum in the opposite horn, because fallen blocks lie below it on the plain. Stepping back from the outer edge of the cliff, I find that a thin layer of limestone, barren of conspicuous fossils, forms a crust on the capstone. The surface is overprinted by pitted patterns of karstic weathering. Across the way, a similar layer probably formed the bench from which we watched the ground-fog's progress.

One thing is certain. Nowhere in the cliffs below are pebbles of Miocene Comondú volcanics incorporated in the thick Upper Pliocene strata. The twin sentries guard a gentle dip slope—a slope inclined in the same direction and at the same angle as the dip of the underlying rocks. It drapes to the southwest through a succession of minor escarpments separated by parallel arroyos draining the mesa on a northwest-by-southeast axis. The vista is something like that from the foot of a staircase, looking up at successive risers, except that in this case the staircase is not fully upright. It lies on its back, as if a master carpenter has just assembled the framework on the ground and has yet to hoist it into place.

Using the compass clinometer, I find that the caprock dips about 5° to the southwest, leading me to think that in crossing the barracks landscape ahead, the layers of a carbonate ramp will be ascended in stratigraphic order from oldest (at the bottom) to youngest (at the top). Is this another paleoisland? If so, where are the telltale conglomerate beds with their evidence of coastal erosion against a central igneous core? If not evident in the exposed base of the stratigraphic succession behind us on the main escarpment—the foot of the stairway—are they any more likely to occur in the steps ahead? I start down the gentle dip slope to the southwest but soon find myself drawn into an arroyo that descends precipitously to intersect at right angles with the first drainage footing the next inner escarpment.

Another landscape greets us at the intersection of the two arroyos. The ridge behind offers shelter from the north wind, but the local vegetation differs markedly from that of the narrow, shady glens on the south side of the Punta Chivato promontory. The exposure here is more open to the sky, and conditions are more arid. There are no tall palo blanco or palo verde trees around. The copal is present, upright but diminutive. A close cousin to the copal, the torote colorado *(Bursera microphylia),* is more common. Larger in stature, this tree is known by its reddish bark and the pungent smell akin to turpentine it gives off when its small, pinnate leaves are crushed.[2] It is pleasant to sit and rest for a few moments against the cool arroyo wall eroded in coarse siltstone and shaded from above by an upright torote. Leaving my pack, I explore the drainage to the northwest. The arroyo embankments rarely exceed 6.5 feet (2 m) in height. No orphan fossils are to be found in the dry streambed. There is some similarity between the strata exposed in this drainage and the massive siltstone face of the principal escarpment traversed at the start of the day, but these layers are composed of coarser, better cemented sediments. Returning upstream, I retrieve my gear and head southwest, up slope now, toward the first internal escarpment or step in the Barracas *cuesta* (map 6).

The soil is riddled with variously sized holes that house spiders, desert mice, and snakes. Now and then, when a shallow burrow collapses under my weight, my boot heels sink into the ground. Here in the open, the vegetation differs yet again from that of the arroyo embankments left behind. The Mormon tea plant *(Ephedra aspera)* has arrowlike leaf shafts that form branchlets up to 3.3 feet (1 m) tall. One or more varieties of the hedgehog cactus (*Echinocereus* sp.) thrive on this well-drained slope. Known locally as *pitayita,* the plant yields a small, edible fruit. Also common are one or more varieties of the cholla cactus (*Opuntia* sp.). These small tree cacti possess a stout woody trunk. The wood is flesh-covered, but in death, the skeletal trunk is hollow and perforated by distinctive diamond-shaped openings. The plant piques my paleontologist instincts, causing me to wonder if I might someday be lucky enough to stumble on a stream deposit bearing its fossil remains. It would be an unusual occurrence requiring rapid burial by flood sediments, but it is a distinct possibility. Fossil trunks and bark are known near El Rosario on the Pacific coast of Baja California from rocks of Cretaceous age, but I am unaware of any younger deposits that might bear traces related to the peninsula's present endemic flora.

The sun casts a harsh light on the rampartlike beige cliff line stretched out ahead. The topographic map indicates our position (map 6) and shows that the escarpment has a linear extent of three-quarters of a mile (1.25 km). There are few eroded fossils to pick through at its base. Little more than 5 feet (1.5 m) thick, the ledge is easy to climb. Scattered throughout are a few internal molds of bivalves and some dark andesite pebbles. Standing on the rampart with my compass, I find that the first internal step in the Mesa Barracas cuesta (denoted on map 6 as S1) follows a bearing of N18°W. This agrees well with the contour line orientation shown on the map. Beyond the adjacent dip slope to the southwest, the next linear rampart rises in the distance, over 1,000 feet (about 0.3 km) away. Beyond that lies yet a third wall. I suspect that this is the first in a series of hogbacks, a colloquial term applied by field geologists to resistant strata that are tilted and exposed in repeated units due to faults located in the intervening valleys. The name derives from swine with sharp and narrow shoulders, though perhaps the term really says more about the crusty prospector types who did field geology in years past. Nonetheless, topographic hogbacks are said to resemble the profiles of thin pigs ranked side by side.

The principal dip slope to the southwest remains constant with a value not exceeding 6°. Again we descend to a drainage established on a northwest-southeast axis. Once more it is necessary to cross an arroyo that terminates the dip slope, although this arroyo is not as deeply entrenched as the first. Again we make our way up the opposite slope, which is covered in soil eroded from softer rocks. The next internal cliff line in Las Barracas is shaped by a more resistant stratum. The landscape's symmetry is similar to that of Punta Cacarizo, seen during the second day. The succession of Pliocene strata is arrayed at a low angle. The eroded cliff face forms the steep edge of the structure in one or a few large steps, while the dip slope falls away on a gentler grade parallel to the bedding plane of the underlying strata. In this terrain, however, it is not easy to maintain a direct course, as it was at Hammerhead Point. Small detours around thickets of spiky Mormon tea plants or prickly cholla cactus are frequent. As I doggedly push my way between two Mormon tea plants, I flush a lone California quail *(Callipepla californicus),* a plump hen dressed in soft brown tones that blend well with the surrounding country. She does not attempt to fly but scurries away to find another hiding place. The male's fancier plumage includes a distinctive black topknot on his head.

At last we stand atop the second low step in Mesa Barracas (S2 on map 6). The topographic map shows the cliff line to extend unbroken for 1.25 miles (2 km). Similar to that of the previous bench, the orientation of this outcrop is N20°W. Bivalve fossil molds are more abundant here than in the previous cliff face. A few pecten shells lie around. I pick up a coarsely ribbed oyster, *Ostrea vespertina,* broadly representative of the Pliocene and now extinct.[3] A few spherical rhodoliths are also scattered about. Coralline red algae are compact with stubby branches; the largest colonies measure about 1.5 inches (4 cm). These specimens are larger but less abundant than the rhodoliths encountered on the Pleistocene seabed behind Playa La Palmita on the first day. There the abandoned embayment is close to present sea level, whereas here we are more than 130 feet (40 m) higher. We have advanced more than a half mile (1 km) from the oyster-encrusted caprock on the principal northeastern escarpment behind us. In doing so, we have also worked our way upward in time through strata that reflect a slightly more offshore ecology. Modern rhodoliths dwell in gulf waters up to about 40 feet (12 m) deep, whereas oyster mounds usually develop in shallower waters.

As before, the strata exposed in this cliff line include only a few dark andesite pebbles. More plentiful are small, lustrous, rusty orange pebbles. Oval in shape, they are no more than three-quarters of an inch (2 cm) long, and the first task is to extract a few samples. Some protrude from the rocks in bas-relief, which attests to their greater hardness in contrast to the entombing limestone. I bring my hammer down on a half-exposed pebble, cracking it so that the fragment falls into my cupped hand. My first surprise is that the rust-orange exterior of the pebble hides beneath it a flat gray material. A second surprise comes when I realize that the fine-grained rock is sedimentary, not igneous, in origin. Although extremely hard with almost a crystalline appearance, the pebble is a carbonate rock akin to limestone. I am reminded of the magnesium-rich rocks visited during the first day, which form the hard dolomite on the south margin of the Pleistocene Bahía Santa Inés. Chemical precipitation from a hydrothermal vent was the suspected source.[4] It strikes me that the same kind of phenomenon might have been at work here, but no comparable dolomite outcrop is nearby. Perhaps the original Pliocene dolomite was eroded by waves and the resulting fragments rounded into pebbles. The small, hard pebbles would be dispersed by currents and incorporated into the soft marine limestone now exposed on this escarpment. This is, of course, only a working hypothesis. For present purposes, it is more important that the odd pebbles serve as a locally unique marker. Until now, our path has not crossed anything quite like them on Mesa Barracas or, for that matter, elsewhere around Punta Chivato.

The third internal escarpment of Las Barracas dominates the near horizon but does not form a continuous rampart. Instead, it is breached by a secondary arroyo running perpendicular to the main northwest-southwest drainage. Geomorphologists refer to streambeds with many right-angle turns as having a trellised pattern. Such a system is sometimes related to topography underlain by folded rocks, which is not the case here. Otherwise, a trellised drainage may be influenced by regularly spaced faults. I am more confident that the morphology of this landscape is due to something other than the eroded edges of beds on a cuesta. The flow's outward direction through the escarpment is S65°W, perpendicular to the escarpment. Through the gap, we glimpse yet a fourth step on the outskirts of Las Barracas. Mexican Highway 1 lies about 5.5 miles (9 km) away. Occasionally, a semitrailer crawls specklike across the plain, more apparent by its deep engine noise than by its movement. In the far distance is the red-hued Sierra de Guadalupe, dressed in its thick mantle of Comondú volcanics. A glance at the topographic map shows that at least three different breaches cut across the third step in Las Barracas, with a particularly large gap situated to the northwest, as indicated by the long indentation on the 130-foot (40-m) contour interval. The feature ahead is small but quite satisfactory as an example of a water gap. How does such a passage come into existence? The contiguous strata on either side of the breech show no apparent offset. The beds on one side seem to match perfectly with those on the other. I think the passage grew from simple beginnings as a natural joint in the limestone to a more sizable crevice. But the germ of an idea has been planted, and I am more inclined to consider faults as a possible explanation for the main axes in the Mesa Barracas drainage system.

Near the gap in the wall, I stop to examine the low limestone cliffs. There are perhaps more fossil molds of bivalves here, but definitely the same scattering of dark andesite pebbles and the peculiar orange-tinted dolomite pebbles. Climbing the low cliff face near the intersecting arroyos, I check my compass for the third step, which is identical to the last escarpment. The southwesterly orientation of the passage is close to a right angle. The fourth and most southwesterly step on Las Barracas is so muted that it does not register on the topographic map with its 65-foot (20-m) contour intervals. Further exploration down-dip hold little promise of finding something new. An abrupt turn at the next principal arroyo leads southeast toward the coast of Bahía Santa Inés.

The change in route brings us imperceptibly down, close to the Palo Verde road. The 65-foot (20-m) contour interval on the topographic map not only marks the southwest corner of Las Barracas but also conforms to the maximum transgression of the Pleistocene embayment against the older Pliocene structure. Just where Las Barracas' cliff line along the Palo Verde road comes into view, it is possible to recognize a variety of Pleistocene marine fossils at our feet. Here and there are rounded lumps of coral *(Porites californica)* or single bivalve shells *(Chione californiensis)*. Occasionally, a cluster of large, finely sculptured bivalve shells belonging to *Codakia distinguenda* is found articulated and in growth position, nestled on the edge of a slight embankment. The thin concentration of shells does not rival the great deposit investigated behind Playa La Palmita during our first day. There are enough here, however, to give the distinct impression of a former shoreline from about 125,000 years ago.

Closer to the Palo Verde road is an oblique view of Las Barracas that immediately recalls the name's origin (fig. 24). The impression of slanted roofs in ranked repetition is readily conveyed by the gently dipping caprocks that are truncated by the Pleistocene shoreline. Undoubtedly, the 1939 Scripps expedition members walked this same ground. From our present vantage, it may be assumed that each step is offset from the next by modest vertical displacement along a fault line, indicating that the pitched roof of one barracks was moved up or down with respect to its neighbor. Another traverse in the opposite direction along this jagged cliff line is useful in order to test the supposition further.

An unrelated aspect of the view still before us concerns the small sand dunes abutting the eastern coastal flank of Las Barracas. One such dune forms a

Figure 24. Mesa Barracas, the "barracks," seen in profile. Photo by author.

distinct lobe rising as much as a third of the way up the side of the more distant barracks on the right (fig. 24). The dune's position is striking because the moving sand makes it difficult for vegetation to take hold. In contrast, desert plants more extensively cover the stable Pliocene slopes. But wait. How could sand dunes form on the sheltered Bahía Santa Inés, out of the north wind?

As we saw yesterday, contemporary dunes above the north beach at Ensenada El Muerto feed material over the lower, western end of the Punta Chivato promontory to spill into the valley between mesas El Coloradito and Atravesada. In fact, a cover of windblown carbonate sand drapes much of the plain west of Mesa El Coloradito. The small dunes on the coastal flank of Las Barracas are situated almost due south, beyond the gap between mesas Atravesada and Ensenada de Muerte. The skewed north-south alignment of Mesa El Coloradito helps to deflect the wind slightly, toward the east face of Las Barracas. Carbonate sand emanating from the north beach rises up and over a 65-foot-high (20-m) saddle, but the gradient is gentle and the winds strong. In short, the coastal flank of Mesa Barracas is exposed to the viento norte's influence, so small dunes hug its coastal exposure.

Our goal is to reach one of the steep, narrow gashes in the cliffs where two barracks adjoin each other. A good prospect is located ahead, against Las Barracas' coastal face about one-third mile (0.5 km) to the northeast along the flats bordering the Pleistocene shoreline. There, a thick succession of strata is well exposed on the east side of the cut, allowing us to work our way slowly to the top while paying close attention to each stratum's contents. My first impression is that the sequence towering above must be quite different from the one climbed early this morning. Here, for example, there are no fossil oysters. Instead, a diverse assemblage of internal molds derived from other bivalves is strewn on the talus slope. Internal molds are represented by sediment that fills the inside of a shell after the animal dies. If the infilling is composed of fine-grained sediment, the mold will faithfully pick up all the inner sculpture of the shells, including the shape of the beaks (where the shells are conjoined) and the position of the various muscle scars. The sediment slowly becomes hardened into rock with time, and later still the original shell of the mollusk is dissolved away by mildly acidic groundwater that percolates through the strata. Once the layers are exposed edgewise in cliff sections, the fossil molds may literally fall out of the rocks, because a thin open space is left where the original shell once existed—nothing firmly attaches the molds to the larger body of rock that encases them. Tumbling off the outcrop, they become part of the talus apron at the base of the cliffs.

To understand this geological story in its proper sequence, it's good to spend some time here. I climb up the talus slope to the base of the cliffs to examine the lowest layers exposed in the pile of strata. Astonishingly, the bottom layers contain almost no fossils at all. Instead, there are two pebble beds, each about 8 inches (20 cm) thick, separated by a layer of limestone. The two beds are very similar, with many elongated and oval pebbles. There is a vague hint that the pebbles are shingled, or slightly overlapping in position, like roof tiles. Such a pattern suggests that the pebbles were shifted by a current. The prevalent orientation, in the case of this particular cliff face, appears to be to the west. A variety of pebbles is present in the outcrop, some of hard gray andesite, others of softer, red andesite, and a few resembling deeply weathered granite. Most peculiar of all are those that seem to be composed of dark tan sandstone. None of the small orange dolomite pebbles discovered atop Las Barracas are in evidence. Nor is there any sign of the parent rocks from which the pebbles were eroded. The igneous rocks of the Comondú Group surely exist some distance below, and the closest large outcrop is Mesa El Coloradito, 1.5 miles (2.5 km) to the northeast. As for the sandstone pebbles, I have seen nothing like them before.

Continuing up through the slope's overlying strata, we encounter the source of the plentiful fossil molds on the hillside. They come from layers of limestone, individually about 3.3 feet (1 m) thick. Each layer is crowded with fossil molds that await their release from the weathered outcrop (fig. 25). The beds rise to a height of at least 33 feet (10 m) before tapering off to reach the sloped crown of the cliff line that belongs to this particular barracks. Collectively, the thick layers comprise a massively dense shell bank. Surprisingly, less than half of the fossils are represented by molds of articulated mollusk shells. Most appear as a downward curved slit in the rocks; each crack denotes the location of a single valve that came to rest on the bank in a concave-down position, like an overturned cup. Due to the seabed's original hydrodynamics, individual bivalves died, their two shells became separated from each other, and the single valves were transported along the bed until they flipped over in a stable position.

Most of the fossil bivalves are large, up to 6 inches (15 cm) in cross section. Their preservation indicates scarcely any breakage due to wave activity. Identifications at the species level are not easy to make from the little that is revealed in cross section, so I backtrack down slope and gather as many of the intact molds as possible from the loose talus. Virtually every species represented by an internal mold can be found living in the Gulf of California today. The first fossil I pick up is a beautiful specimen of a small arc shell *(Arca pacifica)*. Almost immediately, a larger arc shell *(Anadara grandis)* is retrieved; it shows clear signs of bold ribbing indented on the extremities of the mold. The largest mold belongs to the bittersweet shell *(Glycymeris gigantea),* which measures 3.5 inches (9 cm) in length; the paired muscle scars at the shell's opposite ends appear as deep indentations. Another associated bivalve is the cockle *(Laevicardium elatum)*. I am confident that the concave outlines of single valves exposed in the cliff face above can be attributed to these species. Yet another important bivalve mold from this locality belongs to the chocolate shell *(Megapitaria*

Figure 25. Mollusk molds in Pliocene limestone. Photo by author.

squalida). Internal molds are tricky, because half the information about the shell is missing, and the amount of detail regarding features of the inside shell surface depends entirely on the texture of the sediment that filled the empty shell. If the sediment is too coarse, then little other than the general shape of the shell will be preserved. I smile when I see the ovate profile of the chocolate shell, remembering how vexed I was when first confronted with this species' internal mold. There were many ovate shell shapes to choose among in attempting to match the mold with pictures in various shell books. Not until I slipped the Pliocene mold into the valve of a contemporary chocolate shell did I know for certain what I had. The fossil mold fit perfectly.

Few gastropods are present in my little collection. The kernel of a small spindle shell (genus *Fusinus*) catches my eye. The elongate, tapered spire of the mold is quite elegant. It is possible to look down the coiling axis of this specimen and see daylight at the other end, because the infilling sediments were packed firmly around the columella, or central core, of the empty shell. When the shell was later dissolved away, the spiral axis became an intricately mirrored open space. Yes, internal molds are tricky to visualize. I smile again as I recall an odd incident I experienced as a 17-year-old on the outskirts of Lisbon one Saturday morning during the summer I spent as an exchange student living in Portugal.

Knowing of my keen interest in fossils, the Portuguese family who hosted me that summer in 1966 allowed me to find my own way by city bus to the suburbs, where a construction project had cleared away the topsoil from sedimentary layers dating from the Cretaceous Period. The soft sandstone rocks were full of fossil molds, much like the Pliocene material here, although not as well cemented. My host-father loaned me his carpenter's hammer, and I had taken along a few nails to substitute for chisels. By mid-morning I had succeeded in digging out some choice samples of bivalve and gastropod molds. My treasure trove included examples of highly spired gastropods more slender and delicately wrought than the Pliocene *Fusinus* mold I now hold in my fingers. As I continued to work that morning in the middle of the open exposure, I spied an old woman approaching me from the edge of the site. Like nearly all Portuguese women her age, she was dressed from head to foot in black.

The woman was curious to know what I was doing, and I was eager to try out my new language skills. I explained that I was an American visiting her country. So far, I was making myself understood. I tried to explain that I was interested in fossils. She knitted her brow in confusion. The word *fósil* did not register. I tried again, this time extending to her the open palm of my hand, cradling two or three of the delicate gastropod molds I had labored so diligently to recover intact. "Caracol de mar antigo," I attempted. Her face now erupted in comprehension. *Caracol,* she knew, was a snail. Since I had invoked the word for sea, clearly I must be taking about a sea snail, and not the large terrestrial variety some Portuguese are accustomed to enjoy at table. She stretched out her gnarled hand and signaled that I should entrust my precious specimens to her for closer examination. At the same time she began to shake her head from side to side. "Este não é caracol de mar," she strongly insisted in the negative. Then, before I understood what was about to happen, she closed her work-strong hand and crushed the fragile fossils inside her clenched fist. I stared wide-eyed in disbelief as she reopened her hand and the pulverized bits of my hard-won fossils blew away in the breeze. Before I could protest, she launched into a detailed description of precisely which sequence of public buses I should take from here to reach the nearest seawater beach beyond the Tagus estuary. "Now, there, my poor boy, is where you will be able to find genuine sea snails, if that is what you truly desire." She also was hungry for someone to listen to her life story, but I excused myself before she got much beyond the loss of her husband in World War I. When I told my tale of woe at the dinner table that evening, my amiable host-father roared with laughter. She is only an old busybody, he told me. True enough, but she was a busybody in need of better paleontological instruction than I was able to give her. Little more than three centuries ago, many learned scholars believed that fossils were "sports of nature" without any biological affinities. This woman, too, had no reservations about rejecting the vague similarities of my fossil molds to present-day marine invertebrates.

After lunch, the west side of the shaded gully provides a suitable pathway to climb through approximately 80 feet (25 m) of relief and reemerge in the bright sunshine. I want to reexamine the stratified layers that form the second step's caprock, stretching northwest across the plateau. Our morning route took us over the same escarpment, but at a more inland location. Here, now, is an opportunity to study the section nearer to the coastal edge of the plateau, where the layers are exposed through a greater thickness. If I was puzzled by the presence of a few sandstone pebbles in the lower beds on the opposite side of the draw, below the great shell bank I am now completely mystified. The next unusual stratum is only 2.5 feet (75 cm) thick, but it is densely crowded with cobbles of rusty orange sandstone firmly cemented in a matrix of limestone. No mistake about it, a sample under my hand lens reveals that the strange cobbles are composed of fine sandy particles. In order to qualify as fine sand, the individual grains of the rocks must fall within the strict size diameter of 0.005–0.01 inch (one-eighth to one-fourth mm). A cobble is something with a diameter of 2.5–10 inches (64–256 mm). These and related definitions were set forth by a geologist named Charles Wentworth in 1922, and most field geologists have bowed to the convention ever since.[5] An understanding like this is only an informal agreement that allows one geologist to say a thing and be understood implicitly by another who follows the same convention.

When I showed up for my first college course in stratigraphy in the tiered lecture hall on the third floor of Calvin Hall at the University of Iowa, I was thrust into the world of geological conventions the moment I took my seat. The professor in charge did not assign places. I apparently elected to sit in the exact spot where Charles Wentworth sat during his stratigraphy lessons, according to my professor, an experienced man who had come home to Iowa after a distinguished career in the oil fields of Saudi Arabia. Because I occupied Wentworth's chair, it seemed that more might be expected of me than from my fellow students. The thought is amusing to me now as I wrestle with the implications of a conglomerate bed composed of cobbles made of fine-grained sand. I can't do much with these few facts. I desperately need more information. The basic problem is that we have not seen a possible source rock for the cobbles. In our earlier exploration of the carbonate ramps that skirt the Punta Chivato promontory, the origin of the basal conglomerate with andesite boulders and cobbles—the igneous Comondú Group—was unequivocal. During our second day, on the east shore of the promontory, we benefited from a long profile showing the interrelationship between land formed by volcanic rocks and the adjacent carbonate seabed. The textbook clarity of that juxtaposition made the facies concept of Amanz Gressly spring to life. In contrast, where did the fine sandy cobbles in this Upper Pliocene deposit originate?

I retrieve the small plastic bottle that contains a dilute solution of hydrochloric acid (HCl) from my backpack. As soon as I squeeze a tiny amount onto the sample, the wet part of the rock begins to foam, showing the acid's reaction with calcium carbonate. This rock is composed primarily of limestone grains. There are no recognizable vestiges of fossil shells within the cobble, but most of the whole is sure to be composed of individual grains derived from crushed shells. If the sandy cobbles were not ripped up by waves from source rocks directly beneath, then they might have been transported from a source on the margin of the basin. The cobbles are not well rounded, as was characteristic of the andesite conglomerate that formed on the shoreline around the Punta Chivato promontory. If not truly angular in profile, these cobbles are at least lumpy. Clearly, they were delivered rapidly to this spot, and it is unlikely that they moved up slope from a position offshore.

A fresh idea suddenly occurs to me. The profusion of lumpy cobbles might have been derived from fine beach or nearshore sand that began to consolidate into a hardened deposit. If such beds were disturbed, the debris may have been carried offshore, washing down slope away from the coastline. I wonder if the instrument of such a shake-up might have been a shallow earthquake. If we consider the possibility that the barracks are cut by a series of faults that offset the roofline of the structure, then what better source of energy could be imagined? I am beginning to like this idea. Of course, tremors that set off underwater slumps necessarily preceded any earthquakes associated with faults that slice through the conglomerate beds. The pair of thin pebble bands that occur well below us on the other side of the gully could be related to lesser tremors.

The pebble beds examined formerly are distinct entities, as confirmed by their bed size and composition. This is underscored by the fact that only the beds on this side of the gully include the small orange dolomite pebbles also found earlier in the day at a more inland location. Moreover, the basalt or andesite pebbles commonly found below are scarcely present here. The contrasting conglomerate beds on opposite sides of the gully are both succeeded by thick limestone layers replete with fossil molds that represent major shell banks. The gully and associated arroyo on the plateau terminate all strata. No trace of one or the other marker beds is found to extend across this divide. The abrupt separation makes me even more sure that the structure of Las Barracas is accented by a set of parallel faults. It must be that the lesser pair of conglomerate beds is not found on the west side of the gully because they are offset and buried in the ground below. Likewise, it must be that the thicker conglomerate bed is unrecognizable on the east side of the arroyo up top because it is stratigraphically younger than anything else in that sequence and has been eroded away. If this is true, then the strata on the west side of the fault slipped down with respect to strata immediately to the east.

It is also possible that the low-angle dip slope of the barracks captured so dramatically by the caprocks indicates an original ramp system. In this case, the ramp layers dipping to the southwest acquired their slant during deposition and were not tilted afterward by tectonic means. If so, then the faults merely set off one part of the ramp system from neighboring segments along the barracks. Such faults are called *en echelon* faults, due to their parallel arrangement and the overlapping effect they create. In order to suggest the association with topography or hogbacks, only one such fault is positioned on map 6, at the third step on Mesa Barracas. The west side of the fault is marked "down," and the east side "up," to illustrate the kind of relative movement suggested by the disjointed conglomerate beds. To complete the picture, associated en echelon faults would pass through the spots identified as S1 and S2.

For the moment, we have a working hypothesis. The geological relationships in this corner of Punta Chivato seem more complex than others sorted out on previous days. If so, the local development of the Gulf of California assumed a different story line during the later half of the Pliocene Epoch from that of the earlier half. The Lower Pliocene San Marcos Formation to our north tells a simple history of island subsidence and global sea-level rise without too many tectonic complexities. Something more is hinted at by these strata from the Upper Pliocene Marquer Formation.

A nearby jeep track crosses through a low point in the west cliff and over the arroyo at the head of the gully separating the two adjacent barracks structures. We follow the track up the dip slope of the massive shell bank on the other side and continue northeast for more than half a mile (1 km), keeping to the coastal margin of the plateau. No such path existed here in 1995, when I last visited the place with Max Simian. As I look out over the Pleistocene plain below toward Bahía Santa Inés, I count upwards of 40 houses clustering on the shore near Punta El Coloradito, directly east of us (map 6). Not a single one of these dwellings stood there in 1995. The low red rocks of the barely obtrusive point mark a fishing camp operated by the Ejido San Bruno during the winter, when conditions at its village to the north are too windy to launch boats safely. The villagers have not sold the land on the point, which forms the highest shoreline elevation along the curve of Bahía Santa Inés. I pause and sit a while as I retrieve my binoculars and scan the shores and plain below. Inland from Punta El Coloradito more than 2,000 feet (about 650 m) is a tiny mesa that rises to a point 65 feet (20 m) above sea level. The place is marked by a small oval on the topographic map. I focus on the spot with my binoculars. Developers have constructed a water tank on the little mesa's margins. Soon a web of water lines will link the tank with all the new shoreline homes. Progress has come to the bay, but at a rate of expansion that leaves me unsettled. Both wild nature and the people who seek to encamp permanently on its doorstep may suffer when too much development occurs so rapidly.

With its prevailing gentle slopes directed to the southwest, the overall geological disposition of Las Barracas might be interpreted as projecting from the short axis formed by the linkage of Punta El Coloradito and the tiny mesa below us. Without question, if the Barracas plateau were restored beyond its eroded escarpment to the east, its beds would rise up and arch over the line made by the two elevations of Miocene Comondú volcanics. Nowhere in our exploration of the barracks has there been any sign of underlying basement rocks. This should not be surprising, because neither did we find any trace of Pliocene rocks attributable to the older San Marcos Formation. Most likely, lower Pliocene strata and their undergirding Miocene volcanics occur somewhere beneath Las Barracas, out of sight. The little mesa with the water tank and the short bulbous nose of Punta El Coloradito represent the nearest topographic expressions of Comondú rocks that may have formed the central core of another island. The circumstantial evidence of geography and implied paleogeography do not detract from or nullify the working hypothesis about fault lines cutting through the barracks. If the massive shell banks associated with the second and third escarpments of Las Barracas are accepted as the predominant paleoecological fabric of the plateau, then their presence could be the consequence of an offshore ramp in the leeward southwest flank of Pliocene land.

The oyster beds that cap the principal northeast escarpment of Mesa Barracas could be the ultimate shoaling event to overstep an adjacent island complex in later Pliocene time. This is based on an extrapolation in scale from the much younger Pleistocene oyster reef exposed in an arroyo off Playa La Palmita, as seen on day one. Fossils preserved there in growth position are perched atop an oval mound of Pliocene bedrock about 100 feet (some 30 m) in length. This mini-topography suggests that buried Pliocene strata extend outward from the edge of the Miocene volcanics to underlie the loose white carbonates of the Pleistocene seabed behind Playa La Palmita. Scanning the immediate perimeter of the tiny mesa or Punta El Coloradito with binoculars, however, we see no remnants of solid Pliocene strata, but a visit must be made to confirm the impression. The small mesa and Punta El Coloradito could be erosional vestiges of a former and larger island core, reduced in stature during the last interglacial rise in sea level 125,000 years ago. Under this logic, the idea of a Pliocene archipelago in the Punta Chivato region is embellished and enlarged from the island examples so vividly resurrected this morning by the creeping ground-fog.

FEATURE / Roman Fedorovich Hecker and the Birth of Paleoecology

When we understand the organization of marine life in preferred windward or leeward zones around a contemporary island like Isla Requesón in Bahía Concepción, the relationships of the living help guide us to recognize comparable patterns fossilized in the Pliocene-Pleistocene rocks at places like Punta Chivato. Moving between the present and the past in this way, we forge a conceptual link between the ecology of today's world and the paleoecology of former worlds. Paleoecology is, in essence, the study of biological connections among organisms and the physical effects of the environment on those organisms in bygone worlds represented only by rocks, fossils, and their spatial imprint. It is risky to say that a certain person was the first to originate and expedite a new way of thinking about things, but I will argue that the Russian geologist Roman Fedorovich Hecker (1900–1991) did more than any other to establish the discipline of paleoecology. At the very least, the apolitical writings of a dynamic Russian professor personally transformed my teenage life during the height of a cold war that otherwise divided our planet on bitter political and ideological grounds. Hecker, whose family name transliterates from the Russian as Gekker, was the author of a book first published in the Soviet Union in 1957 entitled (in English translation) *Introduction to Paleoecology*.[6] Its straightforward style of writing is appealing and decidedly unpretentious. Hecker's slim book appeared in Chinese and Japanese editions in 1959, a French edition in 1960, and an

English edition in 1965. I first encountered it in the public library of my hometown. Once I devoured its pages, I began to see the marine fossils around me in the cliffs and quarries of eastern Iowa much differently.

Traditionally, fossil collectors sort their material by biological group. All the corals are placed together in the same drawer or cabinet, regardless of place of origin but often sorted by geological age. Likewise, all the subgroups of mollusks, arthropods, and echinoderms are segregated from one another, and so on. Many museum displays are still arranged in this way. After reading Hecker, I organized my growing collections not only by stratigraphic level but also by locality. The simple difference was in the emphasis placed on retaining the natural associations of the different fossil groups with one another as they were in life. A museum diorama that reconstructs a place in terms of the diversity and relative abundance of its plants and animals gives precedence to the ecological story. To my mind, the most appealing museum displays attempt to exhibit the paleoecological information derived from their best fossil collections in precisely the same way.

Hecker wasted no time in exclaiming this particular outlook in the early pages of his book. The Russian geologist, who took his initial professional training in a mining institute in St. Petersburg between 1917 and 1923, listed two fundamental problems as foremost for the budding paleoecologist to consider:

1. Elucidation of the *mode of life* of extinct animals and plants, so as to (a) understand these organisms more completely and profoundly, and (b) determine the influence they may have exercised upon other animals and plants, and upon their inorganic medium of life.
2. Reconstruction of the *life conditions* of various organisms, taken both separately and in association during the geological past, so as to determine the possibilities which then existed for their development as individuals and as associations. [italics in the original][7]

The author concludes that the two problems are inseparable. It is impossible to reconstruct the original life conditions of various organisms associated with one other without first taking the time to investigate the mode of life of each member. Hecker goes on to highlight the basic difference between persons who elect to study ecology and those who will be drawn to consider paleoecology as their life's work:

The basic method of an ecologist (neoecologist) in the study of the world of living organisms is observation of the organisms in their natural environment. Besides this a neoecologist can organize experiments, whereas a paleoecologist cannot do so. However, the whole geological history of the organic world may be regarded as an uninterrupted series of "experiments by nature" affecting the inhabitants of ancient seas and lands, forcing them to shift location with migrating facies and to adapt themselves to new conditions. The methods in a paleoecologist's work are in this respect opposite those used by neoecologists. A neoecologist creates experimental conditions in order to obtain results quite unknown to him in advance, whereas a paleoecologist must undertake to reconstruct the conditions and causes of changes indicated by the preserved fossil material resulting from experiments by nature.[8]

The long-term history of Punta Chivato on the Gulf of California may thus be seen as a grand experiment that began with the initial flooding of the gulf at least 5 million years ago, an experiment that persists today with the added intrusion of a growing human population. How did certain organisms come to be associated with one another to dwell on the wind- and wave-swept north side of the archipelago while others sorted themselves out for life adapted to the sheltered southern lee of the islands? What are the differences in anatomy and mode of life that make the outcome of this experiment inevitable? We have rarely strayed from these questions during our walks about the Punta Chivato area, except to better understand the physical conditions that control wind, waves, variations in water salinity, the erosion of rocky shores, and the transport of beach and dune sands.

To answer these questions, much importance is placed on the distinction between fossil groups preserved in their original mode of growth and those found in deposits that show to varying degrees the breakdown and dispersal of organic materials from one place to another. The shell beds surrounding the phantom island behind Playa La Palmita and the *Porites* reef near the hotel are two examples of Pleistocene life buried intact and preserved undisturbed for more than 100,000 years. The inclusion of intertidal mollusks with the basal conglomerate of carbonate ramps constructed around Punta Chivato typifies a different association that endured rough-water conditions but remained true to its Pliocene ecology of 5 million years past. In the opposite extreme, the development of carbonate beach sand and dunes on the north side of the Punta Chivato promontory represents the thorough recycling of vast shell banks that thrived from the Pliocene to today in the offshore waters of Ensenada El Muerto. The late Pliocene shell banks preserved on Mesa Barracas tell a variation on the same theme, but this time, the raw materials that compose the banks are only moderately disturbed from their original organic form. Hecker was careful to stress the significance of such differences:

A paleoecologist should differentiate between the *place of habitat* of an organism and the *place of its burial,* and in some instances also the *place of its death.* These may coincide, but quite frequently they differ. In any case, a bed containing organic remains represents the location and medium of their burial, but it remains to be proved whether the fossil-bearing bed originated where the organisms lived, or in the place where they perished. [italics in the original][9]

Other aspects of Hecker's writings took much longer for me to appreciate. For example, his book cites an idea he first promulgated in an earlier technical report in 1951—the idea that museum exhibits of the panoramic type mentioned earlier are not always sufficient to illustrate the grand "experiments of nature" related in the rock record. Hecker advocated the development of what he called natural museums, represented by what he considered to be paleoecological monuments. The criteria for development of such monuments he explained as follows:

For paleoecological monuments [there] should be selected those natural exposures which are of paleoecological interest, and which are also rare and may be easily defaced or destroyed by breaking off of specimens, and which in their natural surroundings are more valuable and demonstrative than they could be when transferred to a museum. They can be found and selected in almost any country of the world.[10]

A working example cited by Hecker is Sataplia Preserve near the town of Kutaisi in southern Kazakhstan, where dinosaur tracks are found on a great limestone-bed surface. Dinosaur National Monument in eastern Utah is another example, more familiar to us, of a successful field museum. Dinosaurs are highly popular ambassadors of the fossil world, but the lowly invertebrates also have much to tell us about the intricate ecological systems in which they invested themselves over the last 600 million years.

From Hecker's own field experience in the north desert region of present-day Tajikistan, he offers the example of small islands of old rocks from the Paleozoic Era encrusted with oysters from the much younger Cenozoic Era as yet another potential monument. The 1966 English translation of *Introduction to Paleoecology* provides simple pen-and-ink field sketches of the relationships. Many years later, I plunged myself into Hecker's research on comparable fossil islands that are well exposed in the Kyzil Kum desert of neighboring Uzbekistan.[11] Grainy, black-and-white photos published from an expedition that probably took place in the early 1960s show with surprising clarity the shape and contours of natural basins untouched since the retreat of seas more than

25 million years ago. One photo shows an abandoned sea cliff covered with encrusting oysters. Another illustrates a portion of a seabed strewn with dome-shaped corals that look similar to brain corals. I must struggle to transliterate the photo captions from the original Russian, but the undisturbed landscape speaks for itself in a language I understand. I can easily picture myself at Hecker's side, exploring the ancient shorelines on the remote frontiers of the old Soviet empire, although it is hard to imagine anything like an organized structure for an outdoor museum taking root there. Why not here at Punta Chivato? Over the years, it has slowly dawned on me that the ancient archipelago in this place, now only partially abandoned by the munificent Gulf of California, is an astounding natural monument of precisely the ecological order intimated by Hecker. During these past few days, you have experienced the scale and grandeur of this unfinished experiment in nature. It could never be transposed to a traditional museum. It is best studied and appreciated right here at Punta Chivato.

Roman Fedorovich Hecker was a man of exceptionally wide interests and experience in paleoecology. From 1941 to 1961 he taught paleoecology at the University of Moscow. For most of his long professional career, he was assigned to the Paleontological Institute in Moscow under the Soviet Academy of Sciences. Hecker is said to have been the main organizing force behind most of the paleoecological conferences and field meetings held in the USSR, leading field trips to visit the Lower Paleozoic rocks around St. Petersburg (known as Leningrad during most of his adult life) and in neighboring Estonia and organizing other trips for students and colleagues to the Upper Paleozoic reef rocks in the southern Urals and Mesozoic reef rocks in the Crimea. He was at home in the deserts of middle Asia, where he wandered through the stark topography of abandoned seascapes dating from the early Cenozoic Era. One of my Russian acquaintances tells me that she distinctly remembers Professor Hecker as an intelligent person and a brilliant speaker.[12] She notes that he was a handsome man, always surrounded by admiring female students. Would I have been admitted to Hecker's inner circle, had I been a college student in the Soviet Union in the late 1960s? It is impossible to know. But sitting here overlooking sunlit Bahía Santa Inés, I feel certain that Roman Fedorovich Hecker would have been entirely comfortable at Punta Chivato and eager to promote its considerable charms as an outstanding paleoecological monument.

I rise from my resting spot with a renewed sense of invigoration and purpose. The faint jeep track swings inland, but we must keep to the edge of the coastal escarpment to look for a safe place to alight to the plain below. The strata exposed through this part of the escarpment on the descent will be interesting. Are they similar to those formed by the shell banks ascended to the south at lunchtime, or do they share more in common with the beds visited to the north at the start of the day? Once at the bottom of the cliff line, we must cross over to the tiny mesa on the other side of the Palo Verde road and reevaluate the local Comondú rocks as a possible focal point for a Pliocene island linked to the Mesa Barracas succession. It may also be possible to learn something about the relationship between the small mesa and Punta El Coloradito on the midline of Santa Inés Bay.

The drainage system incised on this part of the barracks is more intricate than the succession of arroyos crossed farther inland this morning. In order to keep to the edge of the escarpment, there is no choice but to cross several small, westward-running arroyos. A small break in the cliff line opens up more than 1,000 feet (0.3 km) to the north, and there it is possible to descend (map 6). Although the passage down is safe, the view directly below provokes some intellectual hesitation on my part. The transition from a Pleistocene shoreline to the base of the Pliocene escarpment, which we tracked from the southwest corner of the barracks, bears no resemblance to the scene now confronting us. We have hypothesized that the primary defining feature of Las Barracas consists of small en echelon faults that strike to the northwest across beds dipping gently to the southwest. Below us at the base of these cliffs is something that resembles a significant fault scarp defined by a shallow valley. On the opposite valley wall are completely different sedimentary rocks, darker beds that dip obviously to the southeast, in marked contrast to the main dip slope of Las Barracas. How could something like this occur just here? I had assumed only a simple erosional escarpment dating from the Pleistocene.

The first objective is to reach the bottom of the high escarpment, having examined the strata that compose it. Gradually I ease my way down talus slopes on a 100-foot (30-m) descent around exposed cliffs. First met is a limey silt-stone with scattered small pectens. These rocks are underlain by a 4-foot (1.25-m) thickness of more resistant siltstone that is extensively burrowed. More precisely, the burrow fillings are well cemented, while the softer surrounding rocks have eroded away, creating a rock unit that looks like macaroni salad, except that the macaroni pieces are not hollow. Most of the solid burrows are horizontal, but here and there it is possible to find a well-preserved vertical burrow that represents a central point of egress (fig. 26; see the cylindrical structure adjacent to the knife). Immediately underlying these rocks is another layer of limey siltstone with scattered small pectens. Except for the absence of an oyster capstone, the succession at this locality is the same as that ascended at

Figure 26. Burrows in Pliocene limestone. Photo by author.

the start of the day. The similarity makes sense, because we are less than half a mile (three-quarters of a kilometer) from where we started up the cliff line this morning, at a position only about 800 feet (one-fourth kilometer) along the principal dip slope of Las Barracas. Our findings confirm that the initial and highest barracks structure in the landscape differs significantly from the successively lower structures with their shell banks to the southwest, so the notion of en echelon faults also makes good sense.

At the bottom of the slope is a trough that maintains a north-south orientation some 20° out of phase with the en echelon faults tentatively mapped on Mesa Barracas. A single fault line on a different compass heading would certainly complicate the story. The shallow valley is so entrenched that the view to the east over the coastal plain on Bahía Santa Inés is blocked. I cross to the other side of the trough and struggle uphill through loose sand to the base of the dark outcrop. It takes me a few moments to collect myself, but I am relieved to find a highly uniform, thick-bedded sandstone that represents a fossil sand dune formerly plastered against the side of the Pliocene escarpment. Before lunch today, we spied an active sand dune from the southwest corner of the barracks (fig. 24). It is difficult to know the age of the dune at this locality, but it is rock solid. Here the beds dip evenly 30° to the southeast through an exposed thickness of about 10 feet (3 m). The trough represents a weak juncture between the dune and the Pliocene escarpment, where preferential erosion took place. The facts add up. Recent dune sand has begun to drift into the trough from the north. We are on a north-south axis directly in line with the wind gap between mesas Atravesada and Ensenada de Muerte (map 6). There is no awkward fault escarpment located here. Instead, there is only an erosional divide between two sets of layered rocks with different dip slopes and different hardnesses. The softer dune sandstone is strictly local, and it adjoins the older Pliocene structure only because it was blown into place. The dip angle within the dune rocks represents nothing more than the original angle of repose.

Our tour of Mesa Barracas is complete. Up slope a short distance through loose sand, we may step across to the highest part of the dune rocks. In clear view, slightly less than one-half mile (1 km) to the east, sits the tiny knob of Comondú volcanics, best reached by striking across country on a direct bearing through the desert scrub. We cross the Palo Verde road halfway there. Upon finally reaching the tiny mesa, which stands about 16 feet (5 m) above the surrounding plain, I am disappointed: the feature has been extensively modified by grading related to the installation of the nearby water tank. Places are few where it is possible to get a clear look at the rocks. Though it is hard to use the compass, the tilted gray andesite layers suggest an orientation of N55°E, with dips that register between 40° and 50° to the northwest. No trace of exposed Pliocene sedimentary rocks exists in the immediate vicinity of the knob.

Our final objective for today is to reach Punta El Coloradito, some 2,000 feet (650 m) to the southeast at the end of a dirt road. The walking is easy and direct, and my steps lighten with the prospect of reaching the cool shade below the cliffs and of once again being near the water. Limited in exposure, the

Comondú rocks at the point are in good condition, offering valuable informa-tion to be collected. They are mainly red, as might be guessed by the name bestowed in Spanish, translated as "Little Red Point." At the rear of the beach, cliffs resembling a conglomerate offer shade. Marine conglomerate typically would consist of wave-rounded pebbles and cobbles. Here there is a crudely layered deposit that contains angular chunks of andesite set in a matrix of finer volcanic material. The technical term for these rocks is volcanic breccia. The materials in these beds were not reworked by water but derived from a hot flow or landslide that slumped down the side of a volcano and picked up the blocky material in its path.

Around to the south side of the outcrop is a place where the orientation and dip of these beds may be measured with the compass. The orientation is N45°E, which is not far from the value obtained inland at the little mesa. The dip of the breccia beds is only 26°, but also to the northwest. Why is this part of the Comondú sequence so different from the andesite exposed at the little mesa? Steno's rules remind us that the various volcanic units in the Comondú Group were originally deposited as fairly flat-lying layers. Why should these volcanic beds have come to rest in a horizontal position if the dune rocks visited only a short time ago are interpreted as having formed naturally at an angle as steep as 30°? The dune sands were blown into place against the side of the escarpment, and individual grains piled on top of one another as steeply as possible before they tumbled downhill to reach a stable resting place. Volcanic flows, on the other hand—even those that occur as hot landslides—behave as fluids, not resting until they pool in a level environment. Although off to one side of the little mesa, the beds at Punta El Coloradito follow a similar orienta-tion; we must mentally restore the dipping beds at both localities to their original horizontal position. Doing so, we realize that the beds close to the bay are stratigraphically below those occurring farther inland at the small mesa. This is an opportune moment to recall from our first day, on the side of Mesa El Coloradito, that the tilted Comondú andesite exposed there was found to have an orientation of N50°E, with a dip to the northwest of 53°. It appears that the Comondú is a very thick package of volcanic rocks showing a rather consistent orientation from place to place in the Punta Chivato area, although dip angles are somewhat variable within the same directional quadrant.

Now comes the most important field measurement we have made all day. I stand at the highest elevation on Punta El Coloradito with my back to Bahía Santa Inés and aim my compass inland toward the tiny mesa. The bearing reads N20°W, which matches or comes close to the orientations of all the internal steps on Mesa Barracas. When the new line is plotted on the topographic map (map 6), it nicely parallels the en echelon faults hypothesized as cutting through the barracks. Furthermore, the new line may be drawn so that it runs from the slight indentation immediately southwest of Punta El Coloradito to a position on the west flank of the tiny mesa and shoots across the narrowest part of the topographic saddle between Mesa El Coloradito and Las Barracas. There are too many coincidences. The most striking factor is that nowhere west of this line within the Punta Chivato area are there any surface outcrops belonging to the Miocene Comondú Group. The rocks surely exist, but they must be in the subsurface, meaning that the delineation represents a significant defining fault. All the rocks on the east side of the fault, including the Miocene and Lower Pliocene of mesas El Coloradito and Atravesada, have moved upward relative to the rocks on the opposite side of the fault. The principal escarpment for Las Barracas occurs on the west side of this fault, below the twin sentry peaks. A fault escarpment was originally situated adjacent to the fault line, but erosion of the soft Upper Pliocene cliffs led to its substantial westward retreat over time. We saw some evidence for this recession early in the morning, in the fallen blocks of oyster capstone.

How much vertical movement took place along the principal fault? It is difficult to know without checking how far the Miocene Comondú rocks lie below the surface on the west side of the fault. Prior to slippage, the Upper Pliocene strata crossed to the east to level out somewhere above Punta El Coloradito, the tiny mesa, and probably the southwest end of Mesa El Coloradito. It is probably in such a sense that the Comondú volcanics on this axis constituted an enlarged island core in later Pliocene time.

The barracks have turned out to be different from any other part of the Punta Chivato area, yet the place fits securely with the rest, just as surely as all the pieces of a jigsaw puzzle conform to their mandated assembly. During this fifth day at Punta Chivato, we have tested our skills at extracting stubborn secrets from the land. As they are known, the facts are few but cumulative. The fossils tell us they belong to one age, and not another. The strata that yield those fossils dip uniformly in one direction, and not another. The same energy released in the form of earthquakes that ruptured the former seabed also brought cascades of rocky debris offshore from the edge of the land. Long after the Pliocene, Pleistocene sea level changes played a hand in truncating the coastal margin of the barracks; the ever-present viento norte brought sand from the Ensenada El Muerto through the wind gap to brush against the structure's eastward face.

The day is advanced but not finished. I am hot and caked with dust. On the return march across Playa La Palmita toward Punta Mezquitito, the temptation grows for a refreshing plunge in the inviting, calm waters of Bahía Santa Inés. What remains to be considered? Each day we have gone out from the center to explore the surrounding landscape in a new direction. Each day we have gradually added to a fund of information that makes sense of an inanimate crust of earth and allows us to visualize its ecological connections to the living world. There is only one direction left to explore. Leaping into the cool waters, we are reminded that the final quadrant of the Punta Chivato area hides its secrets on the Islas Santa Inés and the dark gulf waters beyond.

Offshore: Islas Santa Inés

It is curious that of this so-called solid earth we know little
but the mere skin. All that delights us in green things growing,
from the grass of the field to the cedar of Lebanon, is only that
skin deep.—Walter de la Mare, *Desert Islands*

The life-green vestments of our continents are deceptively thin compared with the earth's solid body. Even the outermost sedimentary and volcanic layers are merely the thinnest veneer tacked onto the underlying crust. Desert places permit us to dispense with the vegetative membrane that obscures the land's outward face. Any flight over Baja California on a clear day leaves the traveler with a profound impression of just how naked and exposed the land is. It is more difficult to appreciate that the deep waters surrounding the peninsula amount to no more than a vaporous film over the concealed oceanic crust. How do we arrive at a better understanding of this great finger of land and the adjacent terrain hidden below the narrow gulf? The gulf islands pose an important part of the answer to the riddle. The federal topographic map relied on for our exploration of Punta Chivato cuts off the uninhabited Islas Santa Inés. The largest of the three lies only 2.8 miles (4.5 km) southwest of Punta Mezquitito, well within our reach.

During my travels in Baja California, I have often flown over Punta Chivato on commercial flights. From the plane, the biggest island has the look of an oversized manta ray cruising the waters off the gulf coast. As I became better acquainted with the Punta Chivato area on the ground, I found myself studying the facing shore of that island whenever I had a good view. The island is little more than a half mile (1 km) in length and two-tenths mile (330 m) in width. It sits low on the water and offers little in the way of an engaging profile. Even with binoculars, I could barely make out tan cliffs with layered rocks toward the light tower at the south end of the island. I was certain those beds must be limestone and guessed they would be Pliocene in age. The islands beckoned, and I had to learn more.

The waters in the channel between Punta Chivato and the Islas Santa Inés are unpredictable. An experienced boatman, Manuel Antonio Romero-Sabin, from Mulegé has agreed to meet me and my students at the boat ramp near the hotel this morning at 8:30. The powerful outboard engine of his panga will propel us rapidly to our destination. He will stay close by and fish while we visit the big island. We agree that at the first sign of deteriorating weather, he will find us and whisk us back to the safety of Punta Mezquitito. The last few days have been relatively calm, but the viento norte could pick up and mar the experience of an otherwise clear and sunny day. As a precaution, extra food and water are packed for today's adventure. I recall a sobering conversation I once held with an American camped south of Mulegé at Playa Santispac, an anchorage sheltered within the mouth of Bahía Concepción. He told me how he left early on a calm morning and crossed to the great bay's opposite shore in an open boat for a day of sport fishing. Later that day, the north wind rose so suddenly that he was marooned on Peninsula Concepción for three days. He could have walked 22 miles (35 km) to reach Mexican Highway 1 but was unwilling to abandon his boat. Without the shelter of a local fishing camp, he surely would have suffered from exposure. On this, our final day at Punta Chivato, the conditions for a boat trip look good, and I am hopeful for a fitting conclusion to our stay.

As promised, Manuel Antonio awaits, his boat moored to the dock along the ramp access to Bahía Santa Inés. He greets us with a broad smile, helps to stow our gear, and makes sure everyone has a life vest. As he engages the engine and casts off, I find myself thinking about different ways of making maps and the astonishing new technology that offers fresh generations of geologists new ways to see through the vegetation and seas cloaking the earth's surface.

Today, we'll use three different maps, each at a different scale and each from a different technological era. The first is a small-scale local map (map 7) depicting the coastline of the Punta Chivato promontory and Bahía Santa Inés, as well as the locations of the three Islas Santa Inés. This map was traced from a satellite image that came from my former student Patrick Russell, now a graduate student well on his way to an advanced degree at Brown University, where he is being trained in remote sensing via satellite reconnaissance. Patrick wondered if he could find a distinctive signature for the carbonate dunes that festoon the north shore of the Punta Chivato promontory and much of the inner plain flanking the west side of Mesa El Coloradito. If such a signature were differentiated from desert scrub, where the composition of windblown sands was known from his field studies as a Williams College student, then it would be possible to locate and map carbonate dunes elsewhere throughout the gulf region. As soon as Patrick acquired the image and began to play with it, he realized that it gave information related to a completely different topic.

Examining the satellite image, Patrick discovered that the rhodolith field and related carbonate sands derived from coralline red algae were visible in the gulf in intricate detail. I smile as I think about my friend Mike Foster and his students from the Moss Landing Labs and their physically demanding survey work using scuba gear. Snapshots of the earth's surface taken from the fringes of outer space using a sensor called the Thematic Mapper cover seven spectral

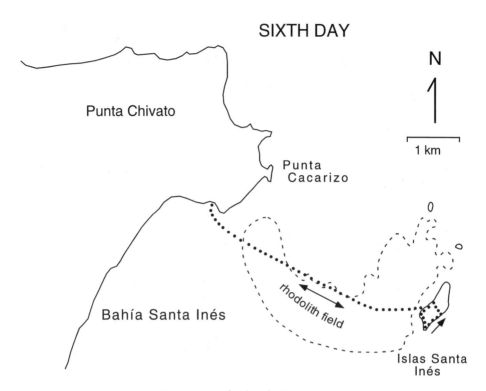

SIXTH DAY

N

Punta Chivato

1 km

Punta
Cacarizo

0

Bahía Santa Inés

0

rhodolith field

Islas Santa
Inés

Map 7. Route for the Islas Santa Inés.

bands from parts of the electromagnetic spectrum that range across visible light to the infrared.[1] Band 1, or the blue part of the spectrum, is usually good for penetrating shallow waters and coastal mapping. In this case, however, Patrick found that Band 2, or the green part of the spectrum, was more effective in highlighting the shape of the active rhodolith field. That band is usually reserved for survey work related to the assessment of vegetation. From Mike's underwater explorations, it is generally known where the rhodolith field exists. The water depth in this area varies between 6 and 42 feet (1.8 and 13 m). The size and shape of the rhodolith field, which stretches across the channel in a crescent pattern with horns pointed north (map 7), is established in fine detail by the image. Onsite mapping under water with the purpose of yielding comparable results would require weeks of effort, sure to be interrupted by windy weather.

Clearing Punta Mezquitito, the boat enters the north-south channel between the gulf coast and the island group. The water is like glass this morning, and Manuel Antonio eases the throttle of the outboard engine wide open. The boat fairly skims across the smooth water. Manuel Antonio follows a direct heading toward the light tower on the big island. His course takes us across the western horn of the rhodolith field and along its northern fringe, where multiple appendages face outward against the channel's strong bottom current. The bright sun penetrates the water and sends back a pale green reflection as lovely and clear as the gemstone peridot. Subtle irregularities in water depth on the margin of the rhodolith field catch the strong sunlight and remit a sublime shimmer. I fix my eyes on the shallow floor of the channel over which we speed. The light's wavering quality plays off the irregular bottom. The boat now slices across the eastern horn of the rhodolith field, and the shores of the big island loom ahead.

Manuel Antonio adjusts his course to aim the boat toward the tan cliffs. On the approach to the coast, large, dark boulders begin to rise from the green glow below, and our helmsman immediately throttles back the boat's engine. The panga eases shoreward toward a black cobble beach at the northern edge of the cliffs. From this distance, the layers in the low bluff look even more like the limestone beds at Punta Cacarizo on the opposite side of the channel. Manuel Antonio cuts the engine, and the panga hits the beach with an abrupt scraping sound.

Once a sheltered spot above the tide line is found to store our gear, Manuel Antonio poles the boat offshore and motors out of sight around the south end of the island. As the sound of his engine fades away, the stillness of a small desert island closes in. There is no trace of human intrusion except for the light tower in the distance to the south. We sit for a moment on the cobble-packed berm, and I take stock of the equipment I need for the rest of the day. The watertight plastic bags come out of my pack, and I retrieve my camera, compass, binoculars, hand lens, pocket notebook, and pencils. I am ready to explore, but for a brief moment I am content to sit and stare lazily back across the channel toward Punta Chivato. The cliffs on this island are unsuitable as a nesting site, but high above over the channel flies a pair of frigate birds *(Fregata magnificens)* on patrol. Their great wingspan, the crook in the slender wings, and the long, forked tail belong to no other bird. In flight, the frigate bird is the ultimate manifestation of grace and agility. Watching one fly is like witnessing a ballet in air. But the frigate bird is also a pirate that attacks other sea birds in midair to steal their food.

According to the geologist Charles Wentworth, rounded rocks larger than 10 inches (25 cm) in diameter qualify as small boulders. The conglomerate outcrop exposed in cross section at the side of the beach is crowded with boulders firmly cemented in a matrix of tan limestone. They range in diameter from about 13 inches (33 cm) to almost 16 inches (40 cm). It is not the size that impresses me so much as the composition of some of them. Many are dark and appear no different from the wave-worn clasts of andesite or basalt that we have become so accustomed to finding in conglomerate beds elsewhere around Punta Chivato. Several larger boulders, however, look remarkably different.

Until now, our explorations in the Punta Chivato area have brought us into contact with only two of the three fundamental classes of rocks, the sedimentary and the igneous. For example, the living rhodolith beds passed over only minutes ago may become fragmented by the waves and currents, compressed into bedded layers, and finally cemented into solid limestone. Under special circumstances, as the Russian paleoecologist Roman Fedorovich Hecker noted, living communities of marine organisms may be buried in their characteristic growth position. Such is the case with the Pleistocene limestone near the pig-pens not far from Hotel Punta Chivato, where an entire coral reef is preserved intact. In the igneous category, we have seen rocks from the Miocene Comondú Group, with its locally tilted basalt and andesite layers. These are volcanic in origin, cooled rapidly from level surface flows. The associated tuff beds are made of explosive volcanic material that accumulated as fallout. Other igneous rocks, like the salt-and-pepper granite cobbles found commonly throughout the area, are plutonic in origin—formed from magma that cooled only slowly, deep within the earth.

The third type of rock is metamorphic. Rocks of this class originate as either sedimentary rocks or igneous rocks but are modified under high temperature and pressure after burial deep within the earth. A sedimentary rock such as limestone, for example, is altered to marble through heat and compression. The change, or metamorphosis, that the rocks undergo is what gives the entire class its name. Here, some of the boulders have a distinctive, banded look. They are the eroded products of a metamorphic rock known as schist. Schist may be derived from granite that is subjected to great pressure. The platy mica minerals that compose these rocks become oriented parallel to one another as a result of tremendous compression, giving the rocks a banded appearance. Although poorly exposed, the unconformity on which the conglomerate bed rests is sufficient to demonstrate that the rocks below are igneous and not metamorphic, indicating that the schist boulders were not quarried by the waves from the rocks immediately at our feet.

The schist bedrock may not be exposed on this island. I wonder if the metamorphic boulders are xenoliths brought to the surface by way of igneous dikes reaching upward from the deep basement rocks below Baja California. From studies by another geologist, I know that massive inclusions of schist are associated with the granite basement rocks exposed near Sierra Gavilanes, about 14 miles (23 km) southeast from here.[2] Because the Miocene Comondú Group in this region is estimated to be more than 13,000 feet (4,000 m) thick, the much older Cretaceous granite must have been brought to the surface in great blocks from considerable depths by uplift along major faults that define the shape of Bahía Concepción. Due to its metamorphic condition, the schist inclusions must have originated in the sub-basement of Baja California. Although nothing comparable occurs around Punta Chivato, this island is well offshore, and its structural alignment with the Concepción Peninsula to the southeast is more favorable. Some tectonic relationship between the geology of the Santa Inés Islands and the Concepción Peninsula most likely exists.

However the schist rocks arrived here, they were subsequently abraded by the waves and incorporated into a cobble beach along an ancient shoreline. The basal conglomerate in which the mixed schist and andesite boulders reside is about 8 feet (2.5 m) thick. Above is a thin cover of limestone, only 1.6 feet (0.5 m) thick, which includes pea-size bits of dark andesite and abundant molds of marine fossils. The limestone and its contents are best evaluated from above, on the gently sloping bedding plane. The preservation of bivalve molds is poor compared with the Upper Pliocene fossils recovered yesterday from Mesa Barracas. Although thin, the bedding planes are extensive. My companions and I fan out to search for recognizable fossils that might help to date this deposit. Finally, after an intense search, a voice rings out. "I've got something." On hands and knees, we crowd around. The fragments belong to the heavy sea biscuit *(Clypeaster bowersi)*. It is the extinct echinoderm encountered on day three at the carbonate ramp on the north shore of Mesa Atravesada (see fig. 14). The shape of this sturdy echinoderm is distinctive, and in cross section the calcite test leaves bold white streaks in the rocks. Once the first specimen is spotted, others are recognized. This particular species is an index fossil for the Lower Pliocene San Marcos Formation, so the limestone on this island is roughly coeval with the sedimentary facies surrounding the Punta Chivato promontory.[3]

I retrieve my compass and determine that the average dip is about 5° to the west. At Punta Cacarizo, on day two, the limestone beds dipped 6° in an easterly direction. This new piece of the puzzle fits into what is known about the rest of the region. A north-south channel lies between the present-day Punta Chivato promontory and the Santa Inés Islands. Carbonate ramps of early Pliocene age occur on both sides of the channel and dip toward one another, so a north-south trough must have existed in the same place during early Pliocene time. If the Punta Chivato promontory was a single large island and the east-facing shore of that island was located at Punta Cacarizo, then the largest of the contemporary Santa Inés Islands was part of a different Pliocene island with a west-facing shore located precisely here. Given the basic alignment of the Santa Inés Islands with the channel's axis, the fifth island in the ancient archipelago encompassed all three Islas Santa Inés and probably even additional territory to the east that eventually was lost to erosion. It appears that the San Marcos limestone at this locality is the only outcrop of its kind intact on any of the three Santa Inés Islands. After visiting this spot in 1995, Max Simian and I decided to bestow the name Santa Inés on the entire Pliocene archipelago, in deference to the only parts of the 5-million-year-old island group that remain true islands today.

The Spanish mariners who anchored in these waters on the saint's day of the martyred Inés, the twenty-first of January, some three and a half centuries ago had no means or inclination to chart ancient seas. They had their own problems to contend with, the most rudimentary being whether or not California was an island. That issue was settled in good time, but many others with geographic ramifications beyond the wildest seventeenth-century mindset remained to be confronted by later-day explorers of the same gulf waters. The origin and future course of geographic evolution in the Gulf of California have yet to be charted in detail, but no one can fail to be impressed by the advances in knowledge achieved steadily, decade by decade, over the last half of the twentieth century. The vistas from this island in the four cardinal directions give us an opportunity to consider how much progress has been made in understanding both the history of this particular body of water, sometimes called the Mar de Cortés, and all the world's oceans.

We repack our lunch and necessary equipment, preparing for a hike around the southern perimeter of the island that will bring us back through its center (map 7). All other supplies are left safely stowed near where we disembarked. The light tower at the south end of the island is only two-tenths of a mile (0.33 km) away, and that is our next destination. The ramped Pliocene limestone that forms the low cliffs on the shore soon disappears to the south. Thereafter, our path leads along loose dark cobbles that form the beach's berm. Identical in design to the light tower at Punta Chivato, the Santa Inés light now rises above us as we pass toward the island's southernmost point. With the water lapping gently at our feet, we enjoy dramatic views looking directly down the throat of Bahía Concepción and squarely onto the adjacent rugged tip of Peninsula Concepción.

Shedding my pack, I seat myself on the beach and pull out the second map to be consulted today (fig. 27). It is a modification of the bathymetric chart for this region compiled by the marine geologist Francis P. Shepard as part of the report from the 1939 and 1940 expeditions to the Gulf of California aboard the *E. W. Scripps*.[4] Issued in 1950 as one of 10 charts covering various parts of the gulf, the original map detailed the coastline and contours of the seabed from San Marcos Island in the north to the inner reaches of Concepcíon Bay in the

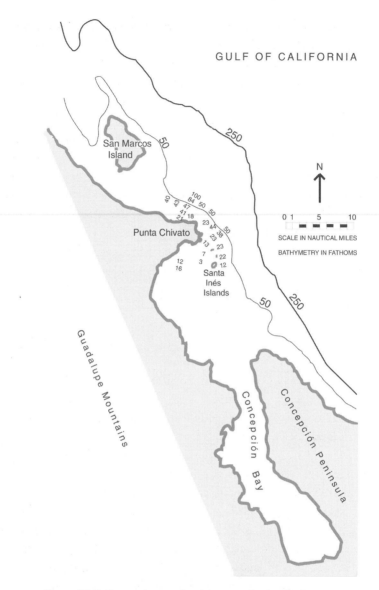

GULF OF CALIFORNIA

San Marcos
Island

250

50

N

100
84
47
50
43
47
41 18
27
23 44
Punta Chivato

23
13 23
7 22
3 12
12
16
Santa
Inés
Islands

50

250

0 1   5   10

SCALE IN NAUTICAL MILES

BATHYMETRY IN FATHOMS

Guadalupe Mountains

Concepción
Bay

Concepción Peninsula

Figure 27. Bathymetric map, San Marcos to Peninsula Concepción.
Modified from Chart 5 by Shepard (1950).

south. Only a few of the 170 soundings taken in the Punta Chivato region are shown in figure 27, in order to give some idea of the range in water depth for the immediate vicinity of the Santa Inés Islands and the Punta Chivato promontory. Altogether, 750 soundings were recorded throughout the region using an instrument called a fathometer. The one aboard the *E. W. Scripps* was basically a device that sent sound waves to the seabed to record the time it took for the echo to travel back to the operator as the ship traveled. (In water, sound travels at a speed of 810 fathoms per second.) The numbers represent water depth in fathoms, with one fathom equaling 6 feet (1.8 m).

Shepard's original chart for this region plotted 18 different isobaths of increasing water depth at intervals of 50 fathoms. An isobath is a continuous line that represents the same water depth, the underwater equivalent of a topographic line on a land map. Our simplified version of the chart features only two isobaths. The location of the 50-fathom (90-m) isobath shows that the coastal waters from San Marcos Island to the Concepción Bay are less than 300 feet (90 m) deep. As noted previously, the waters between Punta Mezquitito and this island are quite shallow, ranging from 3 to 7 fathoms (1.8 to 13 m), and so are those in Bahía Santa Inés, mostly around 12 fathoms (22 m).

The significant line on the Shepard chart is the 250-fathom isobath, at a water depth of 1,500 feet (457 m). What is intriguing is its proximity to the 50-fathom isobath. In Shepard's original chart, three other isobaths squeeze between the 50- and 250-fathom isobaths. On land or beneath the sea, the significance of such closely spaced lines on a map is the same: they denote a steep slope. It is only beyond the 650-fathom isobath (3,900 ft., or 1,188 m) that the submarine slope off the San Marcos–Concepción coastline starts to level out. The maximum water depth recorded by the *E. W. Scripps* in this district is 958 fathoms (5,748 ft., or 1,750 m), due east of San Marcos Island. If the water were drained from the Gulf of California, the change in elevation close by to the east would far surpass that at the Grand Canyon.

Shepard was duly impressed by the rapid drop-off in water depth on the margins of the Gulf of California, especially along the peninsular coast, where nothing resembling a continental shelf is present. He was also struck by the occurrence of deep troughs or trenches parallel to the mountainous margin of the peninsula. The 250-fathom isobath off the San Marcos–Concepcíon shore displays the line bent into segments like a broken stick (fig. 27). The rapidity of the drop-off, together with this type of segmentation, persuaded Shepard that major fault scarps accounted for the nearshore bathymetry of the Gulf of California. In contrast, Bahía Concepción is not deep, but it is an unusually elongated bay with a troughlike shape. Major faults do, in fact, run in broken segments along the east side of the Concepcíon Peninsula. The basement granite and schist exposed in the middle of the peninsula tell us that it was uplifted from considerable depths, whereas the adjacent bay represents an area that was dropped down relative to the peninsula. A block within the earth's upper crust that shifts upward between defining fault scarps is called a horst, and a block that shifts downward between two horsts is termed a graben. Because the linear fault segments on the east side of Bahía Concepción are so well defined, this particular structure is a half graben—a kind of trough in which fault displacement is mostly limited to one side of the structure. The implication is that substantial vertical movement took place between the peninsula and the bay, which dropped down like a trapdoor hinged to the shoreline on the west side of the bay.

Shepard adopted a rhombic construction that entailed two kinds of movement along fault lines as a working model for the origin of submarine basins in the Gulf of California (fig. 28).[5] In principle, the model accommodates basins of two different geometries. Wide basins are represented by two parallel faults, fractures along which vertical displacement takes place due to crustal extension. Literally, the earth's crust is stretched apart; the graben structure that sinks down between two adjacent horsts is called a pull-apart basin. In Shepard's diagram, this divergent tension is represented by two short arrows pointing in opposite directions perpendicular to the fault scarps. Narrow troughs are indicated by more closely spaced faults along which movement is mainly horizontal. In other words, the width of the basin does not change markedly over time because the defining walls of the faults slide past one another in opposite directions. This arrangement, called a strike-slip fault, is depicted by the two long arrows aligned parallel to the faults but pointing in opposite directions.

The broken fault segments, or doglegs, that are traced out by the 250-fathom isobath (fig. 27) strongly resemble the left half of Shepard's rhombic construction (fig. 28). But where is the right half of the rhombus? The complementary set of fault scarps are actually on the opposite side of the gulf, far to the east. Unlike the Grand Canyon, which is 1 mile (1.6 km) deep but only about 5 miles (8 km) wide, the shortest distance across the unusually deep Gulf of California from our present position is 84 miles (135 km) in the direction of Guaymas. Although the vertical scale is comparable, the difference between these two great clefts in the earth's crust is expressed by very different dynamics. The Kaibab Plateau, across which the Grand Canyon of Arizona cuts, is a great dome that has risen slowly like a bubble over the last 15 million to 20 million years while the entrenched Colorado River continued to cut down through the surrounding rocks. In contrast, no such crustal elasticity is apparent in the structural development of the Gulf of California. At the time the Miocene Comondú volcanics began to be deposited, roughly 25 million years ago, no gulf existed, and the Baja California peninsula was firmly attached to the Mexican mainland. Marine waters initially flooded this part of the Gulf of California near the start of the Pliocene Epoch, only 5 million years ago. Since that time, the flooded gulf has grown dramatically in width and length, due to ongoing forces at work within the upper crust.

Shepard's crowning achievement was in stitching the various regional

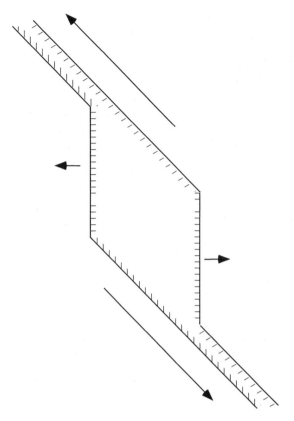

Figure 28. Shepard's rhombic solution to gulf tectonics.

bathymetric charts into a single master chart covering the entire Gulf of California. The composite product drew on a total of 28,000 soundings collected during the 1939 and 1940 expeditions. Reproduced in color, the oversized 1950 chart shows a succession of individual basins that increase in water depth down the axis of the gulf from north to the south.[6] North between Isla Angel de la Guarda and the peninsula, the narrow Salsipuedes Basin registers a depth of only 850 fathoms (5,100 ft., or 1,555 m). The Guaymas Basin, to our immediate east, is indicated with a maximum depth of 1,100 fathoms (6,600 ft., or 2,012 m). Located northeast of Isla Carmen, the Carmen Basin was found to be deeper still, with a depth of 1,530 fathoms (9,180 ft., or 2,800 m). Situated northeast of Isla San José, the last of the large basins in the lower gulf is the Farallon Basin, with a reported maximum depth of 1,750 fathoms (10,500 ft., or 3,200 m). In his structural analysis of the responsible tectonics, Shepard compared the shape and dimensions of the greater Gulf of California to the Imperial Valley and Great Valley in southern California, also bounded by major fault systems. He concluded that "the combination of large-scale vertical movements and horizontal shearing of the San Andreas type" was a plausible explanation for the submarine topography of the Gulf of California. Thus, he drew a clear association between the physiography and tectonic dynamism of southern California and the Gulf of California.

Since 1950, the technical feat of the Shepard map has been eclipsed only modestly, by a two-sheet bathymetric map of the Gulf of California produced in 1989 by the Continental Margins Study Group (CONMAR) at the University of Oregon.[7] The maximum water depths recorded in the various basins by the fathometer on the *E. W. Scripps* and the shapes interpreted for those basins have stood the test of time, while during the intervening years the world of geology was revolutionized by the concept of plate tectonics. Published as a companion to the 1989 bathymetric map by CONMAR is a seismo-tectonic map that plots the epicenters of shallow earthquakes throughout the Gulf of California and reinterprets the individual basin axes as rift zones where the seafloor is actively expanding.[8] Using the same bathymetric base map, we now speak of the Guaymas, Carmen, and Farallon rifts, among others in the gulf. In hindsight, the significance of the Shepard charts as precursors to elements of plate tectonics cannot be overstated.

Also published in 1950 was a best-selling book by Rachel Carson under the title *The Sea Around Us*. In a chapter called "Hidden Lands," she described major physiographic features such as oceanic trenches and mid-ocean ridges in considerable detail but still concluded that "the floor of the deep ocean basins is probably as old as the sea itself."[9] With the application of his rhombic model, Shepard came within a hair's breadth of proclaiming that the Gulf of California was a young, new sea still in the making, and not an archaic holdover from the shrouded beginnings of earth time.

The vista before us, looking south toward Bahía Concepción, is an inspiration. After Punta Chivato, the place I have most enjoyed exploring is the rugged Concepción Peninsula. My colleague Jorge Ledesma and I devoted three seasons of field study during the mid-1990s to the base, tip, and outer coast of the peninsula.[10] The Pliocene story of the Concepción Peninsula is the complete inverse of Punta Chivato's, that story of islands encircled by marine ramps. The Concepción Peninsula features small marine basins almost landlocked by the surrounding high ground of the Miocene Comondú andesite. Lower Pliocene strata comparable in age to the San Marcos Formation occur on the inner tip of the peninsula, barely inside the bay. Upper Pliocene strata coeval with the Marquer Formation of Las Barracas reside in a series of small, interconnected basins at the base of the peninsula, off the bay's southern terminus. From our survey of the outer coast, Jorge and I concluded that the various Pliocene basins on the peninsula were accessible to marine waters only through the mouth of the present Concepción Bay. In short, marine waters flooded the more elevated, inner recesses of the bay a few million years after the entrance to the bay first opened.

Through our reconstruction of coastal geography, Jorge and I found that Bahía Concepcíon has changed little in dimensions since mid-Pliocene time. It was initially established in middle or late Miocene time as a dry valley by the subsidence of a half graben along the major fault segments defining the east side of the bay. There is no evidence for appreciable strike-slip movement along the defining faults or younger parallel faults that cut through the Pliocene deposits on the peninsula. As a large area that was eventually inundated as a consequence of simple vertical movement, the bay is emblematic of an early and mainly extensional phase in the evolution of the gulf. In effect, during the early stages in the development of the gulf, Shepard's rhombus was more a two-sided construct, and most of the tectonic forces were strictly divergent in nature. The piece that became Bahía Concepcíon grew rapidly at first and then ceased to expand altogether. Parallel features that formed east of the 250-fathom isobath, including the prototype of the deep Guaymas Basin, continued to be shaped by extensional stress and accelerated subsidence.

An elegant manifestation of this early phase in the gulf's evolution is fault blocks consisting of Miocene Comondú rocks in the foothills of the Guadalupe Mountains to the southwest, on the Concepción Peninsula to the southeast, and at Mesa Atravesada to the northwest. Indeed, similar Comondú fault blocks are found in the Guaymas area on the opposite side of the gulf to the northeast. Before it was fragmented into blocks by the stretching of the more ductile sub-basement rocks far below, the Comondú succession consisted of layers of andesite, andesite breccia (visited yesterday at Punta El Coloradito), tuff beds, and rare basalt layers. On the whole, these layers conformed to Steno's concept of original horizontality and were deposited as flat-lying units. As the brittle surface layers of the Comondú broke into distinct blocks, the formerly flat beds became tilted, mostly to the east or to the west along fracture zones oriented north-south. On the west side of Mexican Highway 1 south of Mulegé, for example, andesite blocks with distinctly westward dipping layers predominate. On the west margin of the Concepción Peninsula, however, most of the blocks dip to the east. If Shepard's rhombic model operated through equal amounts of extension (stretching in opposite directions across fault lines) and translation (gliding in opposite directions parallel to fault lines), then the orderly arrangement still observed in the various fault blocks of the Punta Chivato–Concepción region would not have been preserved. A rhombus, after all, is a distorted square. Such

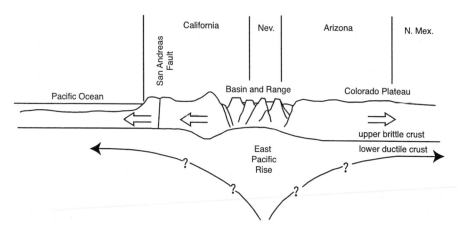

Figure 29. Extensional tectonics beneath the Basin and Range Province.
Cross section modified after Huntoon (1976). Not to scale.

local observations do not invalidate Shepard's model but merely indicate that strike-slip motion was not pervasive in this particular part of the early gulf coast and that major uplift may occur along faults that deviate through doglegs.

Generally speaking, geologists now agree that the Baja California peninsula and adjacent Gulf of California evolved through three sequential phases from the start of Miocene time, about 24 million years ago, to the present.[11] The first lasted until 12 million years ago, when the peninsula was still a part of mainland Mexico and tectonic activity was restricted to the Pacific coast. The second occurred between 10 million and 3.5 million years ago, when the crust stretched widely beneath the western margin of North America. In the United States, particularly from Nevada to southern Idaho, this activity resulted in the development of the Basin and Range physiographic province of horsts and grabens. A cross-sectional panel that cuts through central California to the Colorado Plateau of northern Arizona illustrates the extensional nature of this phase (fig. 29). The north-south orientation of ranges characteristic of the Nevada interval is defined by upthrown horsts relative to downthrown grabens that delineate the separable basins. On a much smaller scale, the oriented fault blocks of the Punta Chivato–Concepción region bear a strong kinship to the Basin and Range Province of the western United States.

Crustal extension continues to play a muted role in Nevada and southern Idaho but was supplanted in the nascent Gulf of California by the third phase of development, which introduced rift zones to the deep gulf basins.[12] Staggered spreading centers interpreted on the 1989 CONMAR maps for the Gulf of California are responsible for northwest-southeast trending fractures along which major strike-slip motion is prevalent. This changeover in tectonic regime began in middle Pliocene time, approximately 3.5 million years ago, and persists in the gulf today. An outgrowth of what geologists call transtensional tectonics is manifested by the San Andreas Fault—something first suggested by Shepard in 1950. This infamous fault arcs across southern California from the northern end of the Gulf of California to San Francisco Bay and beyond to Cape Mendocino on the Pacific shores of northern California. How did Baja California break away from mainland Mexico?

FEATURE / Harry Hammond Hess and the Plate Tectonics Revolution

In one of those odd quirks of history, the perceptiveness of Francis P. Shepard regarding the youthful dynamics of the Gulf of California and the dead end reached by Rachel Carson in her appraisal of the age of the ocean floor owed their separate inspirations to the same person. That person was a remarkable geophysicist who spent nearly his entire professional career working through the ranks in the geology department at Princeton University, except for a critical interlude in the United States Navy during World War II: Harry Hammond Hess (1906–1969). It was on the basis of research abstracted by Hess in 1932 on ocean trenches in the Caribbean Sea that Shepard was inspired to apply the rhombic model of basin configuration to the origin of the Gulf of California.[13] As part of his graduate studies at Princeton, Hess took the opportunity to participate in a gravity survey of the ocean floor in the Lesser Antilles. The work was carried out aboard a submarine belonging to the U.S. Navy. Deep ocean trenches were first discovered the hard way as early as the *Challenger* expedition of 1872–1876, when part of the Marianas Trench in the Philippines was plumbed by piano wire to a depth of 29,520 feet (9,000 m). The Marianas Trench is the deepest spot in the world's oceans; its maximum depth was recorded much later to be 37,772 feet (11,516 m). Due to the extraordinary dents that trenches make in the crust of the ocean floor, gravity readings collected in the water column above those trenches register as abnormally low in value. Hence, the geometry of oceanic trenches may be mapped according to the results of a gravity survey.

Hess speculated that active tectonic forces within the ocean crust influenced the bathymetry of the Lesser Antilles. To expedite his doctoral studies at Princeton during the early 1930s, he took the unusual step of joining the U.S. Naval Reserve.[14] Still a reservist on December 8, 1941, the Princeton professor reported for active duty one day after the United States entered World War II. Eventually, he took command of the attack transport vessel USS *Cape Johnson* in the Pacific theater of war. During the ship's many assignments, which took it back and forth across the Pacific Ocean, Hess operated the depth sounding equipment as often as possible. By the end of the war, he had acquired voluminous data on the locations of about 100 submarine mountains, which are typically conical in shape, but flat topped. Some examples were later found in the North Atlantic, but the vast majority occurs in the Pacific Ocean. The name "guyot" was coined for these features, in commemoration of Arnold Henry Guyot, the nineteenth-century founder of the Princeton geology department. As Hess later recalled, he had considerable difficulty explaining why the guyots of the mid-Pacific region failed to develop as classic atolls, each with a circle of coral reefs that maintained an upward rate of growth commensurate with the gradual rate of "island" subsidence. For this reason, Hess postulated in 1946 that the upper flat surfaces of guyots dated from Precambrian time, prior to the origin of marine invertebrates capable of secreting a calcareous framework like that of corals.[15] Rachel Carson, also relying on Hess's expertise, claimed that "because of this virtual immortality, the oldest oceanic mountains must be infinitely older than any of the ranges left on land."[16]

Nothing could be farther from the truth, but not until 1956 did marine geologists manage to dredge selected guyots and retrieve fossils of a shallow-water origin dating from the Cretaceous Period, near the end of the Mesozoic Era. By other means during the mid-1970s, geologists established that no part of the world's ocean floor is older than about 190 million years. Because the oldest parts of the continents yield a maximum age of almost 4 billion years, the substantially younger ocean floor implies some process of continuous recycling. It was the German scientist Alfred Wegener (1880–1930) who, during the early decades of the twentieth century, developed the concept of continental drift.[17] Although his arguments were intriguing, most members of the geological community rejected the notion that, for example, South America and Africa had fitted snugly together prior to the origin of the South Atlantic Ocean—and this despite the existence of a distinct ocean ridge midway between those two continents that is faithful to the curvaceous outline of the opposing continental-shelf edges. The doubters of continental drift required more rigorous geophysical evidence than the coincidence of matching geometries to substantiate continental mobility.

Rachel Carson gives an accurate description of the great Mid-Atlantic Ridge in *The Sea Around Us,* replete with dimensions for total length (10,000 miles, or 3,000 km) and maximum elevation above the adjacent seafloor (10,000 feet, or 3,280 m). She also notes that the axis of the ridge is the present site of most of the earthquakes in the Atlantic. Nonetheless, she regarded the structure as an archaic and largely quiescent line that originated due to "crustal shifting and rearrangement."[18] She was more expansive in her description of the ring of active volcanoes, deep-sea trenches, and attendant earthquakes that characterize the Pacific rim. What a difference a single decade of research made. More than any other marine geologist of his generation, it was Hess who linked together the mysteries of deep-sea trenches and mid-ocean ridges and thereby opened a rational discourse on the age of the ocean floor and the mobility of continents.

Hess achieved fame due to an eloquent paper first published in 1962 under the title "History of Ocean Basins." In the late 1950s he had submitted it as a possible chapter for a multivolume work called *The Sea* but then withdrew it from consideration. He was hesitant and clearly worried about the reception of his ideas. By 1960, the manuscript had been privately circulated to a wide range of students, colleagues, and other associates affiliated with the Office of Naval Research. The final published product became one of the most influential papers in the history of marine geology. The introduction begins with the following words: "The birth of the oceans is a matter of conjecture, the subsequent history is obscure, and the present structure is just beginning to be understood. Fascinating speculation on these subjects has been plentiful, but not much of it predating the last decade holds much water."[19]

Of course, Hess was forced to reconsider some of his own earlier research in just the same light, but he remained apologetic and almost self-deprecating about his formulation of laws on the dynamic behavior of oceanic crust. In the introduction, he clearly states that he considers his thesis to be an "essay in geopoetry" in need of further substantiation.

Hess intuited that convection cells within the earth's molten mantle feed material upward to the mid-ocean ridges, where new ocean crust cools and solidifies. From these seafloor spreading zones, the solid crust is pushed evenly and symmetrically to the sides. As new crust continues to form at the ridges, old crust is eventually transferred to ocean trenches, where it is returned to the upper mantle and melted. Under the heading "Recapitulation," his paper lists 19 suppositions, some of which I quote here in their original order, but renumbered:

1. Convecting cells have rising limbs under the mid-ocean ridges.
2. Mantle material comes to the surface on the crest of these ridges.
3. Mid-ocean ridges are ephemeral features having a life of 200 to 300 million years (the life of the convection cell).
4. The whole ocean is virtually swept clean (replaced by new mantle material) every 300 to 400 million years.
5. Rising limbs coming up under continental areas move the fragmented parts away from one another at a uniform rate so a truly median ridge forms as in the Atlantic Ocean.
6. The continents are carried passively on the mantle with convection and do not plow through ocean crust.

7. The oceanic crust, buckling down into the descending limb, is heated and loses its water to the ocean.

8. The ocean basins are impermanent features and the continents are permanent, although they may be torn apart or welded together and their margins deformed.[20]

General acceptance of Hess's thesis still required evidence in the form of hard geophysical data, but those data were not long in coming.

As magma rises to the surface and begins to cool, minerals bearing iron, manganese, cobalt, or nickel crystallize and are influenced by the earth's magnetic field. Much like the needle on a compass, the minerals are oriented, or point, toward the north magnetic pole. As the magma continues to cool into a solid igneous rock, whole mineral grains are locked permanently together under magnetic alignment. From time to time, the earth's electromagnetic field switches polarity such that the north and south magnetic poles change place. This was first understood by geologists who discovered that igneous rocks of recent origin conform to magnetic alignment under "normal" polarity, whereas igneous rocks more than about 7,000 years old record specific time intervals of "reversed" polarity.

Less than a year after the publication of Hess's "essay in geopoetry," a note appeared in the prestigious journal *Nature* based on data collected by two young British geophysicists, Fred Vine and Drummond Matthews. Their paper showed that magnetic anomalies are symmetrical to the axis of the Carlsberg Ridge in the Indian Ocean.[21] The ridge crest itself consists of basalt that was found to be normal in its magnetization, but the nearest adjacent flanks are reversed in polarity. Farther away, strips of ocean floor equidistant from the ridge axis were discovered to exhibit normal magnetization, and then reversed polarity, and so on. Upon this extraordinary finding, the geological community blinked, and the plate tectonics revolution reached a zenith during the next few years. Hess had visited Cambridge University in England early in 1962, prior to the publication of his paper, in order to take part in a lecture series on the evolution of the North Atlantic Ocean. Fred Vine was in attendance, which explains how he became an early conscript in the plate tectonics revolution.[22]

The premise of plate tectonics demands that we adopt different geographic units in our way of thinking about the planet's surface. No longer is it germane to divide the physical world into units based on continents versus ocean basins. Under the old geography, North America is flanked by the Atlantic Ocean to the east and the Pacific Ocean to the west. Of course, that reality is still very much the case. Under the new geography, however, the North American plate extends from the axis of the Mid-Atlantic Ridge across most but not quite all of the North American continent. The Mid-Atlantic Ridge, as Hess recognized, is a zone where new ocean crust forms continuously and migrates to the sides. The zone actually passes through Iceland, which means that the western half of that island belongs to the North American plate and the eastern half to the great Eurasian plate. On opposing sides of the ridge, the ocean floor sustains a divergence of almost 1.35 inches (4 cm) per year in the North Atlantic, thus carrying the two halves of Iceland along in opposite directions at half that speed (0.79 inch, or 2 cm, per year).[23] The same pattern of magnetic anomalies first detected by Vine and Matthews in the Indian Ocean is well documented along the entire length of the Mid-Atlantic Ridge.

In contrast to all other tectonic plates, the Pacific plate is the largest solid component formed primarily of ocean crust. Excepting the South Island of New Zealand and the Baja California peninsula, seated in opposite hemispheres, it entails no other continental crust. To the north and west, the Pacific plate is bounded by an interlinked system of deep ocean trenches that arc all the way from the Aleutian Trench off Alaska to the Tonga Trench, which connects with New Zealand. The southeast boundary of the Pacific plate is formed by the East Pacific Rise, another seafloor spreading zone. Compared with the mid-Atlantic, divergence in the eastern Pacific is quite high, reaching 7 inches (18 cm) per year. That means that ocean crust on opposite sides of the rise migrates at a top speed of 3.5 inches (9 cm) per year.[24] The same pattern of magnetic anomalies known from the Atlantic Ocean floor is found astride the East Pacific Rise, except that the symmetrical stripes of alternately normal and reversed polarity are proportionately wider due to more rapid divergence. Some 50 million years ago, the East Pacific Rise cut diagonally across the center of the Pacific Ocean. Since then, approximately 75 percent of the seafloor east of the rise has disappeared into trenches that still endure on the west coast of South and Central America and formerly existed off the west coast of North America.

The relevant boundaries between western North America and the Pacific plate are depicted on the third, and largest-scale, map prepared for today's trip (fig. 30). The southeast shore of the big Santa Inés island leads to solid cliffs that afford a view of the open Gulf of California and a good opportunity to pause and study the map in some detail. Starting from the south, the East Pacific Rise is seen to enter the mouth of the Gulf of California. The ridge from which seafloor spreading emanates is symbolized by parallel solid lines. Within the gulf and beyond, short ridge segments are displaced or set off from one another by perpendicular cuts that terminate as dashed lines. To the north, right-angle cuts also are seen to segment the Gorda Rise and Juan de Fuca Rise situated off northern California, Oregon, and Washington. Marine geologists refer to the offsets as transform faults. Indicated by slender arrows on the map, the ocean

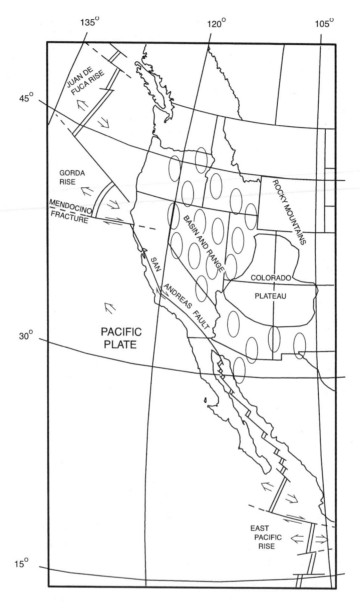

Figure 30. Boundary between the North American and Pacific plates.
Map modified after Huntoon (1976).

floor between two displaced ridges moves in opposite directions on opposing
sides of those fault lines. The faults tend to die out, because at a greater distance
from the offset, the ocean floor moves in the same direction on opposite sides of
the fault trace. This is shown by the placement of the thick arrows on the map.

Within the Gulf of California, most of the basins that incorporate rift zones consist of short segments oriented from southwest to northeast. The Guaymas Basin, hidden beneath the waters in front of us, contains such a rift zone. Long transform faults that show strike-slip motion connect one rift zone to the next in a zigzag fashion up the center of the gulf, always perpendicular to the axes of the short spreading centers. Interestingly, the single elongate basin originally detected by Shepard is the site of a major transform fault, a trough to our north, between Isla Angel de la Guarda and the peninsula. Shepard called this trough the Salsipuedes Basin. On the west side of the Salsipuedes Fault, Bahía de los Angeles moves slowly to the northwest while to the east, Isla Angel de la Guarda moves gradually to the southeast.[25] In fact, the entire Baja California peninsula and the western fringe of California as far north as Cape Mendocino creeps slowly to the northwest. This is well illustrated by the relative motion on opposite sides of the San Andreas Fault, which functions as an extended transform fault linking the north end of the East Pacific Rise with the south end of the Gorda Rise (fig. 30).

The plate-tectonics paradigm reveals that Baja California and a portion of Alto California belong not to the North American plate but to the Pacific plate. The opening of the Gulf of California took place in two critical phases: first, a tectonic phase involving extension over a large sector of western North America, and currently, tension brought about by the encroachment of the East Pacific Rise against North America at an oblique angle. Changeover from one phase to the other transferred Baja California and lands west of the San Andreas Fault from the North American plate to the Pacific plate.

On the big Santa Inés island, the double conundrum of an improbably long and narrow peninsula adjacent to a surprisingly narrow and deep body of water has its natural resolution. Harry Hammond Hess and those inspired by the revolution he helped to spark provided the conceptual framework against which the commerce of young oceans and old continents is understood potentially to result in the splintering of lands and their transfer from one tectonic plate to another. The Malay Peninsula of Indo-China and the Kamchatka Peninsula of Siberia offer up their own mysteries to our intellect, but no other place illustrates quite the same tectonic story as the shores on which we presently stand.

———

Near the midline of the southeast shore, the big Santa Inés island reaches its maximum elevation, girded by bluffs slightly higher than the Pliocene limestone and basal conglomerate inspected early this morning. The thin, gray rock layers stand almost vertically on edge with a north-south orientation. There is again evidence of metamorphic activity. It is almost as if I had been transported to a New England slate quarry. Below, lying prostrate in the tidal zone, are thin slabs of rock that split off the sheer rock face. Thrust upward from the gulf waters, the rocks of these cliffs are strangely exotic, suggesting that a master fault extends north from the tip of the Concepción Peninsula and that the bedrock of the Islas Santa Inés belongs to a horst block brought up from a remote subterranean realm. Nowhere, however, is there any sign of the schist encountered in the boulder conglomerate on the west side of the island.

It is midday and time for our accustomed repast. The best shade available is below the cliffs with a view east over the gulf waters. Manuel Antonio is nowhere in sight; he must have moved the panga to the north end of the island. A faint breeze stirs the air. The sea has lost its flat morning stillness, but there are no whitecaps on the horizon. I begin to think about what lies out there beneath the waves. The depths of the Guaymas Basin have slowly given up their amazing secrets. During my January 1995 visit to Punta Chivato, I met a marine geologist from the University of California at Santa Barbara who was a guest at the hotel for a night or two. Ken Macdonald had been a participant in a 1979 expedition to an area on the East Pacific Rise just outside the entrance to the Gulf of California. The deep-sea research vessel *Alvin* assisted the expedition. Only two years earlier, in 1977, an expedition to the Galapagos Rift off the East Pacific Rise was the first to discover deep-sea geothermal springs.[26] The disclosure drew world attention because associated with the springs is a bizarre community of bottom-dwellers including large clams and giant tube worms, some of which approach more than 8 feet (2.5 m) in length. The animals live in total darkness and thrive on energy derived from bacterial oxidation of sulfurous waters.

Macdonald vividly described to me his first dive on the *Alvin* outside the Gulf of California and the excitement of discovering chimneylike structures rising from the seafloor, belching out hot water clouded with dark sulfide precipitates. The slender chimneys, which stand as tall as 33 feet (10 m) with a diameter of more than 13 inches (40 cm), were named "black smokers." With obvious delight, he told about the first attempts to measure the temperature of the dark fluid issuing from one of the smokers.[27] The thermometer on the *Alvin* was calibrated to 90° F (32° C), a setting believed adequate because the previous record high temperature detected on the ocean floor was only 70° F (21° C). When the probe was inserted into the effluent, the reading plunged off the scale, and when the probe was hastily recovered, it showed signs of partial melting. With a recalibrated thermometer mounted on a reconstructed probe during a subsequent dive, Macdonald discovered that the water had a tempera-

Figure 31. Hydrothermal springs with tube worms, East Pacific Rise. Illustration by Robin M. Gowen/*American Scientist* in Haymon and Macdonald (1985).

ture of 662° F (350° C). He joked that when the upper range of water temperatures around the black smokers was grasped, there was concern about the safety of the *Alvin,* especially the seal around the viewing window on the craft. At sea level, water boils at 212° F (100° C), but the water pressure on the dive site at a depth of 8,692 feet (2,650 m) was roughly 275 times the atmospheric pressure at sea level. Water does not come to a boil under such tremendous pressure, and the occupants of the *Alvin* had no way of knowing they were in danger.

As on the Galapagos Rift, the new locality off the tip of the Baja California peninsula supported the strange biological community of invertebrates that make up a food chain based on chemosynthetic processes. It was found that most of the animals flourished around fissures and hairline cracks in basalt pillows on the seafloor, where the hot water discharged was considerably less than 212° F (100° C).[28] The chimneys forming the black smokers are too hot for life to colonize, but vented mounds called "white smokers" are typically encrusted with the enormous tube worms (fig. 31), which belong to the recently named Phylum Vestimentifera.

The earliest foray into the deep Guaymas Basin occurred in 1977 on the manned submersible *Seacliff,* but exploration was limited to the north trough on the Guaymas Rift, and little of interest beyond talc and massive sulfide deposits was discovered.[29] Scientists from the Scripps Institution of Oceanography returned in 1980 to investigate the south trough on the rift zone. The project was carried out using an unmanned tow with capabilities for remote photography, as well as a more conventional dredge. The tow resulted in photographic evidence of hydrothermal mounds encrusted with tube worms at a depth of about 6,560 feet (2,000 m). The dredge scooped up material from a 164-foot-wide (50-m) patch of the seafloor and recovered samples of the tube worms together with claystone, chunks from a massive sulphide deposit, and other hydrothermal minerals. The expedition made a splash in *Nature* because the recovered material was stained with oil and gave off an odor much like that of diesel fuel.[30] This "hydrothermal petroleum" was immediately recognized to be unique from the ordinary petroleum sought after by commercial interests. The Guaymas oil does not come from older sedimentary rocks buried deep within the earth. Rather, it is the result of young sediments rich in organic matter being cooked on the seafloor by the heat of the active rift zone. Land-derived sediments mixed with the detritus of prolific plankton easily collect in the Guaymas Basin due to its confined geometry. Likewise, the geometry of the basin assures that particulate matter and the high concentration of dissolved silica vented from the smokers in the hydrothermal field are not readily diffused before reaching a level almost 1,000 feet (300 m) above the basin floor. Subsequent expeditions supported by the *Alvin* visited the Guaymas Basin repeatedly throughout the 1980s, and research sponsored by Scripps continued through the 1990s.

I am not a marine geologist and will always remain a peculiar kind of dry-land oceanographer content to walk ancient shorelines and plumb the depths of marine basins now laid out ashore. Yet I am fascinated by the physical-biological dynamics of the thermal springs related to the tectonic rifts in the Gulf of California. Evidence of similar activity is found on land in connection with Pliocene rocks now exposed on the gulf coast. At the base of the Concepción Peninsula, Jorge Ledesma and I studied chert beds that floor one of the enclosed Pliocene basins. We believe the silica was derived, in part, from hydrothermal waters through deep plumbing from the peninsular basement.[31] To the north, near Santa Rosalía, mining geologists have shown me what they believe are Pliocene "black smokers" preserved in the Boleo Formation of the old copper fields. Even here at Punta Chivato, the limited dolomite behind Playa La Palmita and in the hills of Las Barracas probably has a hydrothermal source. One must know where to look, but the powerful dynamics that shaped the Gulf of California also left calling cards scattered throughout the peninsular landscape.

Looking out toward the Guaymas Basin, I can't help thinking of William Beebe, the coinventor of the bathysphere, who reached the Gulf of California in 1936 looking for adventure aboard the yacht *Zaca*. The same Beebe led an expedition to the Galapagos Islands in 1925, where he won renown for his underwater work. The most experienced deep-sea diver of his generation, William Beebe died in 1962 without any knowledge of the amazing world of deep-sea rifts, hydrothermal vents, or vestimentiferan tube worms. Are there any places left, I wonder, where natural wonders of such magnitude still await discovery?

The shortest distance across the island to the west shore is a little more than 1,000 feet (300 m), descending an almost imperceptible slope (map 7). There is no trace of anything like an arroyo where water might run freely after a sudden cloudburst. Thus, there is no exposure of surface rocks on the interior of the island beneath the sparse vegetation and thin soil. All along this leg of the trek, the vista to the north presents itself. In the foreground are the two smaller islands of the Santa Inés group. A gentle breeze moves the air, and Manuel Antonio's panga rides in the lee of the nearest island, 1.25 miles (2 km) away. Visible on the far horizon, 26 miles (42 km) away, stands the volcanic shield of Isla Tortuga. Chemically, the lava flows on the island closely resemble those on other volcanic islands throughout the Pacific Ocean. More specifically, they match the chemistry of ocean-ridge basalt from the East Pacific Rise.[32] There could be no better evidence that the Gulf of California is the true daughter of the East Pacific Rise. According to the 1989 CONMAR maps for the gulf, Isla Tortuga sits directly astride one of the long transform faults that shoots out perpendicularly from the Guaymas Rift. Magma brought near the surface by mantle convection below this short segment of the rise clearly found a structural weakness of which to take advantage. Not surprisingly, the transform fault is called the Tortuga Fault.

A short distance inland from the west coast, a thin deposit of Pleistocene marine shells is spread out on the barren ground. This is another marine terrace, but its dimensions are obscure and its elevation is clearly less than that of terraces on the facing east shore between Punta Cacarizo and Punta Chivato, which typically reach elevations between 28 and 40 feet (8.5 and 12 m) above present sea level. If this deposit is Late Pleistocene in age, then Holocene adjustments in the relative elevations of marine terraces on opposite sides of the channel have occurred. The most unusual elements found here are large pieces of worn coral. Exploring parallel to the shoreline, it is easy to stumble over loose chunks the size of small boulders. Something like a reef once existed here, although these corals are not preserved in growth position like those at the junkyard reef near the hotel. The species is probably *Porites californica,* but the morphology of the coral colonies is robust. Substantial waves along this shore clearly influenced the shape of the corals, although the waves travel parallel to shore from north to south through the adjacent channel. The density of Pleistocene fossils here does not match that of the deposit behind Playa La Palmita. We spread out and make a systematic search. Not surprisingly, the most abundant fossil is a gastropod *(Turbo fluctuosus)* commonly found today in the rocky intertidal zone. After an hour's search, our collection totals 30 species of mollusks. The diversity is considerably less than the junkyard reef's 50 species.

Manuel Antonio is back. He eases his panga through the shallows and shouts at us to move smartly along to the spot where we originally disembarked and left much of our gear. The light breeze has stiffened. Whitecaps dance on the open sea beyond the Islas Santa Inés. He wants to cross the channel and return to Punta Mezquitito as soon as possible. Marching double time along the cobbled berm to the southwest under an air of controlled urgency, I can't prevent myself from paying attention to the rocks that have washed up on the upper beach. I would like to find something else, perhaps a piece of salt-and-pepper granite or a scrap of schist, but the rounded shapes are uniformly dark. Coasting along just offshore, Manuel Antonio urges us on. Travel between any two points should always count for something more than the mere shuffle of feet. In any landscape, there are always valuable kernels of information to be gleaned from the wayside. The cobbled rocks on this beach are overwhelmingly andesite or basalt in composition. Because the bedrock of the island is mainly something else, these rocks must be derived from the channel floor.

As we approach the stockpile of our goods near the Pliocene outcrop, Manuel Antonio cuts the engine and poles the panga onto the beach. In no time, everyone is back on board and we are pointed homeward. Sitting in the bow this time, I feel every slap of the boat as it rides up and over the wave crests. Our helmsman elects to follow a sweeping arc to the southwest and then west, following the natural refraction of the waves around Mesa Atravesada. The growing waves push directly down the long fetch of the channel from the north. By swinging southwest, we manage to ride with them instead of breaking through them at an oblique angle. As a result, the boat suffers less from pitch and roll. Under steady progress, we gradually begin to feel the shelter of Bahía Santa Inés. Below Punta El Coloradito, Manuel Antonio swings his craft to the northwest and brings us closer to shore. He opens the throttle as the boat enters the ever calmer waters of the bay. Mesa Barracas rises on the port side, and we close on Punta El Coloradito. Viewing the familiar barracks profile from offshore, I ponder whether the en echelon faults that slice that landscape are related to the changeover from extensional to transtensional tectonics in the maturing Gulf of California. Our course is adjusted now, on a northeast bearing toward the inner margin of Punta Mezquitito.

With the vista of the Punta Chivato promontory due ahead, thoughts of Nicolaus Steno suddenly come to mind. The landscapes that enfold us are packed with intricate stories about their origins and development. Ahead, I am able to make out patches of reddish color that represent the volcanic core of an old island sheathed in Pliocene limestone. The layered Punta Chivato core is a great, coherent fault block that dips uniformly to the west; its tilting occurred some 10 million years ago during the extensional phase in the gulf's evolution. When marine waters finally reached this area about 5 million years ago, during the early Pliocene, carbonate ramps encircled the main promontory and its neighboring islands. A grand carbonate ramp was consolidated at Las Barracas throughout the later Pliocene, but faults possibly related to the changeover from extensional to transtensional tectonics left their mark on the land sometime during the last 3.5 million years. The advice gleaned from Steno's principles reaches crisply down through the centuries. A story of any kind is only as satisfying as the critical chapter breaks that shape it. We are nearly home.

The Future of Punta Chivato and Baja California

I praise the scoring drought, the flying dust,
The drying creek, the furious animal,
That they oppose us still;
That we are ruined by the thing we kill.
—Judith Wright, *Australia 1970*

Curiosity finally got the better part of him. What could the fellow with the white beard and the two youths be up to? It was January 1995 and we were absorbed in our work, Max, Laura, and I. We were busy laying out a baseline for a map of Playa La Palmita and all the arroyos that cut across the abandoned Pleistocene seabed to the shores of Bahía Santa Inés. I was glad he approached us, because I, too, was a little curious. I had first noticed his motor home parked on the low bluffs overlooking the bay during my first visit to Punta Chivato in 1991. His was the only sign of habitation along the entire sweep of sandy shoreline. Visit after visit, I found the same vehicle precisely in the same location. A cobble-lined path led from the awning on the side of his dwelling down the bluff to the upper beach. A pirate flag always fluttered in the breeze from the short staff attached to one side of the motor home. Now the owner stood in front of me and we shook hands. I told him who we were and explained what we were doing. Steve was his name. Even when you present yourself by your full name and offer your credentials, there are some people who hesitate to reciprocate in kind. I never learned Steve's last name, but he shared with us the essential details of his story.

Steve and his wife had been employed full time and living in the suburbs of Seattle when they decided to stop playing the game of mortgage payments and all that goes with the relentless pursuit of the materialistic world. They chose to cash it all in. They held a garage sale and divested themselves of their extraneous possessions. Then they put their house up for sale. They purchased a motor home with some of the proceeds, paid off their bank loans, and laid the remaining funds aside as investments. They quit their jobs. Eventually, they found their way to Punta Chivato. There, they paid a small annual fee to the Ejido San Bruno to squat on their chosen place overlooking Bahía Santa Inés. Whenever they felt like it, they let down the jacks that leveled their home and drove off to explore another part of Baja California. Like homing pigeons, however, it was to this spot that they faithfully returned. Quite simply, Steve confided in me, Punta Chivato was the finest place they had discovered anywhere on the peninsula.

It's no secret what attracted Steve and his wife to the Gulf of California and, in particular, to Punta Chivato. John Steinbeck covered the territory pretty well in 1940 when he wrote *The Log from the Sea of Cortez*. "One thing impressed us deeply on this little voyage," he wrote; "the great world dropped away very quickly."[1] Steinbeck thought it would be interesting to try explaining to the locals about "our fantastic production of goods that can't be sold, the clutter of possessions which enslave whole populations with debt, the worry and neuroses that go into the rearing and educating of neurotic children who find no place for themselves in this complicated world."[2]

Steinbeck got it right. There is something about the quality of the sunlight here, the special blue of the water, and the stillness of protected embayments like Bahía Santa Inés that enchants the wanderer. The environment is so elemental that it lulls us into feeling we might safely abandon the contrived world of our making, at least for a while. Of course, the societal world is nearby in Mulegé and Santa Rosalía, where the *Western Flyer* paid no port calls. Even in Steinbeck's day, families there struggled to make a living and worried about their children like parents elsewhere in the world. From my earliest impressions, however, the country bounding the Gulf of California struck me as a much smaller but less disturbed variation on the sun-drenched lands surrounding the Mediterranean Sea. Indeed, the coastline of Spanish Andalusía is physically similar to the peninsular shores of Baja California. The choicest embayments on the Gulf of California rival the Bay of Naples for scenic beauty.

But things are changing along the gulf coast. Steinbeck witnessed the first signs of overexploitation in 1940 with regard to commercial fishing, but now modest population pressures are beginning to weigh on the landscape. In the United States, only 3 percent of the landscape is urbanized, but 14 percent of the coast is crowded; it is estimated that by 2025, three out of four Americans will be living in coastal counties.[3] Many of those Americans are seeking prime coastal real estate south of the border. For a decade I have watched while some of the natural wonders of Baja California that so inspired me were irrevocably destroyed by a creeping urbanization. I am deeply torn between conflicting emotions. On one hand, I am mindful of the transpeninsular highway that brought me to this wonderful place. On the other, I am deeply affronted by the expanding roads that carve up destinations like Punta Chivato. Roads are the tangible signs of a certain degree of democratization. The privilege of access that attended visitors like John Steinbeck and Ed Ricketts on the *Western Flyer,* or William Beebe on the *Zaca,* or my geologist predecessors Charles Anderson and J. Wyatt Durham on the *E. W. Scripps,* is now nullified. All those who desire it may come by road. And if they have modest financial means, they may stay as semipermanent residents. What kind of balance should exist between the competing entities of unspoiled nature and the growth of human populations? Why shouldn't the land around the Gulf of California enjoy the growth and development of a human population in proportion to its size relative to the Mediterranean?

In *The Forgotten Peninsula,* Joseph Wood Krutch exclaimed that Bahía Concepción near Punta Chivato was the unrivaled jewel of the entire gulf coast of Baja California. He found it a perfectly proportioned embayment of unsurpassed beauty, equal in size to San Francisco Bay. "The water could not be bluer, the great sandy beaches could not be whiter, and their curves could not be more exquisitely right," he wrote. "The sky is almost as blue as the water and the few palms which here and there dot the open beaches are placed as though they had been put by design just where the eye finds them most effective."[4] Krutch marveled that at the close of the 1950s a great city did not drape itself over the hills that enclose the grand bay. Progress would eventually reach Bahía Concepción, he lamented. "It will be a long time indeed before a city will appropriate this wild area but one can easily (and uneasily) foresee a possibly not very distant future when a good road may make it accessible."[5]

John Steinbeck had set out from Monterey to the Gulf of California with the biologist Ed Ricketts on a privately organized expedition that was intended, in part, to benefit the latter's biological supply business. The work of collecting and preserving marine invertebrates is a repeated theme in *The Log from the Sea of Cortez.* At one point, Steinbeck comments on the fertility of a nudibranch, a shell-less gastropod also known as a sea hare. During its breeding season, a single *Tethys* parent is capable of producing more than 478 million eggs, it is claimed. "Obviously all these eggs cannot mature, all this potential cannot, *must not,* become reality, else the ocean would soon be occupied exclusively by sea-hares," wrote Steinbeck.[6] Larval sea hares form one link in the food chain that supports the greater marine ecosystem both within the Gulf of California and without. Sea hare populations, and all other marine populations, are generally kept in check by the intricacies of such a self-regulating system of resources.

There are more of us humans than ever before, all living off the varied landscapes of the blue planet. Early during the first century of the common era, when the Roman naturalist Pliny the Elder wrote about the magic of *glossoptra,* the world's human population stood at little more than a quarter billion people. By 1667, the year Nicolaus Steno wrote a learned treatise on the dissection of a great white shark to correct Pliny's mistakes, that figure had doubled to about a half billion people. It was not until shortly after 1848, when Robert Chambers published his *Ancient Sea-Margins,* that the human population doubled again to reach a billion people worldwide. In 1900, the year Amadeus W. Grabau earned his doctor of science degree from Harvard University, the world's human population reached about 1.5 billion souls. Within my own lifetime, from 1950 to 2000, the number of *Homo sapiens* seeking daily sustenance to the best of their abilities and varied opportunities grew from something in excess of 2 billion to 6 billion people. The ramifications of Thomas Malthus's dire warning in his famous 1798 study *An Essay on the Principle of Population* are still much debated,[7] but the startling truth cannot be denied that the doubling time in the growth of the human population has steadily gained momentum over the last millennium.

Why should a paleontologist worry about such matters? In their academic work, paleontologists regularly come into contact with the great outdoors. With their geological background, I believe my kind bring something to the table no other experts offer. We are accustomed to seeing environmental change and its impact on species represented by fossils in the geologic record. We are comfortable with the overview of those changes on an epochal time scale. By itself, change is not a thing to be feared or denied. Change is natural, and our planet has undergone astonishing transformations throughout its 4.5 billion years of continuous but sometimes abrupt transition and subsequent development. What is unnerving is the blank realization that the human species constitutes a force for change potentially more catastrophic than any other agent of nature previously experienced on this planet. As the human population expands, it stands to reason that the domesticated animals and cultivated plants favored by humans will occupy space to the maximum extent possible in any given landscape.

On my first visit to Bahía Concepción in January 1990, I was immediately attracted by the pristine state of the rocky shorelines and the lagoons at El Requesón, some 31 miles (50 km) southeast of Punta Chivato. I knew this would be a wonderful place to study, and I returned the following January with a student and my family in tow to take a census of the marine invertebrates in the rocky intertidal zone. We lived in paradise for two weeks while Marshall Hayes and I mapped Isla Requesón and built up an intricate database on the coastal ecosystem using grids to calculate the population size and preferred location of many fixed species. Along the outer, windward shores of the island, the zonation of the rocky intertidal sector was as striking as the individual colors in the Mexican flag. Onshore was the white of the barnacle zone; next came the red of coralline algae that encrusted the boulders and cobbles just offshore; and last came the varied green shades of corals *(Porites californica)* and the matted anemones associated with them. During the quiet morning hours, we could stand on the bluffs overlooking the north side of the island and distinctly see those banded colors rippling in the water like a great pennant waving lazily in the breeze. Large ark shells *(Arca pacifica)* were especially prolific in the coralline algae zone. The water was so clear that I was able to take photographs through 3.3 feet (1 m) of water. On the other side of the island, in lagoons separated at low tide by a long tombolo, large populations of pen shells *(Pinna rugosa)* stood like half-opened Japanese fans discretely hidden in the white carbonate sands. The discarded shells from this species lay in a few great heaps on the edges of the mangroves, attesting to the fact that the lagoons were rich shelling grounds. We worked long hours, but it was not difficult to persuade our few neighbors that we fully enjoyed our labors. Sunrise over the eastern lagoon bathed the entire seascape in a delicious golden glow I have found replicated nowhere else.

In cameo, the living ecology of El Requesón (which includes both the island and its connecting tombolo) prepared me for the bygone Pleistocene and older Pliocene ecosystems of Punta Chivato. Along with Marshall, I learned to recognize the marine invertebrates and their penchants for rough windward waters or calm leeward conditions.[8] When we rolled into Punta Chivato for a reconnaissance at the end of our 1991 field season, I was ready to see the same images cast as sleeping fossils in age-worn stone. That is how my long-standing love affair with Punta Chivato began, without my quite realizing it.

From time to time during subsequent years, I would stop at El Requesón to check on the picture-perfect spit of sand alongside the main highway in Krutch's favorite bay. Nothing seemed amiss. It was during a field course in January 1999, when I planned to spend a full day with students at El Requesón, that I found its rocky shores and lagoons dead by nitrogen strangulation. I should have known what to expect when I saw the tombolo crowded stem to stern with motor homes. I wanted to smell the salt air so badly that I failed to detect the foul odor of rotting algae washed up along the tombolo. I should have drawn a connection with the signs scrawled in English on the plywood walls of several nearby latrines. "No black water," the signs implored. Instead, I hustled my students along for a swim off the north shore, where I had not visited for 10 years. In my mind was fixed the image of a shore teaming with intertidal life. But the waters were not as clear as they once were, and I was unable to find any large arc shells rooted to the stones by their byssal hair. The place was as dead as the lagoons on the opposite side of the island. There, empty pen shells protruded from the white sand, their meat rotted away. They had died in place, never harvested by human hands.

The detective in me should have sprung into action to seek verifiable proof of the murderer. Masses of filmy brown algae, which I should have sampled for later identification, clogged the shallow lagoon waters. I should have organized my students to collect water samples. Instead, I was ready for rough justice. The surface evidence seemed all too clear. Too many people had encamped in a small place. Too many holding tanks were flushed down open holes in the beach. The untreated sewage flowed easily through the carbonate sand to commingle with the zone saturated by marine water below. Large quantities of nitrogen from a strictly human source were being leached directly into the lagoons. People had loved the place to death by their very presence. I could hardly find the words to tell my students that soon there would be precious little left to save here, except the fine evening sunsets and the honey glow of the morning sunrises.

Nowhere else in the district is permanent settlement proceeding faster than at Punta Chivato. With every visit, I find new roads under construction and new vacation homes going up. Slowly but surely, the demand swells for linkage to water delivery via the wells and pipeline originally designed to supply Hotel Punta Chivato. First comes the extension of branch roads that make possible the development of new building sites along the shores of Bahía Santa Inés and the Ensenada El Muerto. Inevitably, once the houses start to go up, trenches are excavated along the roadside to lay new water lines (fig. 32). One by one, each new home puts more strain on the local groundwater supply. In 1996, one of five wells that feeds the Punta Chivato aqueduct (officially designated SG-10) was pumped eight hours a day to yield a flow of 2.6 gallons (10 liters) per second.[9] The water quality has been excellent, and I have never hesitated to recommend the local water, untreated, to my worried students for drinking. Analysis of the Punta Chivato water shows only a negligible trace of nitrates at 4.14 parts per million, which indicates virtually no agricultural or sewage contamination. Already in 1996, however, the chlorides in the drinking water from that well had reached 455 parts per million. It was during my 1999 visit that I first detected a saline taste to the local water.

Not far from well SG-10 are five well heads along Mexican Highway 1 near Palo Verde that service the municipality of Santa Rosalía. As of 2000, one of those wells was already shut down due to the invasion of saline water. The other four wells continued to supply a town of 6,000 people by pumping 14.5 gallons (55 liters) per second on a 24-hour basis. The difficulty is that the average recharge rate of the four online wells is only 4 gallons (15 liters) per second. More water is being removed from the ground for human consumption than is replenished by the natural seepage of rainwater. At the current rate of usage, all wells in the local San José de Magdalena Basin will eventually go saline. More than 530 million gallons (2 million m³) of fresh water is extracted from the San José de Magdalena Basin every year. This exceeds the natural annual recharge of the basin by 109 million gallons (424,000 m³).[10]

Stated bluntly, growth and development within the larger San José de Magdalena Basin has already exceeded the limitations of renewable groundwater supplies. To the average person, the results of overextension are not

Figure 32. New road and water line at Punta Chivato. Photo by author.

immediately obvious. But the outcome may be precisely what happens when a person slowly empties a bank account through withdrawals that exceed deposits. Unless the growth trend is reversed or another source of water is tapped, bankruptcy is the only sure result. The hydrology of the Santa Rosalía district was carefully monitored from 1927 through 1993 (fig. 33).[11] During those years, the maximum rainfall for any single year occurred in 1967—a record 1.4 inches (3.65 cm). Slightly less than half that amount fell during a single 24-hour interval. The least annual rainfall was recorded in 1971—only 0.02 inch (0.05 cm). In 36 out of 63 years, or 57 percent of the time for which data are available, the annual total rainfall amounted to only 0.3 inch (0.75 cm). During 20 of the years (nearly 32 percent of the time), more than half of the annual rainfall arrived in a single 24-hour period. Recharge of local groundwater is a chancy thing. Only a finite amount of renewable fresh water is available from rainfall in the Santa Rosalía district, which includes Punta Chivato.

Living between Santa Rosalía and Punta Chivato, the 300 people who populate the island community of Isla San Marcos have been served since 1996 by a desalinization plant that yields 40,000 gallons (150 m³) of water per day exclusively for drinking.[12] The plant was built for the Compañia Occidental Mexicana, the firm operating the island's gypsum mine, at a cost of 250,000 U.S. dollars. Construction and operational costs of the plant are considered affordable at a payback rate of between U.S.$1.30 and $1.50 per 265 gallons (1 m³) of water. Sooner or later, the hotel and community of American home-owners at Punta Chivato will have little choice but to build their own desalinization plant. Likewise, a proper waste treatment plant cannot wait much longer at the current rate of development. Most environmental ills caused by crowding can be corrected over the long term with care and sufficient investments of capital. In the greater scheme of things, money wisely invested in desalinization and waste treatment plants buys time for the protection of nature.

Yet even with the best possible environmental precautions, the living space and resources available for wild nature are steadily diminished so long as room for the growing human population and its favored agricultural plants and farm animals continues to expand. Global biodiversity suffers as a direct result. If we humans have a natural affinity for the landscapes we share with 10 million or so other species, we should be able to draw a connection between the ecology of the distant past, as embodied in those landscapes, and the wild ecosystems that depend on the same landscapes today. Through intellectual linkage of the remote past and the present, we have the potential to appreciate the long continuum and ongoing evolution of the planet's varied ecosystems across geologic time and into the future.

I sometimes dream about my childhood home in eastern Iowa. I grew up in a town that squeezed its folk into intersecting stream and river valleys but left many of its rocky bluffs relatively undisturbed. As a boy, I enjoyed the freedom to roam far and wide through islands of prairie grass fringed by oaken galleries, which were surrounded, in turn, by urban asphalt. Slowly, almost imperceptibly, those islands shrank, consumed by new housing with manicured lawns.

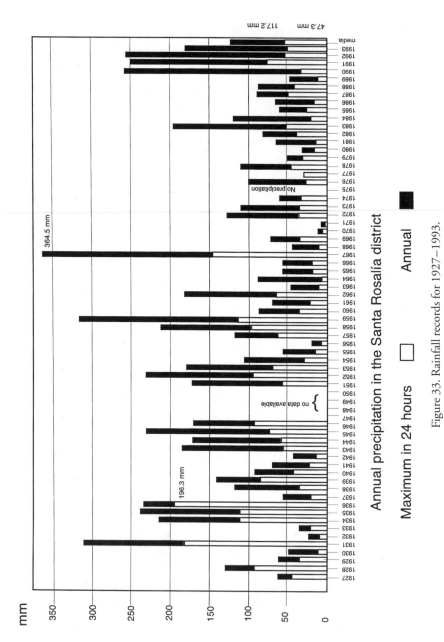

Figure 33. Rainfall records for 1927–1993.

The home in which I grew up was brought into harmony with its adjoining hillside by parents who derived enormous pleasure in restoring native wild-flowers to the abused land. No home is forever. My childhood residence was eventually sold and torn down to make way for something new. In my dreams, I still know exactly where every outdoor path leads and where every wildflower sanctuary blooms. But no other child will have the opportunity to discover the natural retreats I once delighted in. They have vanished forever.

The mass of humanity expands unwaveringly from countless centers all around our artificial human world. The extent and coalescence of these myriad points make an indelible pattern of city lights when viewed as a nighttime snapshot of planet Earth pieced together as a composite satellite image. The National Geographic Society published such a chart in 1998.[13] The effect is startling, especially in the Northern Hemisphere. Seen against the dark background of the oceans, the continents look like so many petri dishes lined up on a laboratory countertop. Each dish cultures the same white mold, but the density of the mold and the thrust of its growth by a web of thin lines into unutilized territory vary from dish to dish.

At odd times, I catch myself staring at that chart mounted on my office wall. The mold, the electric lights—they are symbolic manifestations of *Homo sapiens* in superconcentrations. My eyes glaze over and I perform a devilish thought experiment. I make the chart recede in time through the landscapes and intellectual domains of my predecessors and worthy guides. In an instant, I return to the 1960s and the realm of Harry Hess and Rachel Carson. In another moment I have traveled back a full century to the hopeful world embarked upon by Amadeus Grabau in 1900. The mold retracts, the lights dim. The chart devolves to the seventeenth-century world inhabited by Nicolaus Steno, who looked for beauty and knowledge everywhere in his surroundings. The sad reality, however, will not be assuaged. Like the retreats offered by my childhood home, the opportunities for future generations to be immersed in pristine pockets of wild nature are being obliterated one by one.

The National Geographic chart for 1998 shows Baja California as a still-unblemished land. Like the dark seas around it, most of its night surface remains black, with the obvious exceptions of Tijuana in the north and La Paz and Cabo San Lucas in the south. It requires my hand lens to make a closer inspection and discover no more than 25 tiny points of light dispersed over the entire strip of land. In the year 2000, there still was no unified electrical grid for the Mexican state of Baja California Sur. Diesel-generated plants provide power for Guerrero Negro on the Pacific west coast, the Santa Rosalía to Mulegé area on the gulf, and the La Paz to Cabo San Lucas area at the end of the peninsula. Extension of electrical services to outlying areas has been slow. No power lines cross over the desert from Palo Verde to connect Punta Chivato with the Santa Rosalía grid. Hotel Punta Chivato maintains its own antiquated diesel generator. The wattage produced is too feeble to show up on the National Geographic portrait of our nighttime planet. Indeed, that is one of the special virtues the place holds for me.

The natural edifice of Punta Chivato and its web of ecological connections, past and present, embody another kind of dwelling place. It is a magnificent mansion that I have gradually grown to know inside and out with the same familiarity as my lost childhood home. The landscape and its meanings have ingrained themselves in my mind as recollections, which I hold in intricate detail. I may wander at will from one cerebral vista to the next, anytime I wish. It has been my good fortune to explore the Mesa Atravesada and associated landmarks with perceptive students. I know that they, too, retain a certain measure of the place securely locked in their own memories. No home is forever, but it is my longing that Punta Chivato will continue to host future generations hungry for the meanings of landscapes and the acknowledgment of something greater in their lives than the artificial comforts of a materialistic world. I know of no other spot with the same compact potential to unlock the essential themes identified with the natural history of the Gulf of California. Punta Chivato is the ideal outdoor museum envisioned by the Russian paleo-ecologist Roman Fedorovich Hecker.

When John Steinbeck attempted to sum up the ultimate significance of his voyage to the Gulf of California in 1940, he wrote:

> Our own interest lay in relationships of animal to animal. If one observes in this relational sense, it seems apparent that species are only commas in a sentence, that each species is at once the point and the base of a pyramid, that all life is relational to the point where an Einsteinian relativity seems to emerge. And then not only the meaning but the feeling about species grows misty. One merges into another, groups melt into ecological groups until the time when what we know as life meets and enters what we think of as non-life: barnacle and rock, rock and earth, earth and tree, tree and rain and air. And the units nestle into the whole and are inseparable from it.[14]

Steinbeck was not one to profess faith in what he referred to as a Sunday-school deity, though he conceded that most fellow travelers in this world detest the idea that "a thing is because it is." Nonetheless, his deep spirituality regarding the interrelatedness of the universe is clearly annunciated. The passage of years and the advent of accelerated industrial progress have not yet irredeemably altered the physical and intellectual touchstone that simply exists as Baja

California. It may still be found largely intact, much as Steinbeck experienced it. In places like Punta Chivato, it is still possible to reaffirm the indivisible universe and follow Steinbeck's admonition, "It is advisable to look from the tide pool to the stars, and then back to the tide pool again."[15]

During a March 1996 visit to the Punta Chivato area, I encountered Steve for only the second time. He pulled over on the side of the Palo Verde road in his beach buggy to say hello as I trudged along on foot. He had grown accustomed to me as an annual visitor and greeted me like an old friend. His motor home was no longer parked in its usual place. He and his spouse had moved to the southwest end of the beach, where their home on wheels was parked under the shade of a large, thatched *palapa* that functioned as a protective shed. They had neighbors now. Signs of construction on at least a dozen other plots were tightly knotted near the unobtrusive bulge of Punta El Coloradito. I remarked on all the commotion on Shell Beach and inquired how he liked living in what was fast becoming a small enclave of civilization. Steve gave me a scowl. "You know," he volunteered, "the other day they wanted to organize a block party to celebrate St. Patrick's Day." He continued to ruminate on the possible significance of paper shamrocks in Baja California and the growing colony of strangers on the shores of Bahía Santa Inés who might have a different agenda from his own. It dawned on me that Steve was one of those people who was never meant to have neighbors and who preferred to keep his own counsel and live by his own rules. I never saw him again.

During my subsequent visits, I watched while the oversized palapas clustered at the side of Punta El Coloradito were torn down. In their place came cottages with permanent walls and real roofs. Every year the number of dwellings multiplied. The lonely spot where Steve and his wife first kept their motor home has not been appropriated yet, but it will be in time. I am not entirely certain what happened to the couple who were content to live alone amid the natural splendors of Bahía Santa Inés, but they moved on. Wherever they went, I suspect they chose relative solitude as their companion.

We humans are the only species to give names to things. Things that are conceptual, like the future, require some kind of handle for the exercise of our intellectual dexterity. But I also find great import in the names we bestow on tangible geographic features in the physical world we occupy. We give names to places in order to tame our surroundings. The purely descriptive names are those I value most. Other names, perhaps entirely random in origin, take on their own significance with time. Bahía Santa Inés resides at the calm center of the ancient archipelago landscape of the Punta Chivato area. What does the name of a second-century maiden, real or invented, have to do with this particular place in our own time? Standing on the broad Punta

Chivato promontory, or the narrow Mesa El Coloradito, or the sloping structure of Las Barracas, I struggle with the future of this wondrous place. From those overlooks, I seek some answer from the sheltered waters of the bay that stretch out below to merge with the Gulf of California. Meanings are what we make of them, I conclude.

Oh, Inés! You are the virtuous maiden of my imagination who never brought a single child into the world. Your complete tranquility gives me no peace. The jailer is preoccupied or indifferent. Lithe is your body, but yours, also, is a facile mind. In your eyes are reflected the unbroken connection across deep time from the stars overhead to the tidal pools of our watery home. Let loose the manacles from your thin ankles. Choose life in all its great mystery. Demand your rightful share of schooling so that you may learn all that is known about the world we live in. Nurture life but see to your daughter's education. Encourage her to add to our store of knowledge and our appreciation of beauty. In doing so, give to us all the firm resolve to bring our ravenous kind into a more balanced harmony with the remains of nature.

Notes

Chapter 1. Ancient Shorelines and the Meanings of Landscape

1. John Steinbeck, *The Log from the Sea of Cortez* (New York: Viking Compass, 1962), p. 42.

2. Composed by Bjørnstjerne Bjørnson in 1859, the verses to the Norwegian national anthem are found in *Smørekoppens Visebok* (Trondheim: F. Bruns Bokhandels Forlag, 1971), p. 15. The national anthems of adjacent Sweden and Denmark also feature strong nature themes.

3. John Janovy, Jr., *Vermilion Sea* (Boston: Houghton Mifflin, 1992), pp. 1–10.

4. Details of the Churchill locality are discussed in Markes E. Johnson, David F. Skinner, and Kenneth G. Macleod, Ecological zonation during the carbonate transgression of a late Ordovician rocky shore (northeastern Manitoba, Hudson Bay, Canada), *Palaeogeography, Palaeoclimatology, Palaeoecology,* vol. 65 (1988), pp. 93–114.

5. Markes E. Johnson, Why are ancient rocky shores so uncommon? *Journal of Geology,* vol. 96 (1988), pp. 469–480.

6. The extent of the glacier is described by Bjørn Wold and Leif Ryvarden in *Jostedals-Breen: Norway's Largest Glacier* (Oslo: Boksentreret Forlag, 1996).

7. Cited by Olaf Kortner, Preben Munthe, and Egil Tveterås (editors), *Norge Bilder og Fakta,* Part 2 (Stavanger: Den Norske Bokklubben, 1983), p. 164.

8. The natural-history essayist Stephen Jay Gould qualifies this concept as "methodological uniformitarianism," arguing that its application reflects normal scientific reasoning in any other experimental science. See Stephen Jay Gould, Is uniformitarianism necessary? *American Journal of Science,* vol. 263 (1965), pp. 223–228.

9. The low topography of Australia is discussed by Charles R. Twidale and John D. Pringle in their article on Australia in *Encyclopaedia Britannica* (Chicago, 1991), vol. 4, p. 403.

10. Details of the life of Niels Steensen are related by John G. Winter in his introduction to *The Prodromus of Nicolaus Steno's Dissertation Concerning a Solid Body Enclosed by Process of Nature Within a Solid* (New York: Macmillan, 1916), pp. 175–187.

11. The article is called "A Carcharodon head dissected" (reprint of Latin text of 1667 with English translation by Alex J. Pollock) and is found in *Steno: Geological Papers,* edited by Gustav Scherz (Odense, Odense University Press), pp. 65–131.

12. Winter, *Prodromus of Nicolaus Steno's Dissertation,* pp. 227–230.

13. These are described by Winter, *Prodromus,* pp. 185–186.

14. Steno's introductory lecture as royal anatomist was delivered in Latin at the Copenhagan Anatomical Theatre in 1673 during the dissection of a cadaver. The full lecture is published in Nicolai Stenonis, *Opera Philosophica,* vol. 2 (Copenhagen, 1910), pp. 249–256. The general context of the quotation on beauty is apparent from associated comments. A few lines earlier, Steno argues: "Pursuing the most certain truth by pondering in frequent meditation, let us rather rise from ignorance to knowledge, from imperfection to perfection, and raise in ourselves thoughts worthy of man about his own true dignity." Immediately following the lines quoted in the text, Steno states, "So let us

not dwell further on the senses, but with the mind's eyes, through the bodily eyes, as through a window of a very artistic palace, let us look out over this most delightful meadow in which there are as many flowers as there are parts and as many wonders as there are particles."

15. Steno was familiar with telescopes and celestial observations. He is recorded as having made observations of Jupiter while in Florence on October 23, 1668. See Gustav Scherz, Niels Stensen's geological work, in Scherz, *Steno: Geological Papers,* p. 28.

Chapter 2. South Shore: Playa La Palmita on Bahía Santa Inés

1. Joseph Wood Krutch, *The Forgotten Peninsula* (Tucson: University of Arizona Press, 1986 [1961]), p. 136.

2. Anderson recorded that "one day was available for studies in the headland at the northern end of Santa Inez Bay." Charles A. Anderson, Geology of islands and neighboring land areas, in *1940 E. W. Scripps Cruise to the Gulf of California,* by C. A. Anderson and others (New York: Geological Society of America Memoir 43, Part 1, 1950), p. 33.

3. A detailed biography of Agassiz is provided by Edward Lurie, *Louis Agassiz: A Life in Science* (Chicago: University of Chicago Press, 1960).

4. J. Wyatt Durham, Megascopic paleontology and marine stratigraphy, in *1940 E. W. Scripps Cruise to the Gulf of California,* by C. A. Anderson and others (New York: Geological Society of America Memoir 43, Part 2, 1950), Table 9, Local correlation of strata in Gulf of California area.

5. The interpretation that sea level stood about 6 meters higher 125,000 years ago is based on a survey of abandoned reef tracts and wave-eroded shorelines on islands that are thought to have remained tectonically stable. Two examples of such island groups are Barbados and Bermuda. See M. L. Bender and coauthors, Uranium-series dating of the Pleistocene reef tracts of Barbados, West Indies, *Geological Society of America Bulletin,* vol. 90 (1979), pp. 577–594; and A. C. Neumann and P. J. Hearty, Rapid sea-level changes at the close of the last interglacial (substage 5e) recorded in Bahamian island geology, *Geology,* vol. 24 (1996), pp. 775–778.

6. William Beebe's 1936 visit to Punta Chivato is documented in L. G. Hertlein, Pliocene and Pleistocene fossils from the southern portion of the Gulf of California, *Bulletin of the Southern Academy of Sciences,* vol. 56 (1957), pp. 57–75.

7. The main events and accomplishments of William Beebe's life are addressed in the biographical article by Keir B. Sterling in *American National Biography* (New York: Oxford University Press, 1999), vol. 2, pp. 461–462.

8. Details of the ecology and development of rhodolith beds in the Gulf of California are covered by Michael S. Foster and coauthors, Living rhodolith beds in the Gulf of California and their implications for paleoenvironmental interpretation, *Geological Society of America Special Paper 318* (1997), pp. 127–139.

9. The origin of the name "geoduck" is explained by Eugene C. Harderlie and Donald P. Abbott in chapter 15, Bivalvia: The clams and allies, in *Intertidal Invertebrates of California* (Stanford: Stanford University Press, 1980), p. 388.

10. The geographic range of the geoduck *Panopea globosa* in the Gulf of California is given by A. Myra Keen in *Sea Shells of Tropical West America* (Stanford: Stanford University Press, second edition, 1971), p. 273.

11. Steinbeck, *Log from the Sea of Cortez,* p. 178.

12. Keen, *Sea Shells of Tropical West America,* p. 273.

13. Rainfall on the peninsular coast of the Gulf of California is reviewed by Norman C. Roberts in *Baja California Plant Field Guide* (La Jolla: Natural History Publishing Company, 1989), pp. 15–16.

14. De Maillet's *Telliamed* was edited and translated into English from the third edition of 1755 by Albert V. Carozzi (Urbana: University of Illinois Press, 1968).

15. The scant biographical details of de Maillet's life are covered by Albert V. Carozzi, De Maillet's *Telliamed* (1748): The diminution of the sea or the fall portion of a complete cosmic eustatic cycle, *Geological Society of America Memoir 180* (1992), pp. 17–24.

16. Carozzi, De Maillet's *Telliamed,* p. 126.

17. A 1735 lithograph showing the Nilometer of Cairo is reproduced by Carozzi, De Maillet's *Telliamed,* p. 20. I paid a visit to the locality in 1987.

18. Carozzi, De Maillet's *Telliamed,* p. 87.

19. Carozzi, De Maillet's *Telliamed,* p. 68.

20. Carozzi, De Maillet's *Telliamed,* p. 70.

21. In an earlier publication, I illustrated a fossil barnacle preserved at the entrance to a bivalve boring on the rocky shoreline surrounding the Great Pyramids on the Giza Plateau. See Markes E. Johnson, Hunting for ancient rocky shores, *Journal of Geological Education,* vol. 36 (1988), p. 151.

22. Laura's study was later published as Laura K. Libbey and Markes E. Johnson, Upper Pleistocene rocky shores and intertidal biotas at Playa La Palmita (Baja Californa Sur, Mexico), *Journal of Coastal Research,* vol. 13 (1997), pp. 216–225.

23. Max's study was later published as Maximino E. Simian and Markes E. Johnson, Development and foundering of the Pliocene Santa Inés archipelago in the Gulf of California, Baja California Sur, Mexico, *Geological Society of America Special Paper 318* (1997), pp. 25–38.

Chapter 3. East Shore: Puntas Cacarizo and Cerotito

1. Variations in salinity throughout the Gulf of California are summarized by N. A. Bray, Thermohaline circulation in the Gulf of California, *Journal of Geophysical Research,* vol. 93 (1988), no. C5, pp. 4993–5020. Figure 5 (p. 5020) includes information regarding the Guaymas Basin.

2. Bray, Thermohaline circulation.

3. The shift from counterclockwise to clockwise circulation in the Gulf of California is particularly evident in the seasonal pattern of marine upwelling detected by G. I. Roden and G. W. Groves, Recent oceanographic observations in the Gulf of California, *Journal of Marine Research,* vol. 18 (1959), pp. 10–35.

4. The incident regarding Alexander Agassiz is related by Michael Novacek, *Dinosaurs of the Flaming Cliffs* (New York: Doubleday, 1997), pp. 91–92.

5. The thickness of the Comondú Group was estimated by C. Carew McFall, *Reconnaissance Geology of the Concepcion Bay Area, Baja California, Mexico* (Stanford, Calif.: Stanford University Publications, Geological Sciences, vol. 10, no. 5, 1968).

6. Anderson, *Geology of Islands and Neighboring Land Areas,* p. 33, provides a geological map (fig. 11) and cross section (fig. 12) of San Marcos Island.

7. The depth range of *Porites californica* is given by Alex Kerstitch, *Sea of Cortez Marine Invertebrates* (Monterey, Calif.: Sea Challengers, 1989), p. 27.

8. Data on seasonal changes in wind direction and wind strength are summarized by N. A. Bray and J. M. Robles, Physical oceanography of the Gulf of California, in *The Gulf and Peninsular Province of the Californias,* edited by J. P. Dauphin and B. R. T. Simoneit (American Association of Petroleum Geologists Memoir 47, 1991), pp. 511–553. See especially fig. 2 (p. 514).

9. Patrick's study was later published as Patrick Russell and Markes E. Johnson, Influence of seasonal winds on coastal carbonate dunes from the Recent and Plio-Pleistocene at Punta Chivato (Baja California Sur, Mexico), *Journal of Coastal Research,* vol. 16 (2000), pp. 709–723.

10. The subsurface depth of granite inland from Santa Rosalía is reported by A. López-Hernández and co-authors, Geological and geophysical studies at Las Tres Vírgenes, B.C.S., Mexico, *Transactions of the Geothermal Resources Council,* vol. 18 (1994), pp. 275–280.

11. Amanz Gressly, Observations géologiques sur le Jura soleurois, *Nouveaux Mémoires de la Société Helvétique de Sciences Naturelles* (Neuchatel), vol. 2 (1838), pp. 1–112. The importance of Gressly's contribution is reviewed by Timothy A. Cross and Peter W. Homewood, Amanz Gressly's role in founding modern stratigraphy, *Geological Society of America Bulletin,* vol. 109 (1997), pp. 1617–1630. An appendix to their review provides a translation into English from the original French of Gressly's 1838 paper.

12. Biographical details are covered by Cecil J. Schneer in the entry on Amanz Gressly in *Dictionary of Scientific Biography* (New York: Charles Scribner's Sons, 1972), vol. 5, pp. 533–534.

13. Cross and Homewood, Amanz Gressly's role, p. 1627.

14. Cross and Homewood, Amanz Gressly's role, p. 1627.

15. Cross and Homewood, Amanz Gressly's role, p. 1628.

16. Amanz Gressly, Observations géologiques sur le Jura soleurois. *Nouveaux Mémoires de la Société Helvétique de Sciences Naturelles* (Neuchatel), vol. 4 (1840), pp. 113–241. A reproduction of Gressly's colored map and cross section of the Jura Alps from this volume is available in a review paper by Clifford M. Nelson, Facies in stratigraphy: From "terrains" to "terranes," *Journal of Geological Education,* vol. 33 (1985), pp. 175–187. See his figure 5 on pp. 180–181.

17. Schneer, Amanz Gressly, *Dictionary of Scientific Biography.*

18. Johannes Walther, *Einleitung in die Geologie als historische Wissenschaft* (Jena: Verlag von Gustav Fischer, 1893–1894), three volumes.

19. Interpretation of Walther's law is treated in the context of his original reference material as cited by G. V. Middleton, Johannes Walther's law of the correlation of facies, *Geological Society of America Bulletin,* vol. 84 (1973), pp. 979–988.

20. Russell and Johnson, Influence of seasonal winds.

Chapter 4. Near North Shore: Punta Chivato

1. Latitudinal control of life zones on a global scale is discussed by Robert G. Bailey in *Ecoregions* (New York: Springer, 1998).

2. Steinbeck, *Log from the Sea of Cortez,* p. 71.

3. Cordelia's study is represented by an abstract published in 2000 as Cordelia R. Ransom, Paleoecology of Upper Pleistocene coral reefs based on morphology and fossil assemblages, Baja California Sur, Mexico, *Memorias V, International Meeting on the Geology of the Baja California Peninsula (Loreto, Baja California Sur, April 25– May 1, 2000)* (Ensenada, Mexico: Universidad Autónoma de Baja California, 2000), pp. 36–37.

4. The geographic range of *Divaricella eburnea* in the Gulf of California is given by Keen, *Sea Shells of Tropical West America,* p. 125.

5. Keen, *Sea Shells,* p. 388.

6. Pectens are treated by Keen, *Sea Shells,* pp. 85–94.

7. This is discussed by Markes E. Johnson and Maximino E. Simian, Discrimination between coastal ramps and marine terraces at Punta Chivato on the Pliocene-Pleistocene Gulf of California, *Journal of Geoscience Education,* vol. 44 (1996), pp. 569–575.

8. The interesting case of the fossil coral *Solenastrea fairbanksi* is treated by Ann B. Foster, Environmental variation in a fossil scleractinian coral, *Lethaia,* vol. 12 (1979), pp. 245–264.

9. The geology of El Sombrerito in Mulegé is treated by James R. Ashby and co-authors, Uranium series ages of corals from the upper Pleistocene Mulege terrace, Baja California Sur, Mexico, *Geology,* vol. 15 (1987), pp. 139–141.

10. The 125,000-year-old marine terrace around the Concepción Peninsula is discussed by Markes E. Johnson and Jorge Ledesma-Vázquez, Biological zonation on a rocky-shore boulder deposit: Upper Pleistocene Bahía San Antonio (Baja California Sur, Mexico), *Palaios,* vol. 14 (1999), pp. 569–584. See especially fig. 1, p. 570.

11. Biographical details are covered by Wesley C. Williams in the entry on Robert Chambers in *Dictionary of Scientific Biography* (New York: Charles Scribner's Sons, 1972), vol. 1, pp. 191–193.

12. Robert Chambers, *Ancient Sea-Margins as Memorials of Changes in the Relative Level of Sea and Land* (Edinburgh: W. and R. Chambers, 1848), p. 1.

13. Chambers, *Ancient Sea-Margins,* p. 3.

14. Chambers, *Ancient Sea-Margins,* pp. 10–11.

15. Marine terraces throughout the Gulf of California are summarized by Luc Ortleib, Quaternary vertical movements along the coasts of Baja California and Sonora, in Dauphin and Simoneit, *Gulf and Peninsular Province of the Californias,* pp. 447–480. See especially figure 4, p. 454.

16. Pluvial lakes located south of the Colorado Plateau are treated by R. A. Morrison, Quaternary geology of the southern Basin and Range Province, in *The Geology of North America,* vol. K-2 (Boulder, Colo.: Geological Society of America, 1991), pp. 353–371. See especially figure 1, p. 354.

17. Pluvial lakes located in the Great Basin are treated by R. A. Morrison, Quaternary stratigraphic, hydrologic, and climatic history of the Great Basin, with emphasis on Lakes Lahontan, Bonneville, and Tecopa, in *The Geology of North America,* vol. K-2 (Boulder, Colo.: Geological Society of America, 1991), pp. 283–320. See especially figure 2, p. 287.

18. The toxicity of the desert hollyhock and other related plants is discussed by Roberts, *Baja California Plant Field Guide,* p. 226.

19. Results of growth-ring analysis are given by Russell and Johnson, Influence of seasonal winds, Table 1, p. 715.

20. Santa Inés is treated in volume 54 of the *Enciclopedia Universal Ilustrada Europeo-Americana* (Madrid: Espesa-Calpea, 1975), pp. 1387–1389.

21. Chambers, *Ancient Sea-Margins,* p. 6.

Chapter 5. Far North Shore: Ensenada El Muerto

1. The importance of the September rains at the tip of the Baja California peninsula is cited by Roberts, *Baja California Plant Field Guide,* p. 16. Detailed information on expected bloom times for specific plant species in the cape region is provided by Ann Zwinger in *A Desert Country near the Sea* (Tucson, University of Arizona Press, 1983), pp. 328–358.

2. Quoted from Anderson's description of Carmen Island, *Geology of Islands and Neighboring Land Areas,* p. 20.

3. See Ronald L. Ives, Shell dunes of the Sonoran shore, *American Journal of Science,* vol. 257 (1959), pp. 449–457.

4. The cosmopolitan distribution of the great white shark *(Carcharodon carcharias)* is shown by Peter Benchley in his feature article in *National Geographic,* vol. 194, no. 4 (April 2000), p. 11. Summer visits to the Gulf of California by the great white shark are confirmed by my colleague Gerardo González Barba of the Autonomous University of Baja California Sur (personal communication, March 24, 2000).

5. Steno, A Carcharodon head dissected, pp. 87, 91.

6. Warning on the toxicity of the slipper plant *(Pedilanthus macrocarpus)* is taken from Roberts, *Baja California Plant Field Guide,* p. 178.

7. Mean grain-size data for dunes associated with the far north shore are quoted from Russell and Johnson, Influence of seasonal winds, Table 6, p. 718.

8. Russell and Johnson, Influence of seasonal winds, Tables 6–7, p. 718.

9. Depth ranges are from Keen, *Sea Shells of Tropical West America.* See also Table 5 in Russell and Johnson, Influence of seasonal winds.

10. Loren Eiseley, *The Immense Journey* (New York: Vintage Books, 1957), pp. 15–27.

11. Standing waves, nodal points, and antinodal points are discussed in more detail by William T. Fox in *At the Sea's Edge* (Englewood Cliffs, N.J.: Prentice-Hall, 1983); see especially pp. 83–86 and 138–139.

12. The tendency of the barrel cactus to act as a "compass plant" oriented with respect to the sunlight is commented on by John Minch and co-authors in *Roadside Geology and Biology of Baja California* (Mission Viejo: John Minch and Associates, 1998), p. 56.

13. Russel and Johnson, Influence of seasonal winds, fig. 10 and associated text, pp. 718–719.

14. See Markes E. Johnson, A. W. Grabau's embryonic sequence stratigraphy and eustatic curve, *Geological Society of America Memoir 180* (1992), pp. 43–54.

15. Amadeus W. Grabau, *The Rhythm of the Ages* (Peking; Henry Vetch, 1940), p. vii. A reprint of this historically significant volume is more widely available (New York: Krieger, 1978).

16. Grabau, *Rhythm of the Ages,* p. 50.

17. Some of the biographic details of Grabau's life and career are covered by Markes E. Johnson, A. W. Grabau and the fruition of a new life in China, *Journal of Geological Education,* vol. 33 (1985), pp. 106–111.

18. Johnson, A. W. Grabau, p. 107.

19. Johnson, A. W. Grabau's embryonic sequence stratigraphy, fig. 6, p. 52.

20. The initial key paper from the Exxon research group on global changes in sea level through geologic time was presented by Peter R. Vail and co-authors, Seismic stratigraphy and global changes of sea level, Part 4: Global cycles of relative changes of sea level, in *Seismic Stratigraphy: Applications to Hydrocarbon Exploration,* American Association of Petroleum Geologists Memoir 26 (1977), pp. 83–97. A later version of this work was given by Bilal U. Haq and co-authors, Chronology of fluctuating sea levels since the Triassic, *Science,* vol. 235 (1987), pp. 1156–1167.

21. Ramifications in the Pliocene record of global sea-level changes pertinent to the geological history of Baja California are reviewed by Johnson and Simian, Discrimination between coastal ramps and marine terraces, pp. 569–575. See also J. P. Kennett and D. A. Hodell, Stability or instability of Antarctic ice sheets during warm climates of the Pliocene? *GSA Today,* vol. 5 (1995), pp. 13, 22.

22. Modification of the Exxon sea-level curve of Haq et al. (1987) with specific reference to the late Miocene to early Pliocene interval is treated by S. C. Cande and D. V. Kent, Revised calibration of the geomagnetic polarity time scale for the Late Cretaceous and Cenozoic, *Journal of Geophysical Research,* vol. 100 (1995), pp. 6093–6096.

Chapter 6. Mesa Barracas

1. The place-name "Barracas Table" is in the text and accompanying map in Anderson, *Geology of Islands and Neighboring Land Areas,* pp. 112–113.

2. The torote colorado is described by Roberts, *Baja California Plant Field Guide,* pp. 112–113.

3. The oyster species *Ostrea vespertina* and its stratigraphic range are described by Durham, Megascopic paleontology and marine stratigraphy, p. 59.

4. An inorganic origin for the dolomite on the Pleistocene shoreline at Playa La Palmita is discussed in the section "Abandoned Intertidal Abrasion Platform" in Libbey and Johnson, Upper Pleistocene rocky shores, p. 220.

5. The Wentworth scale for the description of clastic sedimentary rocks was proposed by Charles K. Wentworth, A scale of grade and class terms for clastic sediments, *Journal of Geology,* vol. 27 (1922), pp. 377–392.

6. Some details of the career of Roman Fedorovich Hecker, including the various language editions of his textbook *Introduction to Paleoecology,* are given in an anonymous biography that appeared in the journal *Geologiska Föreningens I Stockholm Föhandlingar,* vol. 102 (1980), p. 234.

7. R. F. Hecker, *Introduction to Paleoecology* (New York: Elsevier, 1965), p. 4.

8. Hecker, *Introduction to Paleoecology,* p. 8.

9. Hecker, *Introduction to Paleoecology,* p. 15.

10. Hecker, *Introduction to Paleoecology,* p. 94.

11. I. A. Pianovskaya and R. F. Hecker, Rocky shores and hard ground of the Cretaceous and Palaeogene seas in central Kyzil Kum and their inhabitants, in *Organisms and Environment in the Geological Past: A Symposium* (Moscow: Nauka, 1966), pp. 222–245 [in Russian]. See their plates 2 and 3 for photographic views of rocky shores exposed in three-dimensional relief under present desert conditions.

12. Personal recollections of R. F. Hecker were provided by the paleontologist Olga K. Bogolepova (personal communication, March 7, 2000).

Chapter 7. Offshore: Islas Santa Inés

1. Essential features of the Multispectral Scanner and Thematic Mapper systems are discussed by Floyd F. Sabins, Jr., in *Remote Sensing: Principles and Interpretation* (New York: W. H. Freeman, second edition, 1987); see especially pp. 78–85.

2. The geology of the Concepción Peninsula was mapped by McFall, Reconnaissance geology. Distribution of the granite basement rocks with schist inclusions are shown by the map in Plate 1.

3. The echinoid species *Clypeaster bowersi* and its stratigraphic range are described by Durham, Megascopic paleontology and marine stratigraphy, pp. 40–41. See also table 9.

4. The original is chart 5 in Francis P. Shepard, Submarine topography of the Gulf of California, in *1940* E. W. Scripps *Cruise to the Gulf of California,* by C. A. Anderson and others (New York: Geological Society of America Memoir 43, Part 3, 1950).

5. Shepard, Submarine topography, fig. 5, p. 18.

6. Shepard, Submarine topography, chart 1.

7. Plates 1 (North Sheet) and 2 (South Sheet), denoted "Bathymetry," are described in an accompanying article by J. Paul Dauphin and Gordon E. Ness, Bathymetry of the Gulf and Peninsula Province of the Californias, in Dauphin and Simoneit, *Gulf and Peninsular Province of the Californias,* pp. 21–23.

8. Plates 7 (North Sheet) and 8 (South Sheet), denoted "Seismo-Tectonics," are described in an accompanying article by Gordon E. Ness and Mitchell W. Lyle, A seismo-tectonic map of the Gulf and Peninsular Province of the Californias, in Dauphin and Simoneit, *Gulf and Peninsular Province of the Californias,* pp. 71–77.

9. Rachel L. Carson, *The Sea Around Us* (New York: Oxford University Press, 1951), p. 61.

10. Results of a multiyear study of the Concepción Peninsula are summarized in Markes E. Johnson and Jorge Ledesma-Vázquez, Pliocene-Pleistocene rocky shorelines trace coastal development of Bahía Concepción, gulf coast of Baja California Sur (Mexico), *Palaeogeography, Palaeoclimatology, Palaeoecology,* vol. 166 (2001), pp. 65–88.

11. The three-stage model for the Baja California peninsula and related Gulf of California was developed through the contributions of several geologists, including Brian P. Hausback, Cenozoic volcanic and tectonic evolution of Baja California, Mexico, in *Geology of the Baja California Peninsula* (Bakersfield, Calif.: Pacific Section, Society of Economic Paleontologists and Mineralogists, 1984), pp. 219–236; Peter Lonsdale, Geology and tectonic history of the Gulf of California, in *The Geology of North America,* vol. N (Boulder: Geological Society of America, 1989), pp. 499–521; and Joann M. Stock and K. V. Hodges, Pre-Pliocene extension around the Gulf of California and the transfer of Baja California to the Pacific plate, *Tectonics,* vol. 8 (1990), pp. 99–115.

12. See Wayne Thatcher and co-authors, Present-day deformation across the Basin and Range Province, western United States, *Science,* vol. 283 (1999), pp. 1714–1718. The schematics in figures 29 and 30, showing extensional tectonics in the southwestern United States, are redrawn from Peter W. Huntoon, The post-Paleozoic structural geology of the eastern Grand Canyon, Arizona, in *Geology of the Grand Canyon,* edited by W. J. Breed and E. Roat (Flagstaff, Ariz.: Museum of Northern Arizona/Grand Canyon Natural History Association, second edition, 1976), pp. 114–115.

13. See Shepard, Submarine topography, p. 18.

14. The main events and accomplishments of Harry Hammond Hess's life are addressed in the biographical article by Elizabeth N. Shore in *American National Biography* (New York: Oxford University Press), vol. 10 (1999), pp. 700–701.

15. Hess's mistaken notion about the Precambrian age of guyots is outlined in his 1946 paper, "Drowned ancient islands of the Pacific Basin," *American Journal of Science,* vol. 244, pp. 772–791.

16. Carson, *The Sea Around Us,* p. 70.

17. See the first English edition: Alfred Wegener, *The Origin of Continents and Oceans* (London: Methuen, 1924).

18. Carson, *The Sea Around Us,* p. 69.

19. H. H. Hess, History of ocean basins, in *Petrologic Studies: A Volume to Honor A. F. Buddington* (Baltimore: Geological Society of America, 1962), p. 599.

20. Hess, History of ocean basins, pp. 617–618.

21. Fred Vine and Drummond Matthews, Magnetic anomalies over oceanic ridges, *Nature,* vol. 199 (1963), pp. 947–949.

22. Hess's visit to Cambridge University in 1962 is described by Robert M. Wood in *The Dark Side of the Earth* (London: Allan and Unwin, 1985), p. 151.

23. Any number of introductory geology textbooks include maps showing the boundaries of the major tectonic plates and the calculated rate of spreading at divergent plate boundaries. An example is Reed Wicander and James S. Monroe, *Historical Geology: Evolution of Earth and Life through Time* (Pacific Grove: Brooks/Cole, third edition, 2000). See figure 6.13 on p. 141.

24. Wicander and Monroe, *Historical Geology,* figure 6.13, p. 141.

25. Movement on the Ballenas-Salsipuedes fault is indicated in Plate 7 (North Sheet), denoted "Seismo-Tectonics," in Dauphin and Simoneit, *The Gulf and Peninsular Province of the Californias.*

26. An account of the 1976–1977 expedition to the Galapagos Rift is given by Joseph Cone in *Fire under the Sea* (New York: William Morrow, 1991), pp. 80–89.

27. The same adventure is related by Ken C. Macdonald and Bruce P. Luyendyk, The crest of the East Pacific Rise, *Scientific American,* vol. 244 (1981), pp. 100–116.

28. Biological relationships to the seafloor hot springs are detailed by Rachel M. Haymon and Ken C. Macdonald, The geology of deep-sea hot springs, *American Scientist,* vol. 73 (1985), pp. 441–449.

29. The results of the 1977 expedition with the *Seacliff* are reviewed by Jan M. Peter and Steven D. Scott, Hydrothermal mineralization in the Guaymas Basin, Gulf of California, in Dauphin and Simoneit, *Gulf and Peninsular Province of the Californias,* pp. 721–741.

30. Bernard R. T. Simoneit and Peter F. Lonsdale, Hydrothermal petroleum in mineralized mounds at the seabed of Guaymas Basin, *Nature,* vol. 295 (1982), pp. 198–202.

31. The Pliocene chert beds from the Concepción Peninsula and their origin are described by Jorge Ledesma-Vázquez and co-authors, El Mono chert: A shallow-water chert from the Pliocene Infierno Formation, Baja California Sur, Mexico, *Geological Society of America Special Paper 318* (1997), pp. 73–81.

32. The geology and origin of Isla Tortuga are described by R. Batiza, Geology, petrology, and geochemistry of Isla Tortuga, a recently formed tholeiitic island in the Gulf of California, *Geological Society of America Bulletin,* vol. 89 (1978), pp. 1309–1324.

Chapter 8. The Future of Punta Chivato and Baja California

1. Steinbeck, *Log from the Sea of Cortez,* p. 210.

2. Steinbeck, *Log from the Sea of Cortez,* p. 208.

3. Population statistics on the crowding of seashore counties in the United States come from Tim Palmer, *The Heart of America* (Washington, D.C.: Island Press/Shearwater Books, 1999), p. 253.

4. Krutch, *Forgotten Peninsula,* p. 139.

5. Krutch, *Forgotten Peninsula,* p. 140.

6. Steinbeck, *Log from the Sea of Cortez,* pp. 133–134.

7. A counter view is mounted by Ronald Bailey in chapter 1, "The progress explosion: Permanently escaping the Malthusian trap," of his *Earth Report 2000* (New York: McGraw-Hill, 2000), pp. 1–21.

8. Observations on marine intertidal zonation at El Requesón were published in a report by Marshall L. Hayes, M. E. Johnson, and W. T. Fox, Rocky-shore biotic associations and their fossilization potential: Isla Requesón (Baja California Sur, Mexico), *Journal of Coastal Research,* vol. 9 (1993), pp. 944–957.

9. Data shared with permission of Francisco Escandón Valle (director general, Project El Boleo) from the company files of Minera Curator, S.A. de C.V., in Santa Rosalía (personal communication dated June 12, 2000). Well data come from a 1996 report, "Estudio de evaluación geohidrológica de las subcuencas hidrológicas de los arroyos la Magdalena, Santa Agueda y Santa Rosalía de la cuenca Trinidad-Mulegé y de la subcuenca del Río San Ignacio, perteneciente a la cuenca San Ignacio–San Raymundo."

10. Compañía Minera Curator hydrological report, p. 27.

11. The rainfall data reproduced in figure 33 were collected for the years 1927–1940 by the U. S. Geological Survey geologist I. F. Wilson; for the years 1941–1946 and 1951–1985 by the Servicio Meteorológico Nacional; and for the years 1986–1993 by the Unidad de Hidrología Operativa, División Hidrométrica, B.C.S. Secretaria de Agricultura y Recursos Hidráulicos.

12. Francisco Escandón Valle, personal communication, June 12, 2000.

13. Population and Resources, Millennium in Maps (Washington, D.C.: National Geographic Society, August 1998).

14. Steinbeck, *Log from the Sea of Cortez,* p. 216.

15. Steinbeck, *Log from the Sea of Cortez,* p. 217.

Glossary of Geological and Ecological Terms

andesite. Igneous rocks of an extrusive origin (volcanic lavas and breccias) that are rich in the minerals silica (53–63%) and plagioclase and contain lesser amounts of pyroxene, hornblende, and/or biotite. Although a freshly broken surface is generally dark gray in color, weathered surfaces often take on a reddish cast due to oxidation of iron content. The name is derived from the Andes, which represent the kind of mountain belt where these rocks occur, owing to ocean-plate subduction against a continental margin.

angular unconformity. A break in the rock record in which older strata below a prominent erosional surface dip at an angle considerably steeper than that of the younger strata deposited above.

arroyo. A streambed, usually with well-defined vertical walls, that carries water only intermittently. In Mexico, dry streambeds are identified on topographic maps as arroyos.

bajada. A continuous apron of coalescent outwash fans consisting of unconsolidated sediments that accumulate on the margin of a plain at its intersection with highlands.

basalt. Igneous rocks of an extrusive origin (flood lavas or submarine pillow lavas) that are rich in the minerals silica (44–50%), calcic plagioclase, pyroxine, and often olivine. These rocks typically form on the ocean floor or in continental rifts. They are dark and generally weather dark.

basement rocks. The intrusive igneous and/or metamorphic rocks that are overlain at depth by sedimentary rocks.

bedding plane. The surface of a layered rock that separates it from the beds or strata above and below.

bedrock. Solid rock, stratified or unstratified, that occurs under soil, gravel, or any other unconsolidated surface materials.

berm. A well-demarcated, level deposit of sand or coarser material that marks the maximum landward extent of reworking by waves. A beach may have more than one berm, depending on the effects of tidal cycles and storms.

binomen. Refers to the formal Latin designation for a species that consists of two names, the genus name (capitalized) followed by the trivial, or species, name (lowercased).

carbonate ramp. A gently sloping surface (generally 5–10°) that forms as a continuum from shallow to deeper water and consists of carbonate sediments when under active construction or limestone when cemented in place. The ramp may sit on an unconformity surface eroded from a preexisting lithology (sedimentary, igneous, or metamorphic) by coastal and nearshore processes.

clast. An individual fragment of rock (varying sizes) eroded from a parent source by the action of wind, waves, or running water.

clinometer. A device, much like a carpenter's level, used to measure the dip in bedded rock layers.

coral. Marine invertebrates that are solitary or colonial and belong to the Phylum Coelenterata. Many species secrete a skeleton of calcium carbonate and are the principle contributors to the construction of reefs.

cuesta. A long, gently dipping plain that is truncated on one side by a steep erosional slope. This landform typically relates to stratified rocks that formed in place as ramp structures or were moderately tilted by uplift after deposition.

dike. A tabular body of igneous rock injected as magma through cracks and fissures in a preexisting body of rock.

echinoderm. Marine invertebrates that are solitary in plan (noncolonial), exhibit five-fold symmetry, and belong to the Phylum Echinodermata. Many species secrete a calcium carbonate test. Common examples include sea urchins, sand dollars, and starfish.

en echelon fault. One in a series of parallel faults that offset adjacent slices of land to effect a repetitiously slanted (or shingled) appearance when viewed in cross section.

escarpment. The steep erosional slope that truncates a cuesta in which moderately tilted strata are exposed.

extensional stress. Force applied to the earth's crust that results in stretching or pulling in opposite directions.

facies. Different but contemporaneous rock and fossil deposits found adjacent to one another or in a lateral relationship indicative of different envrionmental conditions.

fauna. The animals that live in a given area or environment. A faunal list gives the names of those animals (or fossil animals) found in a given area.

fjord. A drowned glacial valley, typically with a sill or raised threshold at its mouth that tends to prevent the circulation of normal marine water at depth within.

geomorphology. The study of physical landforms and the natural processes that lead to their development at the surface of the Earth.

graben. An elongated fault block that is downthrown with respect to the adjacent blocks on either side. The effect is to create a trough-shaped topography.

historical geology. The study of the physical and biological changes (and their interrelationships) that have occurred sequentially through geologic time from Earth's origin to the present day.

Holocene. The last 10,000 years of geological history.

hogbacks. Rustic geological term for ridges that repeat due to patterns of tight folding or faulting of the underlying rocks.

horst. An elongated fault block that is upthrown with respect to the adjacent blocks on either side. The effect is to create a crested topography.

igneous rocks. Rocks cooled from molten material either deep within the Earth's crust (intrusive) or at the Earth's surface (extrusive) as a result of volcanic activity.

inlier. A body of older rocks reduced in size by erosion and subsequently encircled by younger rocks that form an unconformity against the preexisting rocks.

karst. A range of landforms that develop both on and within terrain dominated by limestone cover due to the bedrock's dissolving under a humid climate. The name comes from the Karst district on the coast of the Adriatic Sea.

krummholz. Term derived from German ("twisted wood") that applies to trees or shrubs contorted from normal upright growth to a bent or even ground-hugging posture due to the deleterious effects of salt, sand, or ice crystals carried by the wind.

laterite. Red soil that develops in humid tropical and subtropical regions. It is typically rich in iron and aluminum but depleted in silica.

lithology. The physical characteristics of rocks, primarily their type (i.e., sandstone, shale, limestone, etc.).

limestone. Sedimentary rock consisting of calcium carbonate derived primarily from organic remains of marine invertebrates such as corals, mollusks, echinoderms, and coralline algae.

marine terrace. A narrow coastal rim that usually slopes gently seaward and is veneered by a marine deposit. Formation of the terrace is caused by intertidal erosion, and the position of the terrace depends on changes in global sea level with respect to changes in the local or regional elevation of the coastline.

metamorphic rocks. Rocks that are either sedimentary or igneous in origin but were subsequently altered by heat and pressure due to deep burial in the Earth's crust. Limestone may be altered to marble, for example, and granite may be altered to schist.

Miocene. A geological epoch roughly 19 million years in duration that began about 24 million years ago and terminated a little more than 5 million years ago. All the sedimentary and igneous rocks that originated during this interval are said to belong to the Miocene Series.

mollusk. Marine invertebrates that are solitary in plan (noncolonial) and belong to the Phylum Mollusca. The phylum includes land and sea snails (Class Gastropoda), clams (Class Bivalvia), and squids and the octopus (Class Cephalopoda). In particular, the shelled gastropods and bivalves lend themselves to fossilization.

original horizontality. A geological principle based on the fact that sediment (such as sand, silt, and clay) deposited underwater tends to disperse evenly on the seafloor and form level layers. When sedimentary rock layers are found that are steeply tilted, it is understood that the configuration of the beds was altered due to tectonic forces well after the formation of the strata.

outlier. Isolated bodies of stratified rock that stand detached from the main outcrop due to erosion of the area between the outlier and the rest of the outcrop. Outliers typically form buttes or mesas that may be far removed from similar rocks.

paleontology. The study of prehistoric life.

paleovalley. An ancient valley, preserved as a consequence of sedimentary fill but subject to later exhumation.

Pleistocene. A short geological epoch, less than 2 million years in duration, that bridges the prior Pliocene Epoch and the Holocene (Recent), ending 10,000 years ago. All sedimentary and igneous rocks that originated during this time interval are said to belong to the Pleistocene Series.

Pliocene. A geological epoch roughly 3.5 million years in duration that began more than 5 million years ago and terminated less than 2 million years ago. All the sedimentary and igneous rocks that originated during this interval are said to belong to the Pliocene Series.

pluvial lake. A lake that formed during a geological interval when rainfall was significantly more abundant than it is today. Present desert regions in the Northern Hemisphere typically were subjected to higher rates of rainfall during the various Pleistocene glaciations. When desert conditions returned during the interglacials, the old lake beds and lake terraces were exposed.

red coralline algae. Marine plants that belong to the Phylum Rhodophyta and have the ability to secrete skeletons of calcium carbonate. The adjective *coralline* is applied to indicate that the algae mimic corals in appearance.

rhodolith. A particular kind of red coralline algae that grows unattached on the seafloor. The rhodolith assumes a spherical shape due to frequent movement with wave and current activity during the lifetime of the alga. The alga may colonize a tiny piece of shell or a rock fragment as large as a pebble, thereafter growing outward in a radial pattern.

rift zone. A region, typically linear in demarcation, where a continent has begun to break apart or where ocean crust continues to spread apart in opposite directions.

saltation. Hopping movement of sand grains in a dune due to the translation of energy from one grain to another from inertia and impact in relation to wind transport. The same term is also applied to stream pebbles that are carried along in a skipping movement by currents. From the Latin *saltare*, to jump.

schist. A metamorphic rock that is characterized by strong foliation, or melding out of mineral constituents, due to heat and pressure. The biotite mineral grains scattered evenly throughout granite, for example, may become finely banded in a schist. The term *gneiss* applies to metamorphic rocks in which the banding is coarse.

scree. Jumbled pile of rock waste found at the base of a cliff or a sheet of coarse debris that covers a steep mountainside.

sedimentary rocks. Rocks formed by the burial and cementation of inorganic sediments such as pebbles, sand, silt, and clay, or of the fragments of broken corals and shells that form limestone.

sinkhole. A funnel-shaped depression in the surface of the land, typical of regions where limestone is abundant, due to dissolution.

specific gravity. The ratio of the weight of a given mineral to the weight of the same volume of water. Galena (lead) has a specific gravity of about 7.5, while quartz (SiO_2) has a specific gravity of only 2.6.

strata. Layered sedimentary rocks.

stratigraphy. The study of layered rocks.

stratum. A single layer (or bed) in a sequence of layered sedimentary rocks.

strike-slip fault. A fault in which the net slippage is practically in the direction of the fault strike. That is, movement on opposite sides of the fault trace is seen mainly as lateral, as opposed to vertical. Common synonyms are wrench fault and transcurrent fault.

superposition. In conformity with the concept of original horizontality, the interpretation that the bottom layer in a sequence of stratified rocks is the oldest bed and the top layer is the youngest bed.

transform fault. A major fracture that runs perpendicular to an ocean ridge and along which strike-slip movement predominates.

trellised drainage. A stream pattern in which tributaries merge at right angles to one another. Such a pattern is usually controlled by faulted or folded bedrock.

tombolo. A bar composed of unconsolidated materials (sand) that connects an island with the mainland.

tuff. A rock formed from volcanic ash and small fragments of volcanic rock (usually less than 4 mm, or one-eighth inch, in diameter).

tuffaceous. Adjective for sediments more than 50-percent composed of tuff.

unconformity. A surface of erosion that separates two bodies of rock and represents an interval of time during which deposition ceased, some material was removed, and then deposition resumed again. An *angular unconformity* involves two sets of stratified rocks on opposite sides of the unconformity surface, but other types of unconformities may involve a juncture between sedimentary rocks and igneous or metamorphic rocks.

uniformitarianism. The basic concept that the physical processes we may observe in action today are the same processes that shaped Earth throughout geologic time.

volcanology. The study of volcanoes.

Wentworth scale. A convention established by Charles K. Wentworth in 1922 that sedimentary particles described as cobbles, pebbles, sand, silt, and clay are defined by a specific range of measured diameters. Sand, for example, fits the size category of 2 mm to one-sixteenth mm, although there also are subcategories of very coarse, coarse, medium, fine, and very fine sand.

xenolith. A rock fragment that is foreign to the body of igneous rock in which it occurs. Typically, such fragments are other igneous rocks that are broken off the parent rock by the force of magma moving upward under pressure. The xenolith is carried into fissures that become igneous dikes, or even to the surface, where it may be eroded free from the rock that solidified from the capturing magma.

References

Anderson, C. A. 1950. Geology of islands and neighboring land areas. In *1940* E. W. Scripps *Cruise to the Gulf of California,* by C. A. Anderson et al., Part 1. New York: Geological Society of America Memoir 43.

Anonymous. 1980. Roman Fedorovich Hecker. *Geologiska Foreningens I Stockholm Forhandlingar,* vol. 102, p. 234.

Ashby, J. R., et al. 1987. Uranium series ages of corals from the Upper Pleistocene Mulegé terrace, Baja California Sur, Mexico. *Geology,* vol. 15, pp. 137–141.

Bailey, R. (editor). 2000. *Earth Report 2000: Revisiting the True State of the Planet.* New York: McGraw-Hill.

Bailey, R. G. 1998. *Ecoregions: The Ecosystem Geography of the Oceans and Continents.* New York: Springer.

Batiza, R. 1978. Geology, petrology, and geochemistry of Isla Tortuga, a recently formed tholeiitic island in the Gulf of California. *Geological Society of America Bulletin,* vol. 89, pp. 1309–1324.

Benchley, P. 2000. Great white sharks. *National Geographic,* vol. 194, no. 4, pp. 10–27.

Bender, M. L., et al. 1979. Uranium-series dating of the Pleistocene reef tracts of Barbados, West Indies. *Geological Society of America Bulletin,* vol. 90, pp. 577–594.

Berger, B. 1998. *Almost an Island: Travels in Baja California.* Tucson: University of Arizona Press.

Bjørnson, B. 1971. Verses to the Norwegian national anthem. *Smørekoppens Visebok.* Trondheim: F. Bruns Bokhandels Forlag.

Bray, N. A. 1988. Thermohaline circulation in the Gulf of California. *Journal of Geophysical Research,* vol. 93 (C5), pp. 4993–5020.

Bray, N. A., and J. M. Robles. 1991. Physical oceanography of the Gulf of California. In *The Gulf and Peninsular Province of the Californias,* edited by J. P. Dauphin and B. R. T. Simoneit, pp. 511–553. American Association of Petroleum Geologists Memoir 47.

Brusca, R. C. 1980. *Common Intertidal Invertebrates of the Gulf of California.* Second edition. Tucson: University of Arizona Press.

Cande, S. C., and D. V. Kent. 1995. Revised calibration of the geomagnetic polarity time scale for the Late Cretaceous and Cenozoic. *Journal of Geophysical Research,* vol. 100, pp. 6093–6096.

Carozzi, A. V. (translator). 1968. *Telliamed, or Conversations between an Indian Philosopher and a French Missionary on the Diminution of the Sea.* Urbana: University of Illinois Press.

———. 1992. De Maillet's Telliamed (1748): The diminution of the sea, or the fall portion of a complete cosmic eustatic cycle. *Geological Society of America Memoir 180,* pp. 17–24.

Carson, R. L. 1951. *The Sea Around Us.* New York: Oxford University Press.

Chambers, R. 1848. *Ancient Sea-Margins as Memorials of Changes in the Relative Level of Sea and Land.* Edinburgh: W. and R. Chambers.

Cone, J. 1991. *Fire under the Sea.* New York: William Morrow.

Cross, T. A., and P. W. Homewood. 1997. Amanz Gressly's role in founding modern stratigraphy. *Geological Society of America Bulletin,* vol. 109, pp. 1617–1630.

Dauphin, J. P., and G. E. Ness. 1991. Bathymetry of the Gulf and Peninsula Province of the Californias. In *The Gulf and Peninsular Province of the Californias,* edited by J. P. Dauphin and B. R. T. Simoneit, pp. 21–23. American Association of Petroleum Geologists Memoir 47.

Dauphin, J. P., and B. R. T. Simoneit (editors). 1991. *The Gulf and Peninsular Province of the Californias.* American Association of Petroleum Geologists Memoir 47.

de la Mare, W. 1930. *Desert Islands.* London: Faber and Faber.

Dillard, A. 1975. *Pilgrim at Tinker Creek.* New York: Bantam.

Durham, J. W. 1950. Megascopic paleontology and marine stratigraphy. In *1940* E. W. Scripps *Cruise to the Gulf of California,* by C. A. Anderson et al., Part 2. New York: Geological Society of America Memoir 43.

Eiseley, L. 1957. *The Immense Journey.* New York: Vintage Books.

Foster, A. B. 1979. Environmental variation in a fossil scleractinian coral. *Lethaia,* vol. 12, pp. 245–264.

Foster, M. S., et al. 1997. Living rhodolith beds in the Gulf of California and their implications for paleoenvironmental interpretation. *Geological Society of America Special Paper 318,* pp. 127–139.

Fox, W. T. 1983. *At the Sea's Edge.* Englewood Cliffs, N.J.: Prentice-Hall.

Grabau, A. W. 1940. *The Rhythm of the Ages.* Peking: Henry Vetch. Reprint, New York: Krieger, 1978.

Gressly, A. 1838. Observations géologiques sur le Jura soleurois. *Nouveaux Mémoires de la Société Helvétique de Sciences Naturelles* (Neuchatel), vol. 2, pp. 1–112.

——. 1840. Observations géologiques sur le Jura soleurois. *Nouveaux Mémoires de la Société Helvétique de Sciences Naturelles* (Neuchatel), vol. 4, pp. 113–241.

Gould, S. J. 1965. Is uniformitarianism necessary? *American Journal of Science,* vol. 263, pp. 223–228.

Haq, B. U. 1987. Chronology of fluctuating sea levels since the Triassic. *Science,* vol. 235, pp. 1156–1167.

Haq, B. U., J. Hardenbol, and P. R. Vail. 1988. Mesozoic and Cenozoic chronostratigraphy and cycles of sea-level change. In *Sea-Level Changes: An Integrated Approach,* edited by C. K. Wilgus et al., pp. 71–108. Special Publication no. 42. Tulsa, Okla.: Society of Economic Paleontologists and Mineralogists.

Harderlie, E. C., and D. P. Abbott, 1980. Bivalvia: The clams and allies. In *Intertidal Invertebrates of California,* pp. 355–411. Stanford, Calif.: Stanford University Press.

Hausback, B. P. 1984. Cenozoic volcanic and tectonic evolution of Baja California, Mexico. In *Geology of the Baja California Peninsula,* pp. 219–236. Bakersfield, Calif.: Pacific Section, Society of Economic Paleontologists and Mineralogists.

Hayes, M. L., M. E. Johnson, and W. T. Fox. 1993. Rocky-shore biotic associations and their fossilization potential: Isla Requesón (Baja California Sur, Mexico). *Journal of Coastal Research,* vol. 9, pp. 944–957.

Haymon, R. M., and K. C. Macdonald. 1985. The geology of deep-sea hot springs. *American Scientist,* vol. 73, pp. 441–449.

Hecker, R. F. 1965. *Introduction to Paleoecology.* New York: Elsevier.

Hertlein, L. G. 1957. Pliocene and Pleistocene fossils from the southern portion of the Gulf of California. *Bulletin of the Southern Academy of Sciences,* vol. 56, pp. 57–75.

Hess, H. H. 1946. Drowned ancient islands of the Pacific Basin. *American Journal of Science,* vol. 244, pp. 772–791.

——. 1962. History of ocean basins. In *Petrologic Studies: A Volume to Honor A. F. Buddington,* pp. 599–620. Baltimore: Geological Society of America.

Huntoon, P. W. 1976. The post-Paleozoic structural geology of the eastern Grand Canyon, Arizona. In *Geology of the Grand Canyon,* second edition, edited by W. J. Breed and E. Roat, pp. 82–128. Flagstaff, Ariz.: Museum of Northern Arizona and Grand Canyon Natural History Association.

Ives, R. L. 1959. Shell dunes of the Sonoran shore. *American Journal of Science,* vol. 257, pp. 449–457.

Janovy, J., Jr. 1992. *Vermilion Sea.* Boston: Houghton Mifflin.

Johnson, M. E. 1985. A. W. Grabau and the fruition of a new life in China. *Journal of Geological Eduation,* vol. 33, pp. 106–111.

——. 1988. Hunting for ancient rocky shores. *Journal of Geological Education,* vol. 36, pp. 147–154.

——. 1988. Why are ancient rocky shores so uncommon? *Journal of Geology,* vol. 96, pp. 469–480.

——. 1992. A. W. Grabau's embryonic sequence stratigraphy and eustatic curve. *Geological Society of America Memoir 180,* pp. 43–54.

Johnson, M. E., and J. Ledesma-Vázquez. 1999. Biological zonation on a rocky-shore boulder deposit: Upper Pleistocene Bahía San Antonio (Baja California Sur, Mexico). *Palaios,* vol. 14, pp. 569–584.

——. 2001. Pliocene-Pleistocene rocky shorelines trace coastal development of Bahía Concepción, gulf coast of Baja California Sur (Mexico). *Palaeogeography, Palaeoclimatology, Palaeoecology,* vol. 166, pp. 65–88.

Johnson, M. E., and M. E. Simian. 1996. Discrimination between coastal ramps and marine terraces at Punta Chivato on the Pliocene-Pleistocene Gulf of California. *Journal of Geoscience Education,* vol. 44, pp. 569–575.

Johnson, M. E., D. F. Skinner, and K. G. Macleod. 1988. Ecological zonation during the carbonate transgression of a late Ordovician rocky shore (northeastern Manitoba, Hudson Bay, Canada). *Palaeogeography, Palaeoclimatology, Palaeoecology,* vol. 654, pp. 93–114.

Keen, A. M. 1971. *Sea Shells of Tropical West America.* Second edition. Stanford, Calif.: Stanford University Press.

Kennett, J. P., and D. A. Hodell. 1995. Stability or instability of Antarctic ice sheets during warm climates of the Pliocene? *GSA Today,* vol. 5, pp. 13, 22.

Kerstitch, A. 1989. *Sea of Cortez Marine Invertebrates.* Monterey, Calif.: Sea Challengers.

Kortner, O., P. Munthe, and E. Tveterås (editors). 1983. *Norge Bilder og Fakta.* Stavanger: Den Norske Bokklubben.

Krutch, J. W. 1986 [1961]. *The Forgotten Peninsula: A Naturalist in Baja California.* Tucson: University of Arizona Press.

Ledesma-Vázquez, J., et al. 1997. El Mono chert: A shallow-water chert from the Pliocene Infierno Formation, Baja California Sur, Mexico. *Geological Society of America Special Paper 318,* pp. 73–81.

Libbey, L. K., and M. E. Johnson. 1997. Upper Pleistocene rocky shores and intertidal biotas at Playa La Palmita (Baja California Sur, Mexico). *Journal of Coastal Research,* vol. 13, pp. 216–225.

Lonsdale, P. 1989. Geology and tectonic history of the Gulf of California. In *The Geology of North America,* vol. N, pp. 499–521. Boulder, Colo.: Geological Society of America.

López-Hernández, A., et al. 1994. Geological and geophysical studies at Las Tres Vírgenes, B.C.S., Mexico. *Transactions of the Geothermal Resources Council,* vol. 18, pp. 275–280.

Lurie, E. 1960. *Louis Agassiz: A Life in Science.* Chicago: University of Chicago Press.

Macdonald, K. C., and B. P. Luyendyk. 1981. The crest of the East Pacific Rise. *Scientific American,* vol. 244, pp. 100–116.

McCarthy, C. 1998. *Cities of the Plain.* New York: Vintage Books/Random House.

McFall, C. C. 1968. *Reconnaissance Geology of the Concepción Bay Area, Baja California, Mexico.* Stanford, Calif.: Stanford University Publications in Geological Sciences, vol. 10, no. 5.

McPhee, J. 1980. *Basin and Range.* New York: Farrar, Straus, Giroux.

Middleton, G. V. 1973. Johannes Walther's law of the correlation of facies. *Geological Society of America Bulletin,* vol. 84, pp. 979–988.

Minch, J., et al. 1998. *Roadside Geology and Biology of Baja California.* Mission Viejo, Calif.: John Minch and Associates.

Morrison, R. A. 1991. Quaternary stratigraphic, hydrologic, and climatic history of the Great Basin, with emphasis on Lakes Lahontan, Bonneville, and Tecopa. *The Geology of North America,* vol. K-2, pp. 283–320. Boulder, Colo.: Geological Society of America.

——. 1991. Quaternary geology of the southern Basin and Range Province. *The Geology of North America,* vol. K-2, pp. 353–371. Boulder, Colo.: Geological Society of America.

Nelson, C. M. 1985. Facies in stratigraphy: From "terrains" to "terranes." *Journal of Geological Education,* vol. 33, pp. 175–187.

Ness, G. E., and M. W. Lyle. 1991. A seismo-tectonic map of the Gulf and Peninsular Province of the Californias. In *The Gulf and Peninsular Province of the Californias,* edited by J. P. Dauphin and B. R. T. Simoneit, pp. 71–77. American Association of Petroleum Geologists Memoir 47.

Newman, A. C., and P. J. Hearty. 1996. Rapid sea-level changes at the close of the last interglacial (substage 5e) recorded in Bahamian island geology. *Geology,* vol. 24, pp. 775–778.

Novacek, M. 1997. *Dinosaurs of the Flaming Cliffs.* New York: Doubleday.

Ortleib, L. 1991. Quaternary vertical movements along the coasts of Baja California and Sonora. In *The Gulf and Peninsular Province of the Californias,* edited by J. P. Dauphin and B. R. T. Simoneit, pp. 447–480. American Association of Petroleum Geologists Memoir 47.

Palmer, T. 1999. *The Heart of America.* Washington, D.C.: Island Press/Shearwater Books.

Peter, J. M., and S. D. Scott. 1991. Hydrothermal mineralization in the Guaymas Basin, Gulf of California. In *The Gulf and Peninsular Province of the Californias,* edited by J. P. Dauphin and B. R. T. Simoneit, pp. 721–741. American Association of Petroleum Geologists Memoir 47.

Pianovskaya, I. A., and R. F. Hecker. 1966. Rocky shores and hard ground of the Cretaceous and Palaeogene seas in central Kyzil Kum and their inhabitants. In *Organisms and Environment of the Geological Past: A Symposium* [in Russian], pp. 222–245. Moscow: Nauka.

Ransom, C. R. 2000. Paleoecology of Upper Pleistocene coral reefs based on morphology and fossil assemblages, Baja California Sur, Mexico. *Memorias V, International Meeting on the Geology of the Baja California Peninsula (Loreto, Baja California Sur, April 25–May 1, 2000),* pp. 36–37. Ensenada, Mexico: Universidad Autónoma de Baja California.

Roberts, N. C. 1989. *Baja California Plant Field Guide.* La Jolla, Calif.: Natural History Publishing Company.

Roden, G. I., and G. W. Groves. 1959. Recent oceanographic observations in the Gulf of California. *Journal of Marine Research,* vol. 18, pp. 10–35.

Russell, P., and M. E. Johnson. 2000. Influence of seasonal winds on coastal carbonate dunes from the Recent and Plio-Pleistocene at Punta Chivato (Baja California Sur, Mexico). *Journal of Coastal Research,* vol. 16, pp. 709–723.

Sabins, R. F., Jr. 1987. *Remote Sensing: Principles and Interpretation.* Second edition. New York: W. H. Freeman.

Scherz, G. 1969. Niels Stensen's geological work. In *Steno: Geological Papers,* edited by G. Scherz, p. 28. Odense: Odense University Press.

Schneer, C. F. 1972. Amanz Gressly. *Dictionary of Scientific Biography,* vol. 5, pp. 533–534. New York: Charles Scribner's Sons.

Shepard, F. P. 1950. Submarine topography of the Gulf of California. In *1940 E. W. Scripps Cruise to the Gulf of California,* by C. A. Anderson et al., Part 3. New York: Geological Society of America Memoir 43.

Shore, E. N. 1999. Harry Hammond Hess. *American National Biography,* pp. 700–701. New York: Oxford University Press.

Simian, M. E., and M. E. Johnson. 1997. Development and foundering of the Pliocene Santa Inés archipelago in the Gulf of California, Baja California Sur, Mexico. *Geological Society of America Special Paper 318,* pp. 25–38.

Simoneit, B. R. T., and P. F. Lonsdale. 1982. Hydrothermal petroleum in mineralized mounds at the seabed of Guaymas Basin. *Nature,* vol. 295, pp. 198–202.

Steinbeck, J. 1962. *The Log from the Sea of Cortez.* New York: Viking Compass.

Steno, N. 1969 [1667]. A Carcharodon head dissected [reprint of Latin text of 1667 with English translation by Alex J. Pollock]. In *Steno: Geological Papers,* edited by G. Scherz, pp. 65–131. Odense: Odense University Press.

Stenonis, N. (Nicolaus Steno). 1910 [1673]. *Opera Philosophica,* vol. 2. Edited by Vilhelm Maar. Copenhagen: Vilhelm Tryde.

Sterling, K. B. 1999. William Beebe. *American National Biography,* vol. 2, pp. 461–462. New York: Oxford University Press.

Stock, J. M., and K. V. Hodges. 1990. Pre-Pliocene extension around the Gulf of California and the transfer of Baja California to the Pacific plate. *Tectonics,* vol. 8, pp. 99–115.

Swift, J. 1963. *Gulliver's Travels.* New York: Airmont Books.

Thatcher, W., et al. 1999. Present-day deformation across the Basin and Range Province, western United States. *Science,* vol. 283, pp. 1714–1718.

Twidale, C. R., and J. D. Pringle. 1991. Australia: Physical geography. *Encyclopaedia Britannica,* vol. 4, pp. 418. Chicago.

Vail, P., et al. 1977. Seismic stratigraphy and global changes of sea level, Part 4: Global cycles of relative changes of sea level. In *Seismic Stratigraphy: Applications to Hydrocarbon Exploration,* pp. 83–97. American Association of Petroleum Geologists Memoir 26.

Vine, F., and D. Matthews. 1963. Magnetic anomalies over oceanic ridges. *Nature,* vol. 199, pp. 947–949.

Walther, J. 1893–94. *Einleitung in die Geologie als historische Wissenschaft.* Three vols. Jena: Verlag von Gustav Fischer.

Waterman, J. 1995. *Kayaking the Vermilion Sea: Eight Hundred Miles down the Baja.* New York: Simon and Schuster.

Wegener, A. 1924. *The Origin of Continents and Oceans.* London: Methuen.

Wentworth, C. K. 1922. A scale of grade and class terms for clastic sediments. *Journal of Geology,* vol. 27, pp. 377–392.

Wicander, R., and J. S. Monroe. 2000. *Historical Geology: Evolution of Earth and Life through Time.* Third edition. Pacific Grove, Calif.: Brooks/Cole.

Williams, W. C. 1972. Robert Chambers. *Dictionary of Scientific Biography,* vol. 1, pp. 191–193. New York: Charles Scribner's Sons.

Wilson, E. O. 1992. *The Diversity of Life.* Cambridge, Mass.: Harvard University Press.

Winter, J. G. (translator). 1916. *The Prodromus of Nicolaus Steno's Dissertation Concerning a Solid Body Enclosed by Process of Nature Within a Solid.* New York: Macmillan.

Wold, B., and L. Ryvarden. 1996. *Jostedals-Breen: Norway's Largest Glacier.* Oslo: Boksentreret Forlag.

Wood, R. M. 1985. *The Dark Side of the Earth.* London: Allan and Unwin.

Zwinger, A. 1983. *A Desert Country near the Sea.* Tucson: University of Arizona Press.

Index

Hanna, G. D., 23, 24
heart urchin. *See* sea biscuit
Hecker, Roman Fedorovich, 138–42; bi-
    ography of, 139, 142; and *Introduction*
    to Paleoecology, 138–40; and paleo-
    ecological monument, 141
hedgehog cactus *(Echinocereus* sp., *pita-*
    yita), 125
Hess, Harry Hammond, 163–67, 169;
    biography of, 163; and *History of*
    Ocean Basins, 165–66
high pressure system. *See* weather
Hipponix. See horse-hoof limpet
History of Ocean Basins. See Hess, Harry
    Hammond
Hofmeisteria fasciculata, 86
hogback, 125–26
horse-hoof limpet *(Hipponix),* 75
horst. *See* graben
Hotel Punta Chivato, xiii, 15, 16
Hudson Bay, 7
human population. *See* population
hurricane, tropical, 29
hydrochloric acid, and limestone, 34,
    135
hydrothermal mound. *See* geothermal
    spring/vent

ice age, 8, 19, 21, 28; and glacial re-
    bound, 79, 84
igneous rock, formation of, 153
Inés, Santa, 88, 187–88
inland sea, 6–7
inlier, 115
Introduction to Paleoecology. See Hecker,
    Roman Fedorovich
Iowa, 6–7, 183–84
Isamna dekavi. See shark, mackerel
Isla del Carmen, and wind direction, 91
islands, fossil, xiii, 96, 121–22, 174–75;
    at Islas Santa Inés, 154–55; at Kyril
    Kum, 141–42; near Mesa Barracas,
    137–38, 143; at Phantom Island, 33–
34; at Punta Chivato promontory, 96,
    113, 116
Isla Requesón, 29–31, 43, 179–80
Isla San Marcos, 47, 183
Islas Santa Inés, xiii, 149–57, 169–70,
    173–75
Isla Tortuga, 49, 173
isobath, 157
Ives, Ronald L., 91–92

jackknife clam *(Tegelus californianus,*
    Tegelus politus), 21–22, 25
Janovy, John, 5, 6
Jatropha cuneata. See leatherplant
Johanson, Jim, 15, 39–40
Jostedal Glacier, 8
Juan de Fuca Rise, 167

Kaibab Plateau, 158
karst, 44, 112; at Gascoyne River, 8–9; at
    North Shore, 84–85
krummholz, 50, 85, 86, 112
Krutch, Joseph Wood, 7, 15, 16, 178

Laevicardium elatum. See cockle
lake, pluvial, 84–85; Lake Bonneville,
    84; Lake Cochise, 84
landscape, 4, 13–14; of Arctic Siberia, 5;
    connection to older landscape, 7, 8;
    and karst, 8–9; of Norway, 4–5, 8; and
    prairie, 5, 6
Larus livens. See yellow-footed seagull
laterite, formation of, 8
leatherplant *(Jatropha cuneata),* 50, 85,
    109
limestone ramp. *See* carbonate ramp
Little Horn Point. *See* Punta Cerotito
Little Red Table. *See* Mesa El Coloradito
Lysiloma candida. See palo blanco

Macdonald, Ken, 170–71
Mackintosh, Graham, xv
Maillet, Benoît de. *See* de Maillet, Benoît

Pliny the Elder, 10, 178. *See also* shark, teeth

Podiceps nigricollis. See eared grebe

population: pressure of, 178–85; of world, 178–79, 185

Porites californica. See emerald coral

precipitation. *See* rainfall

preservation, of fossils, 140

Prodromus. See Steno, Nicolaus

pull-apart basin, 158

Pulsation Theory. *See* Grabau, Amadeus William

Punta Cacarizo (Hammerhead Point), 41–49, 62, *62*

Punta Cerotito (Little Horn Point), 49–51, 58–61

Punta Chivato, xiii, 14–16; and geological development, 140; hotel at, 15; light tower at, 75–77, 80–81; structural overview of, 162, 173–74

Punta Chivato promontory. *See* Mesa Atravesada

Punta El Coloradito, 138, 145–47

Punta Mezquitito, 16–20

rainfall: in Baja California, 91; local, 29, 181–83, *184*

razor clam, 25

red coralline algae. *See* rhodolith

red velvet sponge *(Acarnus erithacus)*, 49

regression. *See* sea-level change

remote sensing, 150–51

rhodolith, 26, 27, *27*, 31, 60, 68, 101, 110, 126; formation of, 24–25, 29; in off-shore banks, 29–30, *151*, 151–52, 179; rock forming, 153

Rhythm of the Ages, The. See Grabau, Amadeus William

Ricketts, Ed, 4, 178. *See also* Steinbeck, John

rift zone, 160, 162–63, 168–69, 172

rip current, 107

rocky shore, 46, 54; and associated fauna, 22, 23, 33, 81–82; and fossil sea cliff, 31, 38; and Hudson Bay, 7; and Isla Requesón, 179

Salsipuedes Basin, 159, 169

salt: as condition for precipitation, 44, *45*; and salinity in Gulf of California, 44, 50. *See also* thermohaline circulation

saltation, 59

saltbush *(Atriplex barclayana)*, 86

San Andreas Fault, 163, 169

sand. *See* grain size

sand dollar, 19, *20*; giant keyhole *(Encope grandis)*, 23

sand dune, 59, 91–92, 150; composition of: at Ensenada El Muerto, 112; at Mesa Barracas, 128–30, 145; at Playa El Certito, 59–61, *60*; at southwest flank of Atravesada, 98–100, *99*; fossil windblown, 91, 112, 145

San Marcos Formation, 47, 70, 96–97, 113, 136; and index fossils, 121, 154; relative age of, 117–18

San Marcos Island, 75

Santa Inés Bay. *See* Bahía Santa Inés

Santa Inés Islands. *See* Islas Santa Inés

Sataplia Preserve, 141

schist, formation of, 153–54

Scripps Expedition, 18, 19, 120, 155–57, 160, 171–72

sea biscuit *(Agassizia scorbiculata; Clypeaster bowersi)*, 19, 81–82, 154. *See also* sea urchin

sea cliff, fossil, 31, *32*, 33, 38, 46, 76, 142

sea floor: and age, 164, 165; and spreading zones, 165

sea hare, 178

sea-level change: global, 36, 54, 113, 116–18 (*see also* Exxon curve; Grabau, Amadeus William); and last ice age, 21, 33; and Pleistocene, 100, 138; and

Pliocene, 96; and Pulsation Theory, 114–15; relative, 47, 54, 57, 72, 79–80, 118; and terraces, 75–80

seasonal wind. *See* weather

sea star, pyramid *(Pharia pyramidata),* 48

sea urchin, purple *(Echinometra vanbrunti),* 45, 48. *See also* sea biscuit

sedimentary rock, 102, 153

shantung. *See* Barraboo

shark: great white *(Carcharodon carcharias),* 94; mackerel *(Isurus dekayi),* 94; sand, 94; teeth, 10, 93–95 *(see also* Pliny the Elder)

Shell Beach. *See* Playa La Palmita

Shepard, Francis P., 155–60, 163, 169. See also *Scripps* Expedition

shingled pebbles, and current transport, 130–31

Siberia, and landscape, 24

Slevin, J. R. *See* Hanna, G. D.

slipper plant *(Candelilla; Pedilanthus macrocarpus),* 98

slipper shell *(Crepidula),* 101

Solenastrea fairbanksi, as endemic, 73–74, *74,* 108. *See also* coral

Sphaeralcea ambigua. See desert hollyhock

spindle shell *(Fusinus),* 133

spiny rock shell *(Murex tricoronis),* 23

standing wave, 103–6, *105*

Steensen, Niels. *See* Steno, Nicolaus

Steinbeck, John, 4, 5, 28, 66, 177–78, 186–87

Steno, Nicolaus, 9–15; biography of, 10, 12–13, 178; and law of original horizontality, 11, 35, 111–12; and law of superposition, 11, 35; and *Prodromus,* 10–12, *13,* 35; and shark, 10, 94

storm, tropical (Nora), 69–70

stoss slope, 112

strata, 10

Strombus galeatus, 33. *See also* conch

Strombus gracilior, 22. *See also* conch

Strongylura exilis. See California needlefish

Swift, Jonathan, 61

Tegelus californianus. See jackknife clam

Tegelus politus. See jackknife clam

tellen shell *(Tellina cumingii),* 21

Telliamed. See de Maillet, Benoît

Tellina cumingii. See tellen shell

terrace, marine, 75–79; above Ensenada El Muerto, 108–10; at Islas Santa Inés, 173; and Luc Ortlieb, 79; at Mulegé, 77–78; at Punta Chivato promontory, 75–77, 80, 89; and Robert Chambers, 78–79

Thematic Mapper, 150–51. *See also* remote sensing

thermohaline circulation, 44, 50

Thracia curta, 73. *See also* pholad bivalve

tidal cycle, 104, 107

tidal flat, and associated fauna, 31

tombolo, 43, 180

torote colorado *(Bursera microphylia),* 124–25

Tortuga Fault, 173

trace fossil, 18–19, 121, 143, *144*

Trachycardium consors, 21. *See also* cockle

transgressive. *See* sea-level change

transtensional tectonics, 163

trellised drainage, 127

tube worm *(Vestimentifera),* 170–72

tuff, 41–42; and formation of valley, 86

tun shell *(Malea ringens),* 88–89

turban shell *(Turbo fluctuosus),* 23, 31, 50, 69, 75, 110, 173

Turbo fluctuosus. See turban shell

turkey vulture *(Cathartes aura),* 66–67

Turritella gonostoma. See auger shell

Ulrich, Edward O., 116. *See also* Grabau, Amadeus William

unconformity, 35–38, 67, 117; angular, 39; at Islas Santa Inés, 153; at Punta

About the Author

M arkes E. Johnson studied geology at the University of Iowa and took his advanced training in the Department of Geophysical Sciences at the University of Chicago, where he earned his doctoral degree in 1977. He is the Charles L. MacMillan Professor of Geology at Williams College in Williamstown, Massachusetts, where he has taught historical geology, paleontology, and stratigraphy since 1977. A fascination with ancient shorelines first enticed Professor Johnson to Baja California in 1989. He has subsequently led annual research expeditions and field courses there involving more than 50 Williams students. With colleague Jorge Ledesma-Vázquez (Universidad Autónoma de Baja California, Ensenada), he is the editor of the research volume *Pliocene Carbonates and Related Facies Flanking the Gulf of California, Baja California, Mexico,* published by the Geological Society of America in 1997. Describing himself as a "dry-land oceanographer," Professor Johnson is drawn to landscapes of many improbable places that cloak former changes between the sea and the land. His research on ancient islands of diverse geological ages takes him around the world, to places such as northern China, western Australia, New Zealand, Scandinavia, and Siberia, although Baja California remains his favorite destination. The author lives with his wife and son in Williamstown, Massachusetts.